2003
A BRAND-NEW YEAR—
A PROMISING NEW START

Enter Sydney Omarr's star-studded world of accurate day-by-day predictions for every aspect of your life. With expert readings and forecasts, you can chart a course to romance, adventure, good health, or career opportunities while gaining valuable insight into yourself and others. Offering a daily outlook for 18 full months, this fascinating guide shows you:

- The important dates in your life
- What to expect from an astrological reading
- How the stars can help you stay healthy and fit
- Your lucky lottery numbers
  And more!

Let this expert's sound advice guide you through a year of heavenly possibilities—for today and for every day of 2003!

SYDNEY OMARR'S DAY-BY-DAY
ASTROLOGICAL GUIDE FOR

ARIES—March 21–April 19
TAURUS—April 20–May 20
GEMINI—May 21–June 20
CANCER—June 21–July 22
LEO—July 23–August 22
VIRGO—August 23–September 22
LIBRA—September 23–October 22
SCORPIO—October 23–November 21
SAGITTARIUS—November 22–December 21
CAPRICORN—December 22–January 19
AQUARIUS—January 20–February 18
PISCES—February 19–March 20

IN 2003

SYDNEY OMARR'S

DAY-BY-DAY ASTROLOGICAL GUIDE FOR

SCORPIO

October 23–November 21

2003

A SIGNET BOOK

SIGNET
Published by New American Library, a division of
Penguin Putnam Inc., 375 Hudson Street,
New York, New York 10014, U.S.A.
Penguin Books Ltd, 80 Strand,
London WC2R 0RL, England
Penguin Books Australia Ltd, Ringwood,
Victoria, Australia
Penguin Books Canada Ltd, 10 Alcorn Avenue,
Toronto, Ontario, Canada M4V 3B2
Penguin Books (N.Z.) Ltd, 182–190 Wairau Road,
Auckland 10, New Zealand

Penguin Books Ltd, Registered Offices:
Harmondsworth, Middlesex, England

First published by Signet, an imprint of New American Library,
a division of Penguin Putnam Inc.

First Printing, June 2002
10 9 8 7 6 5 4 3 2 1

Sydney Omarr is syndicated worldwide by
Los Angeles Times Syndicate.

 REGISTERED TRADEMARK—MARCA REGISTRADA

Printed in the United States of America

CONTENTS

INTRODUCTION

Astrology Comes of Age

In times of change, people throughout the ages have looked to astrology for answers and explanations, searching the stars for portents of the future, hoping for a favorable prediction. Today, more people are searching for a deeper, more personal meaning, asking what astrology can tell them about themselves and their purpose in life, and how to handle current events.

Astrology now has evolved into a tool for self-knowledge, which has come of age in our time and is being validated by scholarly research. It is good news for astrology fans that there is an accredited college of astrology in Seattle, which will raise standards and serve as a focal point for the latest research. In France, astrologer Elizabeth Tessier presented her thesis in astrology at the Sorbonne and was granted a degree, making history at this prestigious institution. Internet websites give everyone instant access to sophisticated computer software and the thinking of top astrologers around the world.

Like millions of Americans who turn to astrology for fun, curiosity, or guidance, you're in for a fascinating experience as you explore the cosmos this unique way. Unlike other arts or sciences, astrology can give you specific details on who you are and where you're going, with immediate practical advice on how to deal with the whole range of problems and situations that crop up in daily life. It's no wonder that the lure of discovering a real human connection with the universe has kept people in all walks of life, from tycoons to the man on the street, intrigued with astrology for millennia.

This book is dedicated to helping you make astrology your own. As you discover astrology for yourself, you'll

1

learn that, far from being a vague, intuitive art shrouded in mystery, it is quite a precise language that communicates in a very orderly and specific way. Yet it retains a sense of wonder and mystery. We marvel how those faraway planets can tell us so much about ourselves with such uncanny accuracy!

Haven't there been times when you feel an unexplained "pull" in a certain direction, times when everything seems to be going haywire, times when nobody seems to understand you, and other times when you seem to hit a lucky roll? Astrology offers explanations to these baffling conditions, points out trends and cycles, and suggests solutions to difficulties or alternative courses to take. Astrology brings the happenings in the universe down to human terms without dictating a moral code or involving a religion.

This book will give you basic tools for taking a voyage through your personal galaxy. Your most important tool is your own horoscope, a map of the heavens based on the happenings at the moment you were born. This tells you about your potential in every area of life, what talents to develop, where to look for a profitable career, even what kind of partner to choose for business and love. It can target your trouble spots in relationships, giving you clues about why you have difficulty communicating with someone and how to improve the situation. It offers heavenly help to improve the quality of your life, to make the most of your strengths, protect yourself from stress, even how to decorate your home.

Then there is the matter of timing. Astrology helps you pick the perfect moment to initiate a plan, sign a contract, go to a party, meet someone special, or close a deal. It's all based on an understanding of the way the energies of the planets are acting and interacting at a given time. This book will reveal which planet affects your communications for better or worse and what the 2003 outlook will be. You'll learn which phase of the moon is best for starting new ventures, and when to expect a major transition in your life. Starting with the groundwork of astrology, you'll learn to speak its language and discover what those exotic symbols really mean.

For your day-to-day living, there are eighteen months of

2

personal predictions. Each day, there are highlights of the planetary, lunar, and numerical cycles as they relate to your sign with custom-blended interpretations. What's more, you'll find the daily moon sign and lucky numbers for significant days.

So whether you're new to astrology or a regular reader, let this guide put you on the right celestial path for 2003. May the stars light your way to the happiest, healthiest year ever!

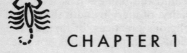

CHAPTER 1

2003: A Year of Changes

Uranus Moves to Pisces

When a slow-moving planet changes astrological signs, it is a major event, marking a total change in direction for at least seven years—a whole new generation. This year, the slow-moving planet Uranus moves into Pisces, bringing about a powerful change in group consciousness. In the astrological drama, Uranus plays the oddball, the rebellious rule breaker who is often called the "Great Awakener," for the way it operates in sudden, surprising ways. Uranus is likely to hit your life when and where you least expect, jolting you out of complacency and comfort. Uranus is also associated with technological experimentation and breakthroughs.

Since 1996, Uranus has been in a power position traveling through Aquarius, the sign it rules. It signaled the rise of the Internet, when the dot coms ruled the stock market and computers became part of our daily lives. As Aquarius is also the sign of social consciousness, associated with the eleventh house of the horoscope, the Uranus transit there has forced us to be aware of the dissension in the global community, with cataclysmic results in the Middle East. The surprise attack on the World Trade Center on September 11, 2001 was a tragic example of Uranus's influence.

Uranus dips its toe into Pisces on March 10, 2003 and spends six months there before retrograding back to Aquarius on September 14. Uranus will move finally into Pisces on December 30, where it will remain until the year 2011. The early six-month visit of Uranus in Pisces gives us a preview of coming trends for the next seven years.

The emphasis now changes to the mysterious mystical sign of Pisces—a sign of secrets, all that is hidden, stealthy, beneath the surface, and behind the scenes. It is a sign of "losing one's self" in spirituality, of merging with the divine via meditation or ecstatic religious practices, of tapping the deep waters of the unconscious. During previous episodes of Uranus in Pisces, great religions and spiritual movements have come into being, most recently Mormonism and Christian fundamentalism.

Pisces is associated with the twelfth house of the horoscope, where we have no limits or boundaries. Athletes know it as the "zone," the euphoria that comes when they feel at one with their sport. Pisces represents places of voluntary or involuntary confinement via monasteries, prisons, and hospitals, where we no longer need take responsibility for our actions. It is where we escape from reality via addictions of all kinds, including alcohol and drugs.

In its most positive mode, Pisces promotes imagination and creativity, the art of illusion in theater and film, the inspiration of great artists. A water sign, Pisces is naturally associated with all things liquid—oceans, oil, alcohol—and with those creatures that live in water—fish, the fishing industry, fish habitats. Pisces also rules the underdog, the enslaved, and the disenfranchised, whose status has been illuminated in previous Uranus in Pisces periods.

The last time Uranus was in Pisces was early in the twentieth century from 1919 to 1927, during the "roaring 20s." Prohibition of alcohol (Pisces-ruled) began in 1920, causing secret bootleg industries and speakeasy clubs where racy dancing and upbeat music signaled the "Jazz Age." A unique American music evolved, with great musicians like Louis Armstrong and George Gershwin. It was a time of creativity in film and theater, which extended to the electronic inventions of radio and television. In literature, the "Lost Generation" of American writers began publishing. Socially, the underdog triumphed. Women finally won the right to vote in 1920. Gandhi began the peaceful noncooperation movement against the British in India. Yet the underworld also thrived, such as the Mafia's secret "Cosa Nostra" and the precursor of the IRA in Ireland.

The nineteenth-century period of Uranus in Pisces, from 1836 to 1843, might also give us a preview of what to expect. At that time, as the Victorian Era began, there were rumblings of women's rights. Victoria Woodhull, who would later be the first female to run for U.S. President, was born. The underdog issues of slavery were coming to a head. The slave ship *Amistad* mutinied and ran aground on Long Island, New York, in 1839. A legal battle ensued that went to the Supreme Court, where former President John Quincy Adams argued for the rebel slaves' freedom and won. The saga of the *Amistad* has inspired books, an opera, and a major film. The Cherokee "Vail of Tears" march to Oklahoma was another dramatic and sorrowful episode. Baseball was invented. Financier J. P. Morgan and John D. Rockefeller, founder of Standard Oil, were born. Many great artists and composers, such as Cézanne, Monet, Renoir, Winslow Homer, and Tchaikovsky, were born. The Cunard Line celebrated its first Atlantic crossing. There were great inventions in photography, such as the stereoscope and the daguerreotype. The Opium Wars erupted in China. Wars between the Afghans and the British resulted in the British being driven from Afghanistan. In America, Mexicans defeated 182 Texans at the Alamo.

These moments from history could give us clues about what to expect. Perhaps the first woman president will be elected, and the emancipation of women in Arab countries will proceed. With the Pisces emphasis this year revved up by Mars, the planet of action and war, which is also transiting Pisces for much of the year, we can expect a continuing emphasis on stealth and terrorist activities. Pisces rules the prenatal phase of life, which is related to regenerative medicine. Researchers dream of replacing body parts with new ones grown from embryonic stem cells. Legal issues, which now present obstacles to this type of research, may be overcome during the Uranus transit. If so, our dream of perfect health may be within reach.

Petroleum issues, both in the oil-producing countries and offshore oil drilling, will come to a head. Uranus in Pisces suggests that development of new hydroelectric sources may provide the power we need to continue our current power-thirsty lifestyle.

In previous eras, there was a flourishing of the arts, particularly new forms such as film, photography, poetry, and painting. We are seeing many new artistic forms developing now, such as computer-created actors and special effects. The sky's the limit on this influence.

Those who have problems with Uranus are those who resist change, so the key is to embrace the future. Those born in early Pisces, February 18 to 20, are most likely to have Uranian changes in their lives this year. Go with the flow!

Pluto in Sagittarius: Religious Intensity

The slow-moving planet Pluto is our guide to life-changing, long-term trends. Pluto brings about a heightened consciousness and transformation of matters related to the sign it is passing through. In Sagittarius until 2008, Pluto is emphasizing everything associated with this sign to prepare us philosophically and spiritually for things to come. Those born from December 10–13 will be feeling the force of Pluto this year.

Perhaps the most pervasive sign of Pluto in Sagittarius over the past few years has been globalization in all its forms. We are re-forming boundaries, creating new forms of travel that will definitely include space travel. At this writing, the $60 billion space station is under way, a joint venture between the United States, Russia, Japan, Europe, and Canada. It is scheduled for completion in 2006 and will be one of the brightest objects in the sky.

In true Sagittarius fashion, Pluto will shift our emphasis away from acquiring wealth to a quest for the meaning of it all, as upward strivers discover that money and power are not enough and religious extremists assert themselves. Sagittarius is the sign of linking everything together. Therefore, the trend will be to find ways to interconnect on a spiritual, philosophical, and intellectual level.

The spiritual emphasis of Pluto in Sagittarius has already filtered down to our home lives. Home altars and private sanctuaries are becoming a part of our personal environment. The oriental art of feng shui has moved westward, giving rise to a more harmonious, spiritual atmosphere in offices and homes, which also promotes luck and prosperity.

Sagittarius are known for their love of animals, especially horses, and people have never been more pet-happy than now. Look for extremes related to animal welfare, such as vegetarianism, which will become even more popular and widespread as a lifestyle. As habitats are destroyed, the care, feeding, and control of wild animals will become a larger issue, especially where there are deer, bears, and coyotes in the backyard.

The Sagittarius love of the outdoors combined with Pluto's power has already promoted extreme sports, especially those that require strong legs, like rock climbing, trekking, or snowboarding. Rugged, sporty all-terrain vehicles continue to be popular. Expect the trend toward more adventurous travel as well as fitness or sports-oriented vacations to accelerate. Exotic hiking trips to unexplored territories, mountain-climbing expeditions, spa vacations, and sports-associated resorts are part of this trend.

Publishing, which is associated with Sagittarius, has been transformed by the new electronic media, with an enormous variety of books available in print and sold over the Internet. The Internet bookstore will continue to prosper under Pluto in Sagittarius. It is fascinating that the online bookstore Amazon.com took the Sagittarius-influenced name of the fierce female tribe of archer–warriors who went to the extreme of removing their right breasts to better shoot their arrows.

Jupiter: Who Is on a Roll This Year?

Good fortune, expansion, and big money opportunities are associated with the movement of Jupiter, the planet that embodies the principle of expansion. Jupiter has a 12-year cycle, staying in each sign for approximately one year.

When Jupiter enters a sign, the fields associated with that sign usually provide excellent opportunities. Areas of speculation associated with the sign Jupiter is passing through will have the hottest market potential—the ones that currently arouse excitement and enthusiasm.

The flip side of Jupiter is that there are no limits. You can expand off the planet under a Jupiter transit, which is why the planet is often called the "Gateway to Heaven." If something is going to burst (such as an artery) or overextend or go over the top in some way, it could happen under a supposedly "lucky" Jupiter transit . . . so be aware.

In 2003, Jupiter will finish its journey through Leo in late August, then move into Virgo for the remainder of the year. So sun sign Leos and Virgos or those with strong Leo or Virgo influence in their horoscopes should have abundant growth opportunities during the year. Those born under Aquarius and Pisces may find their best opportunities working with partners this year, since Jupiter will be transiting their seventh house of relationships.

Tense Times

Be especially cautious in late August. At that time Jupiter, the sun, and Mercury all in Virgo are at odds with Uranus and Mars in Pisces. There may be great impatience to change things, tense boundary issues, and a lack of clear vision. It will be important to communicate well and to understand what each partner in a relationship requires. Most of all, what is needed then is patience. There is still some unfinished business to resolve, which should happen in the fall. There may be responsibilities to others (Aquarius) that must be attended to before you can move ahead and a workable plan for the future can be developed. Play the waiting game.

Saturn Puts on the Brakes in Gemini

Saturn keywords are focus, time, commitment, accomplishment, discipline, restriction. If Jupiter gives you a handout, then Saturn hands you the bill. With Saturn, nothing's free— you work for what you get. So it's always a good idea to find the areas (or houses) of your horoscope where Saturn is passing through in order to learn where to focus your energy on lasting value. With Saturn, you must be sure to finish what you start, be responsible, put in the hard work, and stick with it.

Saturn finishes up its two-year transit of Gemini in June 2003. Over the last two years, the normally light-spirited Geminis have had to deal with a serious, sobering influence of Saturn, just after they enjoyed the expansive period of Jupiter in Gemini in 2000 and 2001. Geminis have to back up the risks they took then, and will be required to deliver on promises made. It'll be a powerful challenge for change-able Geminis, who must now pay the piper.

In the world at large, Saturn in Gemini has impacted communications. Talk must be followed up by action now. We'll be finishing up Gemini issues of lower education and literacy, reforming the lower educational system. Since Gemini is an air sign, which rules the lungs, there will be further controversy and restriction surrounding air pollution, air-born viruses, and the tobacco industry.

After Saturn moves into Cancer on June 3, 2003, the emphasis will switch to Cancer-related issues. Bear in mind that the United States is a Cancer country, born July 4, 1776, and that George W. Bush was born under Cancer (July 7, 1946). So this country is likely to experience the restrictive influence of Cancer.

Other Cancer areas are: domesticity, the home and home-land, the food supply, digestion, motherhood, milk, dairy products, hotels, restaurants, boating, cruise ships, waterways, water-related industries, crabs, sea fowl, the tides, the moon.

Neptune in Aquarius

Where there is Neptune, look for imagination and creativity. And, since Neptune is the planet of deception and illusion, scams and scandals will continue, especially in the high-tech area associated with Aquarius. Neptune is also associated with hospitals, which are acquiring a Neptunian glamour, as well as cutting-edge technology. The atmosphere of many hospitals is already changing from the intimidating sterile surgical environment of the past to that of a health-promoting spa, with alternative therapies such as massage, diet counseling, and aromatherapy. New procedures in plastic surgery, also a Neptunian glamour field, and antiaging therapies should restore the bloom and the body of youth.

There are two Neptune times to watch in 2003: in mid-February and again in the first week of June, when Neptune opposes expansive Jupiter in Leo. There may be a feeling of great optimism on one hand but a lack of direction on the other. Since judgment may be clouded and personal goals are likely unrealistic and too ego-centered, avoid making long-term decisions until the path ahead clears early in 2004. Instead, focus on spiritual growth and on making a positive contribution to the community, be it local or global.

CHAPTER 2

How to Find Your Best Times

Have you ever wanted to coordinate your schedule with the cosmos, as many of the rich and famous who have personal astrologers do? You can practice the art of prediction by studying the movement of the planets, then using this information to pick the perfect time for upcoming events in your life. For instance, when mischievous Mercury creates havoc with communications, you'll back up your vital computer files, read between the lines of contracts, and put off closing that deal until you have double-checked all the information. When Venus in your sign makes you the romantic flavor of the month, you've got maximum sex appeal. Why not get a knockout new outfit or hairstyle, then ask someone you'd like to know better to dinner? Venus timing can also help you win over the competition with a stunning sales pitch or make an offer they won't refuse.

To find out for yourself if there's truth to the saying "timing is everything," mark your own calendar for love, career moves, vacations, and important events, using the information in this chapter and in Chapter 4 on the planets, as well as the moon sign listings under your daily forecast. Here are the happenings to note on your agenda:

- Dates of your sun sign (high-energy period)
- The month previous to your sun sign (low-energy period)
- Dates of planets in your sign this year
- Full and new moons (Pay special attention when these fall in your sun sign)
- Eclipses
- Moon in your sun sign every month, as well as moon in the opposite sign (listed in daily forecast)

- Mercury retrogrades
- Other retrograde periods

Your Annual Prime Time

Every birthday starts a cycle of solar energy for you. You should feel a new surge of vitality as the powerful sun enters your sign. This is the time when predominant energies are most favorable to you. So go for it! Start new projects, make your big moves (especially when the new moon is in your sign, doubling your charisma). You'll get the recognition you deserve now, when everyone is attuned to your sun sign. Look in the tables in this book to see if other planets will also be passing through your sun sign at this time. Venus (love, beauty), Mars (energy, drive), and Mercury (communication, mental sharpness) reinforce the sun and give an extra boost to your life in the areas they affect. Venus will rev up your social and love life, making you seem especially attractive. Mars gives you extra energy and drive. Mercury fuels your brainpower and helps you communicate. Jupiter signals an especially lucky period of expansion.

There are two "down" times related to the sun. During the month before your birthday period, when you are winding up your annual cycle, you could be feeling especially vulnerable and depleted. So at that time get extra rest, watch your diet, and take it easy. Don't overstress yourself. Use this time to gear up for a big "push" when the sun enters your sign.

Another "down" time is when the sun is in a sign opposite your sun sign (six months from your birthday). That's when the prevailing energies are very different from yours. You may feel at odds with the world. You'll have to work harder for recognition because people are not on your wavelength. However, this could be a good time to work on a team, in cooperation with others, or behind the scenes.

Plan Your Day Using the Moon's Phase and Sign

Working with the phases of the moon is as easy as looking up at the night sky. During the new moon, when both the sun and moon are in the same sign, begin new ventures—especially activities that are favored by that sign. Then you'll utilize the powerful energies pulling you in the same direction. You'll be focused outward, toward action, and in a doing mode. Postpone breaking off, terminating, deliberating, or reflecting—activities that require introspection and passive work. These are better suited to a later moon phase.

Get your project under way during the first quarter. Then go public at the full moon, a time of high intensity, when feelings come out into the open. This is your time to shine—to express yourself. Be aware, however, that because pressures are being released, other people will also be letting off steam. Since confrontations are possible, take advantage of this time either to air grievances or to avoid arguments. Traditionally, astrologers often advise against surgery at this time, which could produce heavier bleeding.

From the last quarter of the moon to the next new moon, it's a winding-down phase, a time to cut off unproductive relationships, do serious thinking, and focus on inward-directed activities.

You'll feel some new and full moons more strongly than others, especially those new moons that fall in your sun sign and full moons in your opposite sign. Because that full moon happens at your low-energy time of year, it is likely to be an especially stressful time in a relationship, when any hidden problems or unexpressed emotions could surface.

Full and New Moons in 2003

New Moon—January 2 in Capricorn
Full Moon—January 18 in Cancer

New Moon—February 1 in Aquarius
Full Moon—February 16 in Leo

15

New Moon—March 2 in Pisces
Full Moon—March 18 in Virgo

New Moon—April 1 in Aries
Full Moon—April 16 in Libra

New Moon—May 1 in Taurus
Full Moon—May 15 in Scorpio
New Moon—May 30 in Gemini

Full Moon—June 14 in Sagittarius
New Moon—June 29 in Cancer

Full Moon—July 13 in Capricorn
New Moon—July 29 in Leo

Full Moon—August 11 in Aquarius
New Moon—August 27 in Virgo

Full Moon—September 10 in Pisces
New Moon—September 25 in Libra

Full Moon—October 10 in Aries
New Moon—October 25 in Scorpio

Full Moon—November 8 in Taurus
New Moon—November 23 in Sagittarius

Full Moon—December 8 in Gemini
New Moon—December 23 in Capricorn

Moon Sign Timing

To forecast the daily emotional "weather," to determine your monthly high and low days, or to synchronize your activities with the cycles of the moon, take note of the moon's sign under your daily forecast at the end of the book. Here are some of the activities favored and the moods you are likely to encounter under each moon sign.

Moon in Aries

Get moving! The new moon in Aries is an ideal time to start new projects. Everyone is pushy, raring to go, rather impatient, and short-tempered. Leave details and follow-up for later. Competitive sports or martial arts are great ways to let off steam. Quiet types could use some assertiveness, but it's a great day for dynamos. Be careful not to step on too many toes.

Moon in Taurus

It's time to lay the foundations for success. Do solid, methodical tasks like follow-through or backup work. Make investments, buy real estate, do appraisals, do some hard bargaining. Attend to your property. Get out in the country or spend some time in your garden. Enjoy creature comforts, music, a good dinner, sensual love-making. Forget starting a diet—this is a day when you'll feel self-indulgent.

Moon in Gemini

Talk means action today. Telephone, write letters, fax! Make new contacts, stay in touch with steady customers. You can juggle lots of tasks today. It's a great time for mental activity of any kind. Don't try to pin people down— they, too, are feeling restless. Keep it light. Flirtations and socializing are good. Watch gossip—and don't give away secrets.

Moon in Cancer

This is a moody, sensitive, emotional time. People respond to personal attention, to mothering. Stay at home, have a family dinner, call your mother. Nostalgia, memories, and psychic powers are heightened. You'll want to hang on to people and things (don't clean out your closets now). You could have shrewd insights into what oth-

17

ers really need and want. Pay attention to dreams, intuition, and gut reactions.

Moon in Leo

Everybody is in a much more confident, warm, generous mood. It's a good day to ask for a raise, show what you can do, dress like a star. People will respond to flattery, enjoy a bit of drama and theater. You may be extravagant, treat yourself royally, and show off a bit—don't break the bank! Be careful you don't promise more than you can deliver.

Moon in Virgo

Do practical down-to-earth chores. Review your budget, make repairs, be an efficiency expert. Not a day to ask for a raise. Tend to personal care and maintenance. Have a health checkup, go on a diet, buy vitamins or health food. Make your home spotless. Take care of details and piled-up chores. Reorganize your work and life so they run more smoothly and efficiently. Save money. Be prepared for others to be in a critical, faultfinding mood.

Moon in Libra

Attend to legal matters. Negotiate contracts. Arbitrate. Do things with your favorite partner. Socialize. Be romantic. Buy a special gift, a beautiful object. Decorate yourself or your surroundings. Buy new clothes. Throw a party. Have an elegant, romantic evening. Smooth over any ruffled feathers. Avoid confrontations. Stick to civilized discussions.

Moon in Scorpio

This is a day to do things with passion. You'll have excellent concentration and focus. Try not to get too intense emotionally. Avoid sharp exchanges with loved ones. Others may tend to go to extremes, get jealous, overreact.

Great for troubleshooting, problem solving, research, scientific work—and making love. Pay attention to those psychic vibes.

Moon in Sagittarius

A great time for travel, philosophical discussions, setting long-range career goals. Work out, do sports, buy athletic equipment. Others will be feeling upbeat, exuberant, and adventurous. Risk taking is favored. You may feel like taking a gamble, betting on the horses, visiting a local casino, buying a lottery ticket. Teaching, writing, and spiritual activities also get the green light. Relax outdoors. Take care of animals.

Moon in Capricorn

You can accomplish a lot today, so get on the ball! Attend to business. Issues concerning your basic responsibilities, duties, family, and elderly parents could crop up. You'll be expected to deliver on promises. Weed out the deadwood from your life. Get a dental checkup. Not a good day for gambling or taking risks.

Moon in Aquarius

A great day for doing things with groups—clubs, meetings, outings, politics, parties. Campaign for your candidate. Work for a worthy cause. Deal with larger issues that affect humanity—the environment and metaphysical questions. Buy a computer or electronic gadget. Watch TV. Wear something outrageous. Try something you've never done before. Present an original idea. Don't stick to a rigid schedule—go with the flow. Take a class in meditation, mind control, yoga.

Moon in Pisces

This can be a very creative day, so let your imagination work overtime. Film, theater, music, ballet could inspire you. Spend some time alone, resting and reflecting, reading or writing poetry. Daydreams can also be profitable. Help those less fortunate. Lend a listening ear to someone who may be feeling blue. Don't overindulge in self-pity or escapism, however. People are especially vulnerable to substance abuse now. Turn your thoughts to romance and someone special.

How to Handle Eclipses

One of the most amazing phenomena, which many of us take for granted, is the spatial relationship between the sun and moon. How many of us have ever noticed or marveled that, relative to our viewpoint here on earth, both the largest source of energy (the sun) and the smallest (the moon) appear to be almost exactly the same size? Or wondered what would happen if the moon's orbit became closer to earth or farther away?

This fascinating relationship is most evident to us at the time of the solar eclipse, when the moon is directly aligned with the sun and so nearly covers it that scientists use the moment of eclipse to study solar flares. The darkening of the sun has been used in history and mythology to indicate dire happenings ahead. In some parts of the world, people hide in their homes during the darkening of the sun. When the two most powerful forces in astrology—the sun and moon—are lined up, we're sure to feel the effects both in world events and in our personal lives. Both solar and lunar eclipses are times when our natural rhythms are changed, depending on where the eclipse falls in your horoscope. If the eclipse falls on or close to your birthday, you're going to have important changes in your life, perhaps a turning point.

Lunar Eclipses

Lunar eclipse: A momentary "turn off" that could help us turn our lives around.

A lunar eclipse happens during a full moon when the

earth moves exactly between the sun and moon, breaking their natural monthly opposition. Normally, the earth is not on a level plane; otherwise, eclipses would occur every month. During a lunar eclipse, the earth "short circuits" the connection between the sun and moon. The effect on us can be either confusion or clarity. Our subconscious lunar energies, which normally respond to the rhythmic cycle of opposing sun and moon, are momentarily turned off. This could cause a bewildering disorientation that intensifies our insecurities. On the other hand, this moment of clarity might give us insights that could help change destructive emotional patterns such as addictions.

Solar Eclipses

Solar eclipse: Deep feelings come to the surface.

The solar eclipse occurs during the new moon. This time, the moon blocks the sun's energies as it passes exactly between the sun and the earth. In astrological interpretation, the moon darkens the objective, conscious force, represented by the sun, allowing subconscious lunar forces, which activate our deepest emotions, to dominate. Emotional truths can be revealed or emotions can run wild, as our solar objectivity is cut off. If your sign is affected, you may find yourself beginning a period of work on a deep inner level. And you may have psychic experiences or deep feelings that come to the surface.

You'll start feeling the energies of an upcoming eclipse a few days after the previous new or full moon. The energy continues to intensify until the actual eclipse, then disperses for three or four days. So plan ahead at least a week or more before an eclipse, then allow several days afterward for the natural rhythms to return. Try not to make major moves during this period. (It's not a great time to get married, change jobs, or buy a home, for instance.)

Eclipses in 2003

There are four eclipses this year.

Full Moon and Lunar Eclipse—May 15 in Scorpio

New Moon and Solar Eclipse—May 30 in Gemini
Full Moon and Lunar Eclipse—November 8 in Taurus
New Moon and Solar Eclipse—November 23 in Sagittarius

When the Planets Go Backward

All the planets, except for the sun and moon, have times when they appear to move backward—or retrograde—as it seems from our point of view on earth. At these times, planets do not work as they normally do. So it's best to "take a break" from that planet's energies in our life and to do some work on an inner level.

Mercury Retrograde: Taming the Trickster

Mercury goes retrograde most often, and its effects can be especially irritating. When it reaches a short distance ahead of the sun several times a year, it seems to move backward from our point of view. Astrologers often compare retrograde motion to the optical illusion that occurs when we ride on a train that passes another train traveling at a different speed—the second train appears to be moving in reverse.

What this means to you is that the Mercury-ruled areas of your life—analytical thought processes, communications, scheduling—are subject to all kinds of confusion. Be prepared. People may change their minds, renege on commitments. Communications equipment can break down. Schedules may be changed on short notice. People are late for appointments or don't show up at all. Traffic is terrible. Major purchases malfunction, don't work out, or get delivered in the wrong color. Letters don't arrive or are delivered to the wrong address. Employees will make errors that have to be corrected later. Contracts don't work out or must be renegotiated.

Since most of us can't put our lives on "hold" during Mercury retrogrades, we should learn to tame the trickster and make it work for us. The key is in the prefix *re-*. This is the time to go back over things in your life, *re*flect on what you've done during the previous months. Now you can get deeper insights, spot errors you've missed. So take time to *re*view and *re*evaluate what has happened. *Re*st and *re*ward yourself—it's a good time to take a vacation, especially if you *re*visit a favorite place. *Re*organize your work and finish up projects that are backed up. Clean out your desk and closets. Throw away what you can't *re*cycle. If you must sign contracts or agreements, do so with a contingency clause that lets you *re*evaluate the terms later.

Postpone major purchases or commitments for the time being. Don't get married (unless you're *re*marrying the same person). Try not to *re*ly on other people keeping appointments, contracts, or agreements to the letter; have several alternatives. Double-check and *re*ad between the lines. Don't buy anything connected with communications or transportation (if you must, be sure to cover yourself).

Mercury retrograding through your sun sign will intensify its effect on your life.

If Mercury was retrograde when you were born, you may be one of the lucky people who don't suffer the frustrations of this period. If so, your mind probably works in a very intuitive, insightful way.

The sign in which Mercury is retrograding can give you an idea of what's in store—as well as the sun signs that will be especially challenged.

MERCURY RETROGRADES IN 2003
Mercury has four retrograde periods this year.
  January 2 to January 22 in Capricorn
  April 26 to May 20 in Taurus
  August 28 to September 20 in Virgo
  December 17 to January 6, 2004 in Capricorn

Venus Retrograde

Retrograding Venus can cause your relationships to take a backward step, or it can make you extravagant and impractical. Shopping till you drop and buying what you cannot afford are trip-ups at this time. It's *not* a good time to redecorate—you'll hate the color of the walls later. Postpone getting a new hairstyle. Try not to fall in love either. But if you wish to make amends in an already troubled relationship, make peaceful overtures at this time.

VENUS RETROGRADES IN 2003
There is no Venus retrograde period in 2003.

Mars Tips: When to Push and When to Hold Back!

Mars shows how and when to get where you want to go. Timing your moves with Mars on your side can give you a big push. On the other hand, pushing Mars the wrong way can guarantee that you'll run into frustrations in every corner. Your best times to forge ahead are during the weeks when Mars is traveling through your sun sign or your Mars sign (look these up at the end of Chapter 4 on the planets). Also consider times when Mars is in a compatible sign (fire with air signs, or earth with water signs). You'll be sure to have planetary power on your side.

In 2003, Mars spends six months in Pisces from June 17 to December 16. This is especially significant because the movements of Mars will be activating the volatile planet Uranus (the planet of awakenings), which is in the process of making a major move from Aquarius to Pisces. As Uranus dips its toe in the watery sign of Pisces, Mars will be on hand to give it a warm welcome! This could be quite an unstable time, as we make a leap into the future. Be alert for sudden changes around June 23 and again in mid-September, when these two volatile planets align.

MARS RETROGRADE
Hold your fire when Mars retrogrades in 2003, especially if you are a Pisces. Be especially careful around the ocean or bodies of water. Since this happens during the warm beachtime months of August and September, beware of dangerous tides and prowling sharks. Now is the time to exercise patience. Let someone else run with the ball, especially if it's the opposing team. You may feel you're not accomplishing

24

much, but that's the right idea. Slow down and work off any frustrations at the gym. It's also best to postpone buying mechanical devices, which are Mars-ruled, and to take extra care when handling sharp objects.

Be sure to use the appropriate protective gear when playing sports, especially foot gear. Don't take unnecessary chances. This is not the time for daredevil moves! Pace yourself. Pay extra attention to your health, since you may be especially vulnerable at this time.

MARS RETROGRADES IN 2003

Mars retrogrades in 2003 for almost two months: July 29 to September 27 in Pisces.

When Other Planets Retrograde

The slower-moving planets stay retrograde for months at a time (Saturn, Jupiter, Neptune, Uranus, and Pluto). When Saturn is retrograde, it's an uphill battle with self-discipline. You may feel more like hanging out at the beach than getting things done. Neptune retrograde promotes a dreamy escapism from reality, when you may feel you're in a fog (Pisces will feel this, especially). Uranus retrograde may mean setbacks in areas where there have been sudden changes, when you may be forced to regroup or reevaluate the situation. Since Mars is activating Uranus this year, it could be a significantly unstable time. Think of this as an adjustment period, a time to think things over and allow new ideas to develop. Pluto retrograde is a time to work on establishing proportion and balance in areas where there have been recent dramatic transformations.

When the planets move forward again, there's a shift in the atmosphere. Activities connected with each planet start moving ahead, plans that were stalled get rolling. Make a special note of those days on your calendar and proceed accordingly.

OTHER RETROGRADES IN 2003

The five slower-moving planets all go retrograde in 2003.

Jupiter retrogrades from December 4, 2002 to April 4, 2003 in Leo.

Saturn retrogrades from October 11, 2002 to February 22, 2003, and again from October 25, 2003 to March 7, 2004.

Uranus retrogrades from June 6 in Pisces back to Aquarius on September 15, then turns direct on November 8 in Aquarius.

Neptune retrogrades from May 15 to November 22 in Aquarius.

Pluto retrogrades from March 22 to August 28 in Sagittarius.

CHAPTER 3

A Crash Course in Astrology: What You Need to Know

Could you be your own astrologer? You may be wondering if you can access this special realm of knowledge without years of study. Even though astrology is a very precise art that uses an ancient language of symbols, the basic principles are not difficult to learn. And once you know the basics, you can penetrate beyond the realm of your sun sign into the realm of the other planets. The more you know, the more you'll want to know.

Here's a nontechnical guide to help you find your way around the world of astrology.

Where the Signs Are

First, let's get our "sign language" straight because, for most readers, that's the starting point of astrology.

Signs are actually a type of celestial real estate, located on the *zodiac*, an imaginary 360-degree belt circling the earth. This belt is divided into twelve equal 30-degree portions, and these are the signs. There's confusion about the difference between the *signs* and the *constellations* of the zodiac. Constellations are patterns of stars that originally marked the twelve divisions, like signposts. Though a sign is named after the constellation that once marked the same area, the constellations are no longer in the same place relative to the earth they were centuries ago. Over hundreds of years, the earth's orbit has shifted, so that from our point of view here on earth the constellations moved.

However, the signs remain in place. Most Western astrologers use the twelve-equal-part division of the zodiac. However, there are some methods of astrology that do still use the constellations instead of the signs.

Most people think of themselves in terms of their *sun sign.* A sun sign refers to the sign the sun is orbiting through at a given moment (from our point of view here on earth). For instance "I'm an Aries" means that the sun was passing through Aries when that person was born. However, there are nine other planets (plus asteroids, fixed stars, and sensitive points) that also form our total astrological personality, and some or many of these will be located in other signs. No one is completely "Aries," with all their astrological components in one sign! (Please note that, in astrology, the sun and moon are usually referred to as "planets," though of course they're not.)

As mentioned before, the sun signs are areas on the zodiac. They do not *do* anything (planets are the doers). However, they are associated with many things, depending on their location.

What Makes a Sign Special?

What makes Aries the sign of go-getters, Taurus savvy with money, Gemini talk a blue streak, and Sagittarius footloose? Definitions of the signs are not accidental. They are derived from different combinations of four concepts: a sign's *element, quality, polarity,* and *place (order)* on the zodiac.

Take the element of fire: it's hot, passionate. Then add the active cardinal mode. Give it a jolt of positive energy, and place it first in line. And doesn't that sound like the active, me-first, driving, hotheaded, energetic Aries?

Then take the element of earth: it's practical, sensual, where things grow. Add the fixed, stable mode. Give it energy that reacts to its surroundings, that settles in. Put it after Aries. Now you've got a good idea of how sensual, earthy Taurus operates.

Another way to grasp the idea is to pretend you're doing

a magical puzzle based on the numbers that can divide into twelve (the number of signs): 4, 3, and 2. There are four "building blocks" or elements, three ways a sign operates (qualities), and two polarities. These alternate in turn around the zodiac, with a different combination coming up for each sign.

The Four Elements

First, consider the four elements that describe the physical concept of the sign. Is it *fiery* (dynamic), *earthy* (practical), *airy* (mental), *watery* (emotional)? Therefore, there are three zodiac signs of each of the four elements: *fire* (Aries, Leo, Sagittarius); *earth* (Taurus, Virgo, Capricorn); *air* (Gemini, Libra, Aquarius); *water* (Cancer, Scorpio, Pisces). These are the same elements that make up our planet: earth, air, fire, and water. But astrology uses the elements as *symbols* that link our body and psyche to the rhythms of the planets.

Fire signs spread warmth and enthusiasm. They are able to fire up or motivate others. They have hot tempers. These are people who make ideas catch fire and spring into existence. Earth signs are the builders of the zodiac who follow through after the initiative of fire signs to make things happen. These people are solid, practical realists who enjoy material things and sensual pleasures. They are interested in ideas that can be used to achieve concrete results. Air signs are mental people, great communicators. Following the consolidating earth signs, they'll reach out to inspire others through the use of words, social contacts, discussion, and debate. Water signs complete each four-sign series adding the ingredients of emotion, compassion, and imagination. Water sign people are nonverbal communicators who attune themselves to their surroundings and react through the medium of feelings.

The Three Qualities

The second consideration when defining a sign is how it will operate. Will it take the initiative, or move slowly and deliberately, or adapt easily? It's *quality* (or modality) will tell. There are three qualities and four signs of each quality: cardinal, fixed, and mutable.

Cardinal signs are the start-up signs that begin each season (Aries, Cancer, Libra, Capricorn). These people love to be active, involved in projects. They are usually on the fast track to success, impatient to get things under way. *Fixed signs* (Taurus, Leo, Scorpio, Aquarius) move steadily, always in control. They happen in the middle of a season, after the initial character of the season is established. Fixed signs are naturally more centered. They tend to move more deliberately, do things more slowly but thoroughly. They govern parts of your horoscope where you take root and integrate your experiences. *Mutable signs* (Gemini, Virgo, Sagittarius, Pisces) embody the principle of distribution. These are the signs that break up the cycle, then prepare the way for a change by distributing the energy to the next group. Mutables are flexible, adaptable, communicative. They can move in many directions easily, darting around obstacles.

The Two Polarities

In addition to an element and a quality, each sign has a *polarity,* either a positive or a negative electrical charge that generates energy around the zodiac, like a giant battery. Polarity refers to opposites, which you could also define as masculine/feminine, yin/yang, active/reactive. Alternating around the zodiac, the six fire and air signs are positive, active, masculine, and yang in polarity. These signs are open, expanding outward. The six earth and water signs are reactive, negative, and yin in polarity. They are nurturing and receptive, which allows the energy to develop and take shape. All positive energy would be like a car without brakes. All negative energy would be like a stalled vehicle, going nowhere. Both polarities are needed in balanced proportion.

The Order of the Signs: Their Place

Finally we must consider the *order* of the signs—that is the *place* each sign occupies in the zodiac. This consideration is vital to the balance of the zodiac and the transmission of energy throughout the zodiac. Each sign is quite different from its neighbors on either side. Yet each seems to grow out of its predecessor like links in a chain. And each transmits a synthesis of energy gathered along the chain to the following sign—beginning with the fiery, active, positive, cardinal sign of Aries and ending with the watery, mutable, reactive Pisces.

The table shows how the signs shape up according to the four characteristics discussed.

How the Signs Add Up

Sign	Element	Quality	Polarity	Place
Aries	fire	cardinal	masculine	first
Taurus	earth	fixed	feminine	second
Gemini	air	mutable	masculine	third
Cancer	water	cardinal	feminine	fourth
Leo	fire	fixed	masculine	fifth
Virgo	earth	mutable	feminine	sixth
Libra	air	cardinal	masculine	seventh
Scorpio	water	fixed	feminine	eighth
Sagittarius	fire	mutable	masculine	ninth
Capricorn	earth	cardinal	feminine	tenth
Aquarius	air	fixed	masculine	eleventh
Pisces	water	mutable	feminine	twelfth

The Houses and the Horoscope Chart

A horoscope chart is a map of the heavens at a given moment in time. It looks somewhat like a wheel divided with twelve spokes. In between each of the "spokes" is a section called a *house*. Each house deals with a different area of life and is influenced by a special sign and a planet. In addition, the house is governed by the sign passing over the spoke (or cusp of the house) at that particular moment. For example, the first house is naturally associated with Aries and Mars. However, if Capricorn was the sign passing over the house cusp at the time the chart was cast, that house would have a Capricorn influence as well.

The houses start at the left center spoke (the number 9 position if you were reading a clock) and are read *counterclockwise* around the chart. Astrologers look at the houses to tell in what area of life an event is happening or about to happen.

The First House: Home of Aries and Mars

This is the house of "firsts"—the first impression you make, how you initiate matters, the image you choose to project. This is where you advertise yourself, where you project your personality. Planets that fall here will intensify the way you come across to others. Often the first house will project an entirely different type of personality than the sun sign. For instance, a Capricorn with Leo in the first house will come across as much more flamboyant than the average Capricorn. The sign passing over the first house at the time of your birth is known as your *ascendant,* or *rising sign.*

The Second House: Home of Taurus and Venus

This house is where you experience the material world— what you value. Here are your attitudes about money, possessions, finances, whatever belongs to you, and what you own, as well as your earning and spending capacity. On a deeper level, this house reveals your sense of self-worth, the inner values that draw wealth in various forms.

The Third House: Home of Gemini and Mercury

This house describes how you communicate with others, how you reach out to others nearby, and how you interact with the immediate environment. It shows how your thinking process works and the way you express your thoughts. Are you articulate or tongue-tied? Can you think on your feet? This house also shows your first relationships, your experiences with brothers and sisters, and how you deal with people close to you such as your neighbors or pals. It's where you take short trips, write letters, or use the telephone. It shows how your mind works in terms of left-brain logical and analytical functions.

The Fourth House: Home of Cancer and the Moon

The fourth house shows the foundation of life, the psychological underpinnings. At the bottom of the chart, this house shows how you are nurtured and made to feel secure—your roots! It shows your early home environment and the circumstances at the end of your life (your final "home") as well as the place you call home now. Astrologers look here for information about the parental nurturers in your life.

The Fifth House: Home of Leo and the Sun

The fifth house, the Leo house, is where the creative potential develops. Here you express yourself and procreate in the sense that children are outgrowths of your creative ability. But this house most represents your inner childlike self who delights in play. If your inner security has been established by the time you reach this house, you are now free to have fun, romance, and love affairs and to give of yourself. This is also the place astrologers look for playful love affairs, flirtations, and brief romantic encounters (rather than long-term commitments).

The Sixth House: Home of Virgo and Mercury

The sixth house has been called the "repair and maintenance" department. This house shows how you take care of your body and organize yourself to perform efficiently in the world. Here is where you get things done, where you look after others, and fulfill service duties such as taking care of pets. Here is your daily survival, your "job" (as opposed to your career, which is the domain of the tenth house), your diet, and your health and fitness regimens.

The Seventh House: Home of Libra and Venus

This house shows your attitude toward partners and those with whom you enter commitments, contracts, or agreements. Here is the way you relate to others, as well as your close, intimate, one-on-one relationships (including open enemies—those you "face off" with). Open hostilities, lawsuits, divorces, and marriages happen here. If the first house represents the "I," the seventh or opposite house is the "not-I"—the complementary partner you attract by the way you come across. If you are having trouble with partnerships, consider what you are attracting by the energies of your first and seventh house.

The Eighth House: Home of Scorpio and Pluto (also Mars)

The eighth house refers to how you merge with something or someone, and how you handle power and control. This is one of the most mysterious and powerful houses, where your energy transforms itself from "I" to "we." As you give up power and control by uniting with something or someone, two kinds of energies merge and become something greater, leading to a regeneration of the self on a higher level. Here are your attitudes toward sex, shared resources, taxes (what you share with the government). Because this house involves what belongs to others, you face issues of control and power struggles, or undergo a deep psychological transformation as you bond with another. Here you transcend yourself with dreams, drugs, and occult or psychic experiences that reflect the collective unconscious.

The Ninth House: Home of Sagittarius and Jupiter

The ninth house shows your search for wisdom and higher knowledge—your belief system. As the third house represents the "lower mind," its opposite on the wheel, the ninth house, is the "higher mind"—the abstract, intuitive, spiritual mind that asks "big" questions like "Why are we here?" After the third house has explored what was close at hand, the ninth stretches out to broaden you mentally with higher education and travel. Here you stretch spiritually with religious activity. Since you are concerned with how everything is related, you tend to push boundaries, take risks. Here is where you express your ideas in a book or thesis, where you pontificate, philosophize, or preach.

The Tenth House: Home of Capricorn and Saturn

The tenth house is associated with your public life and high-profile activities. Located directly overhead at the "high noon" position on the horoscope wheel, this is the most "visible" house in the chart, the one where the world sees you. It deals with your career (but not your routine "job") and your reputation. Here is where you go public, take on responsibilities (as opposed to the fourth house, where you stay home). This will affect the career you choose and your "public relations." This house is also associated with your father figure or the main authority figure in your life.

The Eleventh House: Home of Aquarius and Uranus

The eleventh house is where you extend yourself to a group, a goal, or a belief system. This house is where you define what you really want, the kinds of friends you have, your political affiliations, and the kind of groups you identify with as an equal. Here is where you become concerned with "what other people think" or where you rebel against social conventions. Here is where you could become a socially conscious humanitarian or a partygoing social butterfly. It's where you look to others to stimulate you and discover your kinship to the rest of humanity. The sign on this house can help you understand what you gain and lose from friendships.

The Twelfth House: Home of Pisces and Neptune

The twelfth house is where the boundaries between yourself and others become blurred, and you become selfless. Old-fashioned astrologers used to put a rather negative spin on this house, calling it the "house of self-undoing." When we "undo ourselves," we surrender control, boundaries, limits, and rules. But instead of being self-undoing, the twelfth house can be a place of great creativity and talent. It is the place where you can tap into the collective unconscious, where your imagination is limitless.

In your trip around the zodiac, you've gone from the "I" of self-assertion in the first house to the final house symbolizing the dissolution that happens before rebirth. It's where accumulated experiences are processed in the unconscious. Spiritually oriented astrologers look to this house for evidence of past lives and karma. Places where we go for solitude or to do spiritual or reparatory work such as retreats, religious institutions, and hospitals belong to the twelfth house. Here is also where we withdraw from society voluntarily or involuntarily, put to prison because of antisocial activity. Selfless giving through charitable acts is part of this house, as is helpless receiving or dependence on charity.

In your daily life, the twelfth house reveals your deepest intimacies, your best-kept secrets, especially those you hide from yourself and keep repressed deep in the unconscious. It is where we surrender a sense of a separate self to a deep feeling of wholeness, such as selfless service in religion or any activity that involves merging with the greater whole. Many sports stars have important planets in the twelfth house that enable them to play in the "zone," finding an inner, almost mystical, strength that transcends their limits.

Who's Home in Your Houses?

Houses are stronger or weaker depending on how many planets are inhabiting them. If there are many planets in a given house, it follows that the activities of that house will be especially important in your life. If the planet that rules the house is also located there, this too adds power to the house.

In the next chapter we will visit the planets.

CHAPTER 4

The Guide to Your Galaxy: Visit All Your Planets

Your personal galaxy includes nine other planets besides the sun (the moon is also regarded as a "planet"). Each planet represents a basic force in your life, and the sign where it is placed represents how this force will manifest. Visit all your planets, not just your sun sign, for a complete picture of your astrological personality.

It may be easiest to imagine the planet as a person with a choice of twelve different roles to play. In some roles the planet will be more outgoing and aggressive; in other roles the more thoughtful or spiritual side of its nature will be expressed.

Whether a planet will play a starring or supporting role depends on its position in your horoscope. A planet in the first house, especially one that's close to your rising sign, is sure to be a featured player. Planets that are grouped together usually operate like a team, playing off each other, rather than expressing their energy singularly. A planet that stands alone, away from the others, is usually outstanding and sometimes calls the shots.

Each planet has two signs where it is especially at home. These are called its *dignities*. The most favorable place for a planet is in the sign or signs it rules; the next best place is in a sign where it is *exalted*, or especially harmonious. On the other hand, there are places in the horoscope where a planet has to work harder to play its role. These places are called the planets *detriment* and *fall*. The sign opposite a planet's rulership, which embodies the opposite area of life, is its *detriment*. The sign opposite its exaltation is its *fall*. Though these terms may suggest unfortunate circumstances for the planet, that is not always true. In fact, a planet that is debilitated can actually be more complete because it must stretch itself to meet the challenges of living in a more difficult sign. Like world leaders who've had to struggle for greatness, this planet may actually develop great strength and character.

Here's a list of the best places for each planet to be. Note that, as new planets were discovered, they replaced the traditional rulers of signs which best complemented their energies.

ARIES—Mars
TAURUS—Venus, in its most sensual form
GEMINI—Mercury, in its communicative role
CANCER—the moon
LEO—the sun
VIRGO—also Mercury, this time in its more critical capacity
LIBRA—also Venus, in its more aesthetic, judgmental form
SCORPIO—Pluto, replacing Mars, the sign's original ruler
SAGITTARIUS—Jupiter
CAPRICORN—Saturn
AQUARIUS—Uranus, replacing Saturn, its original ruler
PISCES—Neptune, replacing Jupiter, its original ruler

A person who has many planets in exalted signs is lucky indeed, for here is where the planet can accomplish the most and be its most influential and creative.

SUN—exalted in Aries, where its energy creates action
MOON—exalted in Taurus, where instincts and reactions operate on a highly creative level
MERCURY—exalted in Aquarius, where it can reach analytical heights
VENUS—exalted in Pisces, a sign whose sensitivity encourages love and creativity
MARS—exalted in Capricorn, a sign that puts energy to work productively
JUPITER—exalted in Cancer, where it encourages nurturing and growth

39

SATURN—at home in Libra, where it steadies the scales of justice and promotes balanced, responsible judgment

URANUS—powerful in Scorpio, where it promotes transformation

NEPTUNE—especially favored in Cancer, where it gains the security to transcend to a higher state

PLUTO—exalted in Pisces, where it dissolves the old cycle to make way for transition to the new

The Sun Is Always Top of the List

Your sun sign is the part of you that shines brightest. Then other planets add special coloration that sets you apart from other members of your sign. If you know a person's sun sign, you already know some useful generic qualities. But when you know all the planets, you have a much more accurate profile and can predict more accurately how that individual will act. The sun is just one card in your hand. When you know the other planets, you can really play to win!

Since the sun is always the first consideration, it is important to treat it as the star of the show. It is your conscious ego. It is always center stage, even when sharing a house or a sign with several other planets. This is why sun sign astrology works for so many people. In chart interpretations, the sun can also play the parental role.

The sun rules the sign of Leo, gaining strength through the pride, dignity, and confidence of this fixed, fiery personality. It is exalted in "me-first" Aries. In its detriment, Aquarius, the sun ego is strengthened through group participation and social consciousness rather than through self-centeredness. Note how many Aquarius people are involved in politics, social work, public life, and follow the demands of their sun sign to be spokesperson for a group. In its fall, Libra, the sun needs the strength of a partner—an "other"—to enhance balance and self-expression.

Like your sun sign, each of the other nine planet's personalities is colored by the sign it is passing through at the time. For example, Mercury, the planet that rules the way you communicate, will express itself in a dynamic, head-strong Aries way if it is passing through the sign of Aries when you were born. You will communicate in a much different way if it is passing through the slower, more patient sign of Taurus. And so on through the list. Here's a rundown of the planets and how they behave in every sign.

The Moon Expresses Your Inner Feelings

The moon can teach you about the inner side of yourself, your needs and secrets, as well as those of others. It is your most personal planet—the receptive, reflective, female, nurturing side of you. And it reflects who you were nurtured by—the "mother" or mother figure in your chart. In a man's chart, the moon position also describes his female, receptive, emotional side as well as the woman in his life who will have the deepest effect. (Venus reveals the kind of woman who attracts him physically.)

The sign the moon was passing through at your birth reflects your instinctive emotional nature, what appeals to you subconsciously. Since accurate moon tables are too extensive for this book, check through these descriptions to find the moon sign that feels most familiar. Or, better yet, have your chart calculated by a computer service to get your accurate moon placement.

The moon rules maternal Cancer and is exalted in Taurus—both comforting, home-loving signs where the natural emotional energies of the moon are easily and productively expressed. But when the moon is in the opposite signs—in its Capricorn detriment and its Scorpio fall—it leaves the comfortable nest and deals with emotional issues of power and achievement in the outside world. Those of you with the moon in these signs will find your emotional role more challenging in life.

Moon in Aries

You are an idealistic, impetuous person who falls in and out of love easily. This placement makes you both independent and ardent. You love a challenge, but could cool once your quarry is captured. You should cultivate patience and tolerance. Otherwise, you might gravitate toward those who treat you rough, just for the sake of challenge and excitement.

Moon in Taurus

You are a sentimental soul who is very fond of the good life. You gravitate toward solid, secure relationships. You like displays of affection and creature comforts—all the tangible trappings of a cozy, safe, calm atmosphere. You are sensual and steady emotionally, but very stubborn and determined. You can't be pushed and tend to dislike changes. You should make an effort to broaden your horizons and to take a risk sometimes.

Moon in Gemini

You crave mental stimulation and variety in life, which you usually get through an ever-varied social life or the excitement of flirtation, or multiple professional involvements—or all of these. You may marry more than once and have a rather chaotic emotional life due to your difficulty with commitment and settling down. Be sure to find a partner who is as outgoing as you are. You will have to learn at some point to focus your energies because you tend to be somewhat fragmented—to do two things at once, to have two homes, even to have two lovers. If you can find a creative way to express your many-faceted nature, you'll be ahead of the game.

Moon in Cancer

This is the most powerful lunar position. It is sure to make a deep imprint on your character. Your needs are very much associated with your reaction to the needs of others. You are very sensitive and self-protective, though some of you may mask this with a hard shell. This placement also gives an excellent memory, keen intuition, and an uncanny ability to perceive the needs of others. All of the lunar phases will affect you, especially full moons and eclipses, so you would do well to mark them on your calendar. Because you're happiest at home, you may work at home or turn your office into a second home where you can nurture and comfort people. (You may tend to "mother the world.") With natural psychic and intuitive ability, you might be drawn to occult work in some way. Or you may get professionally involved with providing food and shelter to others.

Moon in Leo

This warm, passionate moon takes everything to heart. You are attracted to all that is noble, generous, and aristocratic in life (and may be a bit of a snob). You have an innate ability to take command emotionally, but you do need strong support, loyalty, and loud applause from those you love. You are possessive of your loved ones and your turf, and will roar if anyone threatens to take over your territory.

Moon in Virgo

You are rather cool until you decide if others measure up. But once someone or something meets your ideal standards, you hold up your end of the arrangement perfectly. You may, in fact, drive yourself too hard to attain some notion of perfection. Try to be a bit easier on yourself and others. Don't always act the censor! You love to be the teacher. You are drawn to situations where you can change others for the better, but sometimes you must learn to accept others for what they are. Enjoy what you have!

Moon in Libra

A partnership-oriented moon, you may find it difficult to be alone or to do things alone. After you have learned emotional balance by leaning on yourself first, you can have excellent relationships. It is best for you to avoid extremes, which set your scales swinging and can make your love life precarious. You thrive in a rather conservative, traditional, romantic relationship where you receive attention and flattery—but not possessiveness—from your partner. You'll be your most charming in an elegant, harmonious atmosphere.

Moon in Scorpio

This is a moon that enjoys and responds to intense, passionate feelings. You may go to extremes and have a very dramatic emotional life, full of ardor, suspicion, jealousy, and obsession. It would be much healthier to channel your need for power and control into meaningful work. This is a good position for anyone in the fields of medicine, police work, research, the occult, psychoanalysis, or intuitive work, because life-and-death situations don't faze you. However, you do take personal disappointments very hard.

Moon in Sagittarius

You take life's ups and downs with good humor and the proverbial grain of salt. You'll love 'em and leave 'em, taking off on a great adventure at a moment's notice. "Born free" could be your slogan. Attracted by the exotic, you have wanderlust mentally and physically. You may be too much in search of new mental and spiritual stimulation to ever settle down.

Moon in Capricorn

Are you ever accused of being too cool and calculating? You have an earthy side, but you take prestige and position very seriously. Your strong drive to succeed extends to your romantic life where you will be devoted to improving your lifestyle and rising to the top. A structured situation where you can advance methodically makes you feel wonderfully secure. You may be attracted to someone older or very much younger or from a different social world. It may be difficult to look at the lighter side of emotional relationships. However, the "up" side of this moon in the sign of its detriment is that you tend to be very dutiful and responsible to those you care for.

Moon in Aquarius

You are a people collector with many friends of all backgrounds. You are happiest surrounded by people and may feel uneasy when left alone. Though you usually stay friends with lovers, intense emotions and demanding one-on-one relationships turn you off. You don't like anything to be too rigid or scheduled. Though tolerant and understanding, you can be emotionally unpredictable and may opt for an unconventional love life. With plenty of space, you will be able to sustain relationships with liberal, freedom-loving types.

Moon in Pisces

You are very responsive and empathetic to others, especially if they have problems or are the underdog. (Be on guard against attracting too many people with sob stories!) You'll be happiest if you can express your creative imagination in the arts or in the spiritual or healing professions. Because you may tend to escape in fantasies or overreact to the moods of others, you need an emotional anchor to help you keep a firm foothold in reality. Steer clear of too much escapism (especially in alcohol) or reclusiveness. Places near water soothe your moods. Working in a field that gives you emotional variety will also help you be productive.

Close Neighbors: Mercury, Venus, and Mars

These planets work in your immediate personal life.

Mercury affects how you communicate and how your mental processes work. Are you a quick study who grasps information rapidly? Or do you learn more slowly and thoroughly? How is your concentration? Can you express yourself easily? Are you a good writer? All these questions can be answered by your Mercury placement.

Venus shows what you react to. What turns you on? What appeals to you aesthetically? Are you charming to others? Are you attractive to look at? Your taste, your refinement, your sense of balance and proportion are all Venus-ruled.

Mars is your outgoing energy, your drive and ambition. Do you reach out for new adventures? Are you assertive? Are you motivated? Self-confident? Hot-tempered? How you channel your energy and drive is revealed by your Mars placement.

Mercury Says It All

Since Mercury never travels far from the sun, read Mercury in your sun sign, then the sign preceding and following it. Then decide which reflects the way your mind works.

Mercury in Aries

Your mind is very active and assertive. You never hesitate to say what you think, never shy away from a battle. In fact, you may relish a verbal confrontation. Tact is not your strong point, so you may have to learn not to trip over your tongue.

Mercury in Taurus

Though you may be a slow learner, you have good concentration and mental stamina. You want to make your ideas really happen. You'll attack a problem methodically and consider every angle thoroughly, never jumping to conclusions. You'll stick with a subject until you master it.

Mercury in Gemini

You are a wonderful communicator with great facility for expressing yourself both verbally and in writing. You talk and talk, and you love gathering all kinds of information. You probably finish other people's sentences, and talk with hand gestures. You can talk to anybody anytime . . . and probably have phone and e-mail bills to prove it. You read anything from sci-fi to Shakespeare, and might need an extra room just for your book collection. Though you learn fast, you may lack focus and discipline. Watch a tendency to jump from subject to subject.

Mercury in Cancer

You rely on intuition more than logic. Your mental processes are usually colored by your emotions, so you may seem shy or hesitant to voice your opinions. However, this placement gives you the advantage of great imagination and empathy in the way you communicate with others.

Mercury in Leo

You are enthusiastic and very dramatic in the way you express yourself. You like to hold the attention of groups, and could be a great public speaker. Your mind thinks big, so you prefer to deal with the overall picture rather than with the details.

Mercury in Virgo

This is one of the best places for Mercury. It should give you critical ability, attention to details, and thorough analysis. Your mind focuses on the practical side of things. This type of thinking is very well suited to being a teacher or editor.

Mercury in Libra

You're either a born diplomat who smoothes over ruffled feathers or a talented debater. However, since you're forever weighing the pros and cons of a situation, you may vacillate when making decisions.

Mercury in Scorpio

This is an investigative mind that stops at nothing to get the answers. You may have a sarcastic, stinging wit or a gift for the cutting remark. There's always a grain of truth to your verbal sallies, thanks to your penetrating insight.

Mercury in Sagittarius

You are a supersalesman with a tendency to expound. Though you are very broad-minded, you can be dogmatic when it comes to telling others what's good for them. You won't hesitate to tell the truth as you see it, so watch a tendency toward tactlessness. On the plus side, you have a great sense of humor. This position of Mercury is often considered by astrologers to be at a disadvantage because Sagittarius opposes Gemini, the sign Mercury rules, and squares off with Virgo, another Mercury-ruled sign. What often happens is that Mercury in Sagittarius oversteps its bounds and loses sight of the facts in a situation. Do a reality check before making promises you may not be able to deliver.

Mercury in Capricorn

This placement endows good mental discipline. You have a love of learning and a very orderly approach to your subjects. You will patiently plod through the facts and figures until you have mastered the tasks. You grasp structured situations easily, but may be short on creativity.

Mercury in Aquarius

An independent, original thinker, you'll have more cutting-edge ideas than the average person. You will be quick to check out any unusual opportunities. Your opinions are so well-researched and grounded that once your mind is made up, it is difficult to change.

Mercury in Pisces

You have the psychic and intuitive mind of a natural poet. Learn to make use of your creative imagination. You may think in terms of helping others, but check a tendency to be vague and forgetful of details.

Venus Relates

Venus tells how you relate to others and to your environment. It shows where you receive pleasure, what you love to do. Find your Venus placement from the charts at the end of this chapter (pages 78–85) by looking for the year of your birth in the left-hand column. Then follow the line of that year across the page until you reach the time period of your birthday. The sign heading that column will be your Venus. If you were born on a day when Venus was changing signs, check the signs preceding or following that day to determine if that sign feels more like your Venus nature.

Venus in Aries

You can't stand to be bored, confined, or ordered around. But a good challenge, maybe even a rousing row, turns you on. Confess—don't you pick a fight now and then just to get someone stirred up? You're attracted by the chase, not the catch, which could cause some problems in your love life if the object of your affection becomes too attainable. You like to wear red and be first with the latest fashion. You'll spot a trend before anyone else.

Venus in Taurus

All your senses work in high gear. You love to be surrounded by glorious tastes, smells, textures, sounds, and visuals. Austerity is not for you! Neither is being rushed. You like time to enjoy your pleasures. Soothing surroundings with plenty of creature comforts are your cup of tea. You like to feel secure in your nest, with no sudden jolts or surprises. You like familiar objects—in fact, you may hate to let anything or anyone go.

Venus in Gemini

You are a lively, sparkling personality who thrives in a situation that affords a constant variety and a frequent change of scenery. A varied social life is important to you, with plenty of stimulation and a chance to engage in some light flirtation. Commitment may be difficult, because playing the field is so much fun.

Venus in Cancer

An atmosphere where you feel protected, coddled, and mothered is best for you. You love to be surrounded by children in a cozy, homelike situation. You are attracted to those who are tender and nurturing, who make you feel secure and well provided for. You may be quite secretive about your emotional life, or attracted to clandestine relationships.

Venus in Leo

First-class attention in large doses turns you on, and so does the glitter of real gold and the flash of mirrors. You like to feel like a star at all times, surrounded by your admiring audience. The side effect is that you may be attracted to flatterers and tinsel, while the real gold requires some digging.

Venus in Virgo

Everything neatly in its place? On the surface, you are attracted to an atmosphere where everything is in perfect order, but underneath are some basic, earthy urges. You are attracted to those who appeal to your need to teach, to be of service, or to play out a Pygmalion fantasy. You are at your best when you are busy doing something useful.

Venus in Libra

Elegance and harmony are your key words. You can't abide an atmosphere of contention. Your taste tends toward the classic, with light harmonies of color—nothing clashing, trendy, or outrageous. You love doing things with a partner, and should be careful to pick one who is decisive but patient enough to let you weigh the pros and cons. And steer clear of argumentative types!

Venus in Scorpio

Hidden mysteries intrigue you. In fact, anything that is too open and aboveboard is a bit of a bore. You surely have a stack of whodunits by the bed, along with an erotic magazine or two. You like to solve puzzles, and may also be fascinated with the occult, crime, or scientific research. Intense, all-or-nothing situations add spice to your life, and you love to ferret out the secrets of others. But you could get burned by your flair for living dangerously. The color black, spicy food, dark wood furniture, and heady perfume all get you in the right mood.

Venus in Sagittarius

If you are not actually a world traveler, your surroundings are sure to reflect your love of faraway places. You like a casual outdoor atmosphere and a dog or two to pet. There should be plenty of room for athletic equipment and suitcases. You're attracted to kindred souls who love to travel and who share your freedom-loving philosophy of life. Athletics and spiritual or New Age pursuits could be other interests.

Venus in Capricorn

No fly-by-night relationships for you! You want substance in life, and you are attracted to whatever will help you get where you are going. Status objects turn you on. And so do those who have a serious, responsible, businesslike approach as well as those who remind you of a beloved parent. It is characteristic of this placement to be attracted to someone of a different generation. Antiques, traditional clothing, and dignified behavior favor you.

Venus in Aquarius

This Venus wants to make friends more than to make love. You like to be in a group, particularly one pushing a worthy cause. You feel quite at home surrounded by people, remaining detached from any intense commitment. Original ideas and unpredictable people fascinate you. You don't like everything to be planned out in advance, preferring spontaneity and delightful surprises.

Venus in Pisces

This Venus loves to give of yourself, and you find plenty of takers. Stray animals and people appeal to your heart and your pocketbook, but be careful to look at their motives realistically once in a while. You are extremely vulnerable to sob stories of all kinds. Fantasy, theater, and psychic or spiritual activities also speak to you.

Mars Moves and Shakes

Mars is the mover and shaker in your life. It shows how you pursue your goals, whether you have energy to burn or proceed in a slow, steady pace. It will also show how you get angry. Do you explode or do a slow burn or hold everything inside, then get revenge later?

To find your Mars, turn to the charts on pages 86–94. Then find your birth year in the left-hand column and trace the line across horizontally until you come to the column headed by the month of your birth. There you will find an abbreviation of your Mars sign. If the description of your Mars sign doesn't ring true, read the description of the sign preceding and following it. You may have been born on a day when Mars was changing signs, and your Mars would then be in the adjacent sign.

Mars in Aries

In the sign it rules, Mars shows its brilliant fiery nature. You have an explosive temper and can be quite impatient. On the other hand, you have tremendous courage, energy, and drive. You'll let nothing stand in your way as you race to be first! Obstacles are met head-on and broken through by force. However, those that require patience and persistence can have you exploding in rage. You're a great starter, but not necessarily around for the finish.

Mars in Taurus

Slow, steady, concentrated energy gives you staying power. You have great stamina, and you never give up. Your tactic is to wear away obstacles with your persistence. Often you come out a winner because you've had the patience to hang in there. When angered, you do a slow burn.

Mars in Gemini

You can't sit still for long. This Mars craves variety. You often have two or more things going on at once—it's all an amusing game to you. Your life can get very complicated, but that only adds spice and stimulation. What drives you into a nervous, hyper state? Boredom, sameness, routine, and confinement. You can do wonderful things with your hands, and you have a way with words.

Mars in Cancer

You rarely attack head-on. Instead, you'll keep things to yourself, make plans in secret, and always cover your actions. This might be interpreted by some as manipulative, but you are only being self-protective. You get furious when anyone knows too much about you. But you do like to know all about others. Your mothering and feeding instincts can be put to good use if you work in the food, hotel, or child-care businesses. You may have to overcome your fragile sense of security, which prompts you not to take risks and to get physically upset when criticized. Don't take things so personally!

Mars in Leo

You have a very dominant personality that takes center stage. Modesty is not one of your traits, nor is taking a backseat. You prefer giving the orders, and have been known to make a dramatic scene if they are not obeyed. Properly used, this Mars confers leadership ability, endurance, and courage.

Mars in Virgo

You are the faultfinder of the zodiac. You notice every detail. Mistakes of any kind make you very nervous. You may worry, even if everything is going smoothly. You may not express your anger directly, but you sure can nag. You have definite likes and dislikes, and you are sure you can do the job better than anyone else. You are certainly more industrious and detail-oriented than other signs. Your Mars energy is often most positively expressed in some kind of teaching role.

Mars in Libra

This Mars will have a passion for beauty, justice, and art. Generally, you will avoid confrontations at all costs. You prefer to spend your energy finding diplomatic solutions or weighing pros and cons. Your other techniques are passive aggression or exercising your well-known charm to get people to do what you want.

Mars in Scorpio

This is a powerful placement, so intense that it demands careful channeling into worthwhile activities. Otherwise, you could become obsessed with your sexuality or might use your need for power and control to manipulate others. You are strong-willed, shrewd, and very private about your affairs, and you'll usually have a secret agenda behind your actions. Your great stamina, focus, and discipline would be excellent assets for careers in the military or medical fields, especially research or surgery. When angry, you don't get mad—you get even!

Mars in Sagittarius

This expansive Mars often propels people into sales, travel, athletics, or philosophy. Your energies function well when you are on the move. You have a hot temper, and are inclined to say what you think before you consider the consequences. You shoot for high goals—and talk endlessly about them—but you may be weak on groundwork. This Mars needs a solid foundation. Watch a tendency to take unnecessary risks.

Mars in Capricorn

This is an ambitious Mars with an excellent sense of timing. You have an eye for those who can be of use to you, and you may dismiss people ruthlessly when you're angry. But you drive yourself hard and deliver full value. This is a good placement for an executive. You'll aim for status and a high material position in life, and you'll keep climbing despite the odds. A great Mars to have!

Mars in Aquarius

This is the most rebellious Mars. You seem to have a drive to assert yourself against the status quo. You may enjoy provoking people, shocking them out of traditional views. Or this placement could express itself in an offbeat sex life. Somehow you often find yourself in unconventional situations. You enjoy being a leader of an active group, which pursues forward-looking studies, politics, or goals.

Mars in Pisces

This Mars is a good actor who knows just how to appeal to the sympathies of others. You create and project wonderful fantasies, or you use your sensitive antennae to crusade for those less fortunate. You get what you want through creating a veil of illusion and glamour. This is a good Mars for someone in the creative fields—a dancer, performer, photographer, or someone in motion pictures. Many famous film stars have this placement. Watch a tendency to manipulate by making others feel sorry for you.

Jupiter Gives You the Breaks

Jupiter is the planet in your horoscope that makes you want *more*. This big, bright, swirling mass of gases is associated with abundance, prosperity, and the kind of windfall you get without too much hard work. You're optimistic under Jupiter's influence, when anything seems possible. You'll travel, expand your mind with higher education, and publish to share your knowledge widely. On the other hand, Jupiter's influence is neither discriminating nor disciplined. It represents the principle of growth without judgment. Therefore, if not kept in check, it could result in extravagance, weight gain, laziness, and carelessness.

Be sure to look up your Jupiter in the tables in this book. When the current position of Jupiter is favorable, you may get that lucky break. This is a great time to try new things, take risks, travel, or get more education. Opportunities seem to open up easily, so take advantage of them.

Once a year, Jupiter changes signs. That means you are due for an expansive time every twelve years, when Jupiter travels through your sun sign. You'll also have "up" periods every four years, when Jupiter is in the same element as your sun sign.

Jupiter in Aries

You are the soul of enthusiasm and optimism. Your luckiest times are when you are getting started on an exciting project or selling an idea that you really believe in. You may have to watch a tendency to be arrogant with those who do not share your enthusiasm. You follow your impulses, often ignoring budget or other commonsense limitations. To produce real, solid benefits, you'll need patience and follow-through wherever this Jupiter falls in your horoscope.

Jupiter in Taurus

You'll spend on beautiful material things, especially those that come from nature—items made of rare woods, natural fabrics, or precious gems, for instance. You can't have too much comfort or too many sensual pleasures. Watch a tendency to overindulge in good food, or to overpamper yourself with nothing but the best. Spartan living is not for you! You may be especially lucky in matters of real estate.

Jupiter in Gemini

You are the great talker of the zodiac, and you may be a great writer, too. But restlessness could be your weak point. You jump around, talk too much, and could be a jack-of-all-trades. Keeping a secret is especially difficult, so you'll also have to watch a tendency to spill the beans. Since you love to be at the center of a beehive of activity, you'll have a vibrant social life. Your best opportunities will come through your talent for language—speaking, writing, communicating, and selling.

Jupiter in Cancer

You are luckiest in situations where you can find emotional closeness or deal with basic security needs such as food, nurturing, or shelter. You may be a great collector. Or you may simply love to accumulate things—you are the one who stashes things away for a rainy day. You probably have a very good memory and love children. In fact, you may have many children to care for. The food, hotel, child-care, and shipping businesses hold good opportunities for you.

Jupiter in Leo

You are a natural showman who loves to live in a larger-than-life way. Yours is a personality full of color that always finds its way into the limelight. You can't have too much attention or applause. Show biz is a natural place for you, and so is any area where you can play to a crowd. Exercising your flair for drama, your natural playfulness, and your romantic nature brings you good fortune. But watch a tendency to be overly extravagant or to monopolize center stage.

Jupiter in Virgo

You actually love those minute details others find boring. To you, they make all the difference between the perfect and the ordinary. You are the fine craftsman who spots every flaw. You expand your awareness by finding the most efficient methods and by being of service to others. Many of you will be drawn to medical or teaching fields. You'll also have luck in publishing, crafts, nutrition, and service professions. Watch out for a tendency to overwork.

Jupiter in Libra

This is an other-directed Jupiter that develops best with a partner. The stimulation of others helps you grow. You are also most comfortable in harmonious, beautiful situations, and you work well with artistic people. You have a great sense of fair play and an ability to evaluate the pros and cons of a situation. You usually prefer to play the role of diplomat rather than adversary.

Jupiter in Scorpio

You love the feeling of power and control, of taking things to their limit. You can't resist a mystery. Your shrewd, penetrating mind sees right through to the heart of most situations and people. You have luck in work that provides for solutions to matters of life and death. You may be drawn to undercover work, behind-the-scenes intrigue, psychotherapy, the occult, and sex-related ventures. Your challenge will be to develop a sense of moderation and tolerance for other beliefs. This Jupiter can be fanatical. You may have luck in handling other people's money—insurance, taxes, and inheritance can bring you a windfall.

Jupiter in Sagittarius

Independent, outgoing, and idealistic, you'll shoot for the stars. This Jupiter compels you to travel far and wide, both physically and mentally, via higher education. You may have luck while traveling in an exotic place. You also have luck with outdoor ventures, exercise, and animals, particularly horses. Since you tend to be very open about your opinions, watch a tendency to be tactless and to exaggerate. Instead, use your wonderful sense of humor to make your point.

Jupiter in Capricorn

Jupiter is much more restrained in Capricorn, the sign of rules and authority. Here, Jupiter can make you overwork and heighten any ambition or sense of duty you may have. You'll expand in areas that advance your position, putting you farther up the social or corporate ladder. You are lucky working within the establishment in a very structured situation where you can show off your ability to organize and reap rewards for your hard work.

Jupiter in Aquarius

This is another freedom-loving Jupiter, with great tolerance and originality. You are at your best when you are working for a humanitarian cause and in the company of many supporters. This is a good Jupiter for a political career. You'll relate to all kinds of people on all social levels. You have an abundance of original ideas, but you are best off away from routine and any situation that imposes rigid rules. You need mental stimulation!

Jupiter in Pisces

You are a giver whose feelings and pocketbook are easily touched by others, so choose your companions with care. You could be the original sucker for a hard-luck story. Better find a worthy hospital or a charity that will appreciate your selfless support. You have a great creative imagination. You may attract good fortune in fields related to oil, perfume, pharmaceuticals, petroleum, dance, footwear, and alcohol. But beware of overindulgence in alcohol—focus on a creative outlet instead.

Saturn Puts on the Brakes

Jupiter speeds you up with *lucky breaks,* then along comes Saturn to slow you down with the *disciplinary brakes.* Saturn has unfairly been called a malefic planet, one of the bad guys of the zodiac. On the contrary, Saturn is one of our best friends, the kind who tells you what you need to hear even if it's not good news. Under a Saturn transit, we grow up, take responsibility for our lives, and emerge from whatever test this planet has in store as far wiser, more capable, and mature human beings.

When Saturn hits a critical point in your horoscope, you can count on an experience that will make you slow up, pull back, and reexamine your life. It is a call to eliminate what is not working and to shape up. By the end of its twenty-eight-year trip around the zodiac, Saturn will have tested you in all areas of your life. The major tests happen in seven-year cycles, when Saturn passes over the *angles* of your chart—your rising sign, midheaven, descendant, and nadir. This is when the real life-changing experiences happen. But you are also in for a testing period whenever Saturn passes a *planet* in your chart or stresses that planet from a distance. Therefore, it is useful to check your planetary positions with the timetable of Saturn to prepare in advance, or at least to brace yourself.

When Saturn returns to its location at the time of your birth, at approximately age twenty-eight, you'll have your first Saturn return. At this time, a person usually takes stock or settles down to find his or her mission in life and assumes full adult duties and responsibilities.

Another way Saturn helps us is to reveal the karmic lessons from previous lives and to give us the chance to overcome them. So look at Saturn's challenges as much-needed opportunities for self-improvement. Under a Jupiter influence, you'll have more fun. But Saturn gives you solid, long-lasting results.

Look up your natal Saturn in the tables in this book for clues on where you need work.

Saturn in Aries

Saturn here puts the brakes on Aries natural drive and enthusiasm. You don't let anyone push you around, and you know what's best for yourself. Following orders is not your strong point, and neither is diplomacy. You tend to be quick to go on the offensive in relationships, attacking first, before anyone attacks you. Because no one quite lives up to your standards, you often wind up doing everything yourself. You'll have to learn to cooperate and tone down self-centeredness.

Saturn in Taurus

A big issue is getting control of the cash flow. There will be lean periods that can be frightening, but you have the patience and endurance to stick them out and the methodical drive to prosper in the end. Learn to take a philosophical attitude, like Ben Franklin who also had this placement and who said, "A penny saved is a penny earned."

Saturn in Gemini

You are a serious student of life, but you may have difficulty communicating or sharing your knowledge. You may be shy, speak slowly, or have fears about communicating, like Eleanor Roosevelt. You dwell in the realms of science, theory, or abstract analysis—even when you are dealing with the emotions, like Sigmund Freud who also had this placement.

Saturn in Cancer

Your tests come with establishing a secure emotional base. In doing so, you may have to deal with some very basic fears centering on your early home environment. Most of your Saturn tests will have emotional roots in those early childhood experiences. You may have difficulty remaining objective in terms of what you try to achieve. So it will be especially important for you to deal with negative feelings such as guilt, paranoia, jealousy, resentment, and suspicion. Galileo and Michelangelo also navigated these murky waters.

Saturn in Leo

This is an authoritarian Saturn—a strict, demanding parent who may deny the pleasure principle in your zeal to see that rules are followed. Though you may feel guilty about taking the spotlight, you are very ambitious and loyal. You have to watch a tendency toward rigidity, also toward overwork and holding back affection. Joseph Kennedy and Billy Graham share this placement.

Saturn in Virgo

This is a cautious, exacting Saturn. You are intensely hard on yourself. Most of all, you give yourself the roughest time with your constant worries about every little detail, often making yourself sick. You may have difficulties setting priorities and getting the job done. Your tests will come in learning tolerance and understanding of others. Charles de Gaulle, Mae West, and Nathaniel Hawthorne had this meticulous Saturn.

Saturn in Libra

Saturn is exalted here, which makes this planet an ally. You may choose very serious, older partners in life, perhaps stemming from a fear of dependency. You need to learn to stand solidly on your own before you commit to another. You are extremely cautious as you deliberate every involvement—with good reason. It is best that you find an occupation that makes good use of your sense of duty and honor. Steer clear of fly-by-night situations. Both Khrushchev and Mao Tse-tung had this placement.

Saturn in Scorpio

You have great staying power. This Saturn tests you in situations involving the control of others. You may feel drawn to some kind of intrigue or undercover work, like J. Edgar Hoover. Or there may be an air of mystery surrounding your life and death, like Marilyn Monroe and Robert Kennedy who both had this placement. There are lessons to be learned from your sexual involvements. Often sex is used for manipulation or is somehow out of the ordinary. The Roman emperor Caligula and the transvestite Christine Jorgensen are extreme cases.

Saturn in Sagittarius

Your challenges and lessons will come from tests of your spiritual and philosophical values, as happened to Martin Luther King and Gandhi. You are high-minded and sincere with this reflective, moral placement. Uncompromising in your ethical standards, you could become a benevolent despot.

Saturn in Capricorn

With the help of Saturn at maximum strength, your judgment will improve with age. And, like Spencer Tracy's screen image, you'll be the gray-haired hero with a strong sense of responsibility. You advance in life slowly but steadily, always with a strong hand at the helm and an eye for the advantageous situation. Like Pat Robertson, you're likely to stand for conservative values. Negatively, you may be a loner, prone to periods of melancholy.

Saturn in Aquarius

Your tests come from relationships with groups. Do you care too much about what others think? Do you feel like an outsider, like Greta Garbo? You may fear being different from others and therefore slight your own unique, forward-looking gifts. Or, like Lord Byron and Howard Hughes, you may take the opposite tack and rebel in the extreme. You can apply discipline to accomplish great humanitarian goals, as Albert Schweitzer did.

Saturn in Pisces

Your fear of the unknown and the irrational may lead you to the safety and protection of an institution. You may go on the run like Jesse James, who had this placement, to avoid looking too deeply inside. Or you might go in the opposite, more positive direction and develop a disciplined psychoanalytic approach, which puts you more in control of your feelings. Some of you will take refuge in work with hospitals, charities, or religious institutions. Queen Victoria, who had this placement, symbolized an era when institutions of all kinds were sustained. Discipline applied to artistic work, especially poetry and dance, or to spiritual work, such as yoga or meditation, might be helpful.

Uranus, Neptune, and Pluto Affect Your Whole Generation

These three planets remain in signs such a long time that a whole generation bears the imprint of the sign. Mass movements, great sweeping changes, fads that characterize a generation, even the issues of the conflicts and wars of the time are influenced by these "outer three" planets. When one of these distant planets changes signs, there is a definite shift in the atmosphere, the feeling of the end of an era.

Since these planets are so far away from the sun—too distant to be seen by the naked eye—they pick up signals from the universe at large. These planetary receivers literally link the sun with distant energies, and then perform a similar function in your horoscope by linking your central character with intuitive, spiritual, transformative forces from the cosmos. Each planet has a special domain, and will reflect this in the area of your chart where it falls.

Uranus Wakes You Up

There is nothing ordinary about this quirky green planet that seems to be traveling on its side, surrounded by a swarm of moons. Is it any wonder that astrologers assigned it to Aquarius, the most eccentric and gregarious sign? Uranus seems to wend its way around the sun, marching to its own tune.

Significantly, Uranus follows Saturn, the planet of limitations and structures. Often we get caught up in the structures we have created to give ourselves a sense of security. However, if we lose contact with our spiritual roots, then Uranus is likely to jolt us out of our comfortable rut and wake us up.

Uranus energy is electrical, happening in sudden flashes. It is not influenced by karma or past events, nor does it regard tradition, sex, or sentiment. The Uranian key words are surprise and awakening. Suddenly, there's that flash of inspiration, that bright idea, that totally new approach to revolutionize whatever scheme you were undertaking. A Uranus event takes you by surprise; it happens from out of the blue, for better or for worse. The Uranus place in your life is where you awaken and become your own person, leaving the structures of Saturn behind. And it is probably the most unconventional place in your chart.

Look up the sign of Uranus at the time of your birth and see where you follow your own tune.

Uranus in Aries

Birth Dates:
   March 31, 1927–November 4, 1927
   January 13, 1928–June 6, 1934
   October 10, 1934–March 28, 1935

Your generation is original, creative, pioneering. It developed the computer, the airplane, and the cyclotron. You let nothing hold you back from exploring the unknown, and you have a powerful mixture of fire and electricity behind you. Women of your generation were among the first to be liberated. You were the unforgettable style-setters. You have a surprise in store for everyone. Like Yoko Ono, Grace Kelly, and Jacqueline Onassis, your life may be jolted by sudden and violent changes.

Uranus in Taurus

Birth Dates:
   June 6, 1934–October 10, 1934
   March 28, 1935–August 7, 1941
   October 5, 1941–May 15, 1942

World War II began during your generation. You are probably self-employed or would like to be. You have original ideas about making money, and you brace yourself for sudden changes of fortune. This Uranus can cause shake-ups, particularly in finances, but it can also make you a born entrepreneur.

Uranus in Gemini

Birth Dates:
    August 7, 1941–October 5, 1941
    May 15, 1942–August 30, 1948
    November 12, 1948–June 10, 1949

You were the first children to be influenced by television. Now, in your adult years, your generation stocks up on answering machines, cell phones, computers, and fax machines—any new way you can communicate. You have an inquiring mind, but your interests may be rather short-lived. This Uranus can be easily fragmented if there is no structure and focus.

Uranus in Cancer

Birth Dates:
    August 30, 1948–November 12, 1948
    June 10, 1949–August 24, 1955
    January 28, 1956–June 10, 1956

This generation came at a time when divorce was becoming commonplace, so your home image is unconventional. You may have an unusual relationship with your parents; you may have come from a broken home or an unconventional one. You'll have unorthodox ideas about parenting, intimacy, food, and shelter. You may also be interested in dreams, psychic phenomena, and memory work.

Uranus in Leo

Birth Dates:
  August 24, 1955–January 28, 1956
  June 10, 1956–November 1, 1961
  January 10, 1962–August 10, 1962

This generation understood how to use electronic media. Many of your group are now leaders in the high-tech industries, and you also understand how to use the new media to promote yourself. Like Isadora Duncan, you may have a very eccentric kind of charisma and a life that is sparked by unusual love affairs. Your children, too, may have traits that are out of the ordinary. Where this planet falls in your chart, you'll have a love of freedom, be a bit of an egomaniac, and show the full force of your personality in a unique way, like tennis great Martina Navratilova.

Uranus in Virgo

Birth Dates:
  November 1, 1961–January 10, 1962
  August 10, 1962–September 28, 1968
  May 20, 1969–June 24, 1969

You'll have highly individual work methods. Many of you will be finding newer, more practical ways to use computers. Like Einstein, who had this placement, you'll break the rules brilliantly. Your generation came at a time of student rebellions, the civil rights movement, and the general acceptance of health foods. Chances are, you're concerned about pollution and cleaning up the environment. You may also be involved with nontraditional healing methods. Heavyweight champ Mike Tyson has this placement.

Uranus in Libra

Birth Dates:
  September 28, 1968–May 20, 1969
  June 24, 1969–November 21, 1974
  May 1, 1975–September 8, 1975

Your generation will be always changing partners. Born during the era of women's liberation, you may have come from a broken home and have no clear image of what a marriage entails. There will be many sudden splits and experiments before you settle down. Your generation will be much involved in legal and political reforms and in changing artistic and fashion looks.

Uranus in Scorpio

Birth Dates:
  November 21, 1974–May 1, 1975
  September 8, 1975–February 17, 1981
  March 20, 1981–November 16, 1981

Interest in transformation, meditation, and life after death signaled the beginning of New Age consciousness. Your generation recognizes no boundaries, no limits, and no external controls. You'll have new attitudes toward death and dying, psychic phenomena, and the occult. Like Mae West and Casanova, you'll shock 'em sexually, too.

Uranus in Sagittarius

Birth Dates:
  February 17, 1981–March 20, 1981
  November 16, 1981–February 15, 1988
  May 27, 1988–December 2, 1988

Could this generation be the first to travel in outer space? An earlier generation with this placement included Charles Lindbergh and a time when the first Zeppelins and the Wright Brothers were conquering the skies. Uranus here forecasts great discoveries, mind expansion, and long-distance travel. Like Galileo and Martin Luther, those born in these years will generate new theories about the cosmos and man's relation to it.

Uranus in Capricorn

Birth Dates:
   December 20, 1904–January 30, 1912
   September 4, 1912–November 12, 1912
   February 15, 1988–May 27, 1988
   December 2, 1988–April 1, 1995
   June 9, 1995–January 12, 1996

This generation, now growing up, will challenge traditions with the help of electronic gadgets. In these years, we got organized with the help of technology put to practical use. The Internet was born following the great economic boom of the 1990s. Great leaders, who were movers and shakers of history, like Julius Caesar and Henry VIII, were born under this placement.

Uranus in Aquarius

Birth Dates:
   January 30, 1912–September 4, 1912
   November 12, 1912–April 1, 1919
   August 16, 1919–January 22, 1920
   April 1, 1995–June 9, 1995
   January 12, 1996–March 10, 2003
   September 15, 2003–December 30, 2003

The last generation with this placement produced great innovative minds such as Leonard Bernstein and Orson Welles. The next will become another radical breakthrough generation, much concerned with global issues that involve all humanity. Already this is a time of experimentation on every level, when home computers are becoming as ubiquitous as television.

Uranus in Pisces

Birth Dates:
    April 1, 1919–August 16, 1919
    January 22, 1920–March 31, 1927
    November 4, 1927–January 12, 1928
    March 10, 2003–September 15, 2003
    December 30, 2003–May 28, 2010

Uranus moves into Pisces during 2003, ushering in a new generation that will surely spark new intuitions, innovations, and creativity in the arts as well as in the sciences. In the past century, Uranus in Pisces focused attention on the rise of such electronic entertainment as radio and the cinema as well as on the secretiveness of Prohibition. This produced a generation of idealists exemplified by Judy Garland's theme, "Somewhere Over the Rainbow."

Neptune Takes You Out of This World

Under Neptune's influence, you see what you want to see. But Neptune also encourages you to create, to let your fantasies and daydreams run free. Neptune is often maligned as the planet of illusions, drugs, and alcohol where you can't bear to face reality. But it also embodies the energy of glamour, subtlety, mystery, and mysticism. It governs anything that takes you beyond the mundane world, including out-of-body experiences.

Neptune acts to break through and transcend your ordinary perceptions to take you to another level of reality where you experience either confusion or ecstasy. Neptune's force can pull you off course, but only if you allow this to happen. Those who use Neptune wisely can translate their daydreams into poetry, theater, design, or inspired moves in the business world, avoiding the tricky "con artist" side of this planet.

Find your Neptune listed below.

Neptune in Cancer

Birth Dates:
  July 19, 1901–December 25, 1901
  May 21, 1902–September 23, 1914
  December 14, 1914–July 19, 1915
  March 19, 1916–May 2, 1916

Dreams of the homeland, idealistic patriotism, and glamorization of the nurturing assets of women characterized this time. You who were born here have unusual psychic ability and deep insights into basic needs of others.

Neptune in Leo

Birth Dates:
  September 23, 1914–December 14, 1914
  July 19, 1915–March 19, 1916
  May 2, 1916–September 21, 1928
  February 19, 1929–July 24, 1929

Neptune in Leo brought us the glamour and high living of the 1920s and the big spenders of that time. Neptunian temptations of gambling, seduction, theater, and lavish entertaining distracted from the realities of the age. Those born in that generation also made great advances in the arts.

Neptune in Virgo

Birth Dates:
  September 21, 1928–February 19, 1929
  July 24, 1929–October 3, 1942
  April 17, 1943–August 2, 1943

Neptune in Virgo encompassed the Great Depression and World War II. Those born under this placement spread the gospel of health and fitness as they matured in a changing world. This generation's devotion to spending hours at the office inspired the term "workaholic."

Neptune in Libra

Birth Dates:
  October 3, 1942–April 17, 1943
  August 2, 1943–December 24, 1955
  March 12, 1956–October 19, 1956
  June 15, 1957–August 6, 1957

Neptune in Libra was the romantic generation who would later be concerned with relating. As this generation matured, there was a new trend toward marriage and commitment. Racial and sexual equality become important issues, as they redesigned traditional roles to suit modern times.

Neptune in Scorpio

Birth Dates:
  December 24, 1955–March 12, 1956
  October 19, 1956–June 15, 1957
  August 6, 1957–January 4, 1970
  May 3, 1970–November 6, 1970

Neptune in Scorpio brought in a generation that would become interested in transformative power. Born in an era that glamorized sex, drugs, rock and roll, and Eastern religion, they matured in a more sobering time of AIDS, cocaine abuse, and New Age spirituality. As they evolve, they will become active in healing the planet from the results of the abuse of power.

Neptune in Sagittarius

Birth Dates:
  January 4, 1970–May 3, 1970
  November 6, 1970–January 19, 1984
  June 23, 1984–November 21, 1984

Neptune in Sagittarius was the time when space and astronaut travel became a reality. The Neptune influence glamorized new approaches to mysticism, religion, and mind expansion. This generation will take a new approach to spiritual life, with emphasis on visions, mysticism, and clairvoyance.

Neptune in Capricorn

Birth Dates:
   January 19, 1984–June 23, 1984
   November 21, 1984–January 29, 1998

Neptune in Capricorn brought a time when delusions about material power were first glamorized, then dashed on the rocks of reality. It was also a time when the psychic and occult worlds spawned a new category of business enterprise, and sold services on television.

Neptune in Aquarius

Birth Dates:
   January 29, 1998–April 4, 2111

This should continue to be a time of breakthroughs. Here the creative influence of Neptune reaches a universal audience. This is a time of dissolving barriers, of globalization—when we truly become one world.

Pluto Transforms You

Pluto is a mysterious little planet with a strange elliptical orbit that occasionally runs inside the orbit of its neighbor Neptune. Because of its eccentric path, the length of time Pluto stays in any given sign can vary from thirteen to thirty-two years. It covered only seven signs in the last century. Though it is a tiny planet, its influence is great. When Pluto zaps a strategic point in your horoscope, your life changes dramatically.

This little planet is the power behind the scenes. It affects you at deep levels of consciousness, causing events to come to the surface that will transform you and your generation. Nothing escapes, or is sacred, with this probing planet. Its purpose is to wipe out the past so something new can happen. The Pluto place in your horoscope is where you have invisible power (Mars governs the visible power)—where you can transform, heal, and affect the unconscious needs of the masses. Pluto tells lots about how your generation projects power, what makes it seem "cool" to others. And when Pluto changes signs, there's a whole new concept of what's "cool."

Pluto in Gemini

Birth Dates:
   Late 1800s–May 28, 1914

This was a time of mass suggestion and breakthroughs in communications, a time when many brilliant writers such as Ernest Hemingway and F. Scott Fitzgerald were born. Henry Miller, D. H. Lawrence, and James Joyce scandalized society by using explicit sexual images and language in their literature. "Muckraking" journalists exposed corruption. Pluto-ruled Scorpio President Theodore Roosevelt said, "Speak softly, but carry a big stick." This generation had an intense need to communicate and made major breakthroughs in knowledge. A compulsive restlessness and a thirst for a variety of experiences characterized many of this generation.

Pluto in Cancer

Birth Dates:
   May 26, 1914–June 14, 1939

Dictators and mass media arose to wield emotional power over the masses. Women's rights was a popular issue. Deep sentimental feelings, acquisitiveness, and possessiveness characterized these times and people. Most of the great stars of the Hollywood era that embodied the American image were born during this period: Grace Kelly, Esther Williams, Frank Sinatra, Lana Turner, etc.

Pluto in Leo

Birth Dates:
   June 14, 1939–August 19, 1957

The performing arts played on the emotions of the masses. Mick Jagger, John Lennon, and rock and roll were born at this time. So were "baby boomers" like Bill and Hillary Clinton. Those born here tend to be self-centered, powerful, and boisterous. This generation does its own thing, for better or for worse.

Pluto in Virgo

Birth Dates:
  August 19, 1957–October 5, 1971
  April 17, 1972–July 30, 1972

This is the "yuppie" generation that sparked a mass movement toward fitness, health, and career. It is a much more sober, serious, driven generation than the fun-loving Pluto in Leo. During this time, machines were invented to process detail work efficiently. Inventions took a practical turn with answering machines, fax machines, car phones, and home office equipment—all making the workplace far more efficient.

Pluto in Libra

Birth Dates:
  October 5, 1971–April 17, 1972
  July 30, 1972–November 5, 1983
  May 18, 1984–August 27, 1984

A mellower generation, people born at this time are concerned with partnerships, working together, and finding diplomatic solutions to problems. Marriage is important to this generation, and they will redefine it by combining traditional values with equal partnership. This was a time of women's liberation, gay rights, ERA, and legal battles over abortion, all of which transformed our ideas about relationships.

Pluto in Scorpio

Birth Dates:
  November 5, 1983–May 18, 1984
  August 27, 1984–January 17, 1995

Pluto was in its ruling sign for a comparatively short period of time. In 1989, it was at its perihelion, or closest point to the sun and earth. We have all felt the transforming power somewhere in our lives. This was a time of record achievements, destructive sexually transmitted diseases, nuclear power controversies, and explosive political issues. Pluto destroys in order to create new understanding—the phoenix rising from the ashes—which should be some consolation for those of you who felt Pluto's force before 1995. Sexual shockers were par for the course during these intense years when black clothing, transvestites, body piercing, tattoos, and sexually explicit advertising pushed the boundaries of good taste.

Pluto in Sagittarius

Birth Dates:
  January 17, 1995–April 20, 1995
  November 10, 1995–January 27, 2008

During our current Pluto transit, we are being pushed to expand our horizons, to find deeper spiritual meaning in life. Pluto's opposition with Saturn in 2001 brought an enormous conflict between traditional societies and the forces of change.

For many of us, this Pluto transit will mean rolling down the information superhighway into the future. For others, it signals a time of spiritual emphasis when religious convictions will exert more power in our political life as well.

Since Sagittarius is the sign that rules travel, there's a good possibility that Pluto, the planet of extremes, will make space travel a reality for some of us. Discovery of life on Mars, traveling here on meteors, could transform our ideas about where we came from.

New dimensions in electronic publishing, concern with animal rights and the environment, and an increasing emphasis on extreme forms of religion are other signs of these times. Look for charismatic religious leaders to arise now. We'll also be developing far-reaching philosophies designed to elevate our lives with a new sense of purpose.

VENUS SIGNS 1901–2003

	Aries	Taurus	Gemini	Cancer	Leo	Virgo
1901	3/29–4/22	4/22–5/17	5/17–6/10	6/10–7/5	7/5–7/29	7/29–8/23
1902	5/7–6/3	6/3–6/30	6/30–7/25	7/25–8/19	8/19–9/13	9/13–10/7
1903	2/28–3/24	3/24–4/18	4/18–5/13	5/13–6/9	6/9–7/7	7/7–8/17 9/6–11/8
1904	3/13–5/7	5/7–6/1	6/1–6/25	6/25–7/19	7/19–8/13	8/13–9/6
1905	2/3–3/6 4/9–5/28	3/6–4/9 5/28–7/8	7/8–8/6	8/6–9/1	9/1–9/27	9/27–10/21
1906	3/1–4/7	4/7–5/2	5/2–5/26	5/26–6/20	6/20–7/16	7/16–8/11
1907	4/27–5/22	5/22–6/16	6/16–7/11	7/11–8/4	8/4–8/29	8/29–9/22
1908	2/14–3/10	3/10–4/5	4/5–5/5	5/5–9/8	9/8–10/8	10/8–11/3
1909	3/29–4/22	4/22–5/16	5/16–6/10	6/10–7/4	7/4–7/29	7/29–8/23
1910	5/7–6/3	6/4–6/29	6/30–7/24	7/25–8/18	8/19–9/13	9/13–10/6
1911	2/28–3/23	3/24–4/17	4/18–5/12	5/13–6/8	6/9–7/7	7/8–11/8
1912	4/13–5/6	5/7–5/31	6/1–6/24	6/24–7/18	7/19–8/12	8/13–9/5
1913	2/3–3/6 5/2–5/30	3/7–5/1 5/31–7/7	7/8–8/5	8/6–8/31	9/1–9/26	9/27–10/20
1914	3/14–4/6	4/7–5/1	5/2–5/25	5/26–6/19	6/20–7/15	7/16–8/10
1915	4/27–5/21	5/22–6/15	6/16–7/10	7/11–8/3	8/4–8/28	8/29–9/21
1916	2/14–3/9	3/10–4/5	4/6–5/5	5/6–9/8	9/9–10/7	10/8–11/2
1917	3/29–4/21	4/22–5/15	5/16–6/9	6/10–7/3	7/4–7/28	7/29–8/21
1918	5/7–6/2	6/3–6/28	6/29–7/24	7/25–8/18	8/19–9/11	9/12–10/5
1919	2/27–3/22	3/23–4/16	4/17–5/12	5/13–6/7	6/8–7/7	7/8–11/8
1920	4/12–5/6	5/7–5/30	5/31–6/23	6/24–7/18	7/19–8/11	8/12–9/4
1921	2/3–3/6 4/26–6/1	3/7–4/25 6/2–7/7	7/8–8/5	8/6–8/31	9/1–9/25	9/26–10/20
1922	3/13–4/6	4/7–4/30	5/1–5/25	5/26–6/19	6/20–7/14	7/15–8/9
1923	4/27–5/21	5/22–6/14	6/15–7/9	7/10–8/3	8/4–8/27	8/28–9/20
1924	2/13–3/8	3/9–4/4	4/5–5/5	5/6–9/8	9/9–10/7	10/8–11/12
1925	3/28–4/20	4/21–5/15	5/16–6/8	6/9–7/3	7/4–7/27	7/28–8/21

Libra	Scorpio	Sagittarius	Capricorn	Aquarius	Pisces
8/23–9/17	9/17–10/12	10/12–1/16	1/16–2/9	2/9–3/5	3/5–3/29
			11/7–12/5	12/5–1/11	
10/7–10/31	10/31–11/24	11/24–12/18	12/18–1/11	2/6–4/4	1/11–2/6
					4/4–5/7
8/17–9/6	12/9–1/5			1/11–2/4	2/4–2/28
11/8–12/9					
9/6–9/30	9/30–10/25	1/5–1/30	1/30–2/24	2/24–3/19	3/19–4/13
		10/25–11/18	11/18–12/13	12/13–1/7	
10/21–11/14	11/14–12/8	12/8–1/1/06			1/7–2/3
8/11–9/7	9/7–10/9	10/9–12/15	1/1–1/25	1/25–2/18	2/18–3/14
	12/15–12/25	12/25–2/6			
9/22–10/16	10/16–11/9	11/9–12/3	2/6–3/6	3/6–4/2	4/2–4/27
			12/3–12/27	12/27–1/20	
11/3–11/28	11/28–12/22	12/22–1/15			1/20–2/4
8/23–9/17	9/17–10/12	10/12–11/17	1/15–2/9	2/9–3/5	3/5–3/29
			11/17–12/5	12/5–1/15	
10/7–10/30	10/31–11/23	11/24–12/17	12/18–12/31	1/1–1/15	1/16–1/28
				1/29–4/4	4/5–5/6
11/19–12/8	12/9–12/31		1/1–1/10	1/11–2/2	2/3–2/27
9/6–9/30	1/1–1/4	1/5–1/29	1/30–2/23	2/24–3/18	3/19–4/12
	10/1–10/24	10/25–11/17	11/18–12/12	12/13–12/31	
10/21–11/13	11/14–12/7	12/8–12/31		1/1–1/6	1/7–2/2
8/11–9/6	9/7–10/9	10/10–12/5	1/1–1/24	1/25–2/17	2/18–3/13
	12/6–12/30	12/31			
9/22–10/15	10/16–11/8	1/1–2/6	2/7–3/6	3/7–4/1	4/2–4/26
		11/9–12/2	12/3–12/26	12/27–12/31	
11/3–11/27	11/28–12/21	12/22–12/31		1/1–1/19	1/20–2/13
8/22–9/16	9/17–10/11	1/1–1/14	1/15–2/7	2/8–3/4	3/5–3/28
		10/12–11/6	11/7–12/5	12/6–12/31	
10/6–10/29	10/30–11/22	11/23–12/16	12/17–12/31	1/1–4/5	4/6–5/6
11/9–12/8	12/9–12/31		1/1–1/9	1/10–2/2	2/3–2/26
9/5–9/30	1/1–1/3	1/4–1/28	1/29–2/22	2/23–3/18	3/19–4/11
	9/31–10/23	10/24–11/17	11/18–12/11	12/12–12/31	
10/21–11/13	11/14–12/7	12/8–12/31		1/1–1/6	1/7–2/2
8/10–9/6	9/7–10/10	10/11–11/28	1/1–1/24	1/25–2/16	2/17–3/12
	11/29–12/31				
9/21–10/14	1/1	1/2–2/6	2/7–3/5	3/6–3/31	4/1–4/26
	10/15–11/7	11/8–12/1	12/2–12/25	12/26–12/31	
11/13–11/26	11/27–12/21	12/22–12/31		1/1–1/19	1/20–2/12
8/22–9/15	9/16–10/11	1/1–1/14	1/15–2/7	2/8–3/3	3/4–3/27
		10/12–11/6	11/7–12/5	12/6–12/31	

VENUS SIGNS 1901–2003

	Aries	Taurus	Gemini	Cancer	Leo	Virgo
1926	5/7–6/2	6/3–6/28	6/29–7/23	7/24–8/17	8/18–9/11	9/12–10/5
1927	2/27–3/22	3/23–4/16	4/17–5/11	5/12–6/7	6/8–7/7	7/8–11/9
1928	4/12–5/5	5/6–5/29	5/30–6/23	6/24–7/17	7/18–8/11	8/12–9/4
1929	2/3–3/7 4/20–6/2	3/8–4/19 6/3–7/7	7/8–8/4	8/5–8/30	8/31–9/25	9/26–10/19
1930	3/13–4/5	4/6–4/30	5/1–5/24	5/25–6/18	6/19–7/14	7/15–8/9
1931	4/26–5/20	5/21–6/13	6/14–7/8	7/9–8/2	8/3–8/26	8/27–9/19
1932	2/12–3/8	3/9–4/3	4/4–5/5 7/13–7/27	5/6–7/12 7/28–9/8	9/9–10/6	10/7–11/1
1933	3/27–4/19	4/20–5/28	5/29–6/8	6/9–7/2	7/3–7/26	7/27–8/20
1934	5/6–6/1	6/2–6/27	6/28–7/22	7/23–8/16	8/17–9/10	9/11–10/4
1935	2/26–3/21	3/22–4/15	4/16–5/10	5/11–6/6	6/7–7/6	7/7–11/8
1936	4/11–5/4	5/5–5/28	5/29–6/22	6/23–7/16	7/17–8/10	8/11–9/4
1937	2/2–3/8 4/14–6/3	3/9–4/13 6/4–7/6	7/7–8/3	8/4–8/29	8/30–9/24	9/25–10/18
1938	3/12–4/4	4/5–4/28	4/29–5/23	5/24–6/18	6/19–7/13	7/14–8/8
1939	4/25–5/19	5/20–6/13	6/14–7/8	7/9–8/1	8/2–8/25	8/26–9/19
1940	2/12–3/7	3/8–4/3	4/4–5/5 7/5–7/31	5/6–7/4 8/1–9/8	9/9–10/5	10/6–10/31
1941	3/27–4/19	4/20–5/13	5/14–6/6	6/7–7/1	7/2–7/26	7/27–8/20
1942	5/6–6/1	6/2–6/26	6/27–7/22	7/23–8/16	8/17–9/9	9/10–10/3
1943	2/25–3/20	3/21–4/14	4/15–5/10	5/11–6/6	6/7–7/6	7/7–11/8
1944	4/10–5/3	5/4–5/28	5/29–6/21	6/22–7/16	7/17–8/9	8/10–9/2
1945	2/2–3/10 4/7–6/3	3/11–4/6 6/4–7/6	7/7–8/3	8/4–8/29	8/30–9/23	9/24–10/18
1946	3/11–4/4	4/5–4/28	4/29–5/23	5/24–6/17	6/18–7/12	7/13–8/8
1947	4/25–5/19	5/20–6/12	6/13–7/7	7/8–8/1	8/2–8/25	8/26–9/18
1948	2/11–3/7	3/8–4/3	4/4–5/6 6/29–8/2	5/7–6/28 8/3–9/7	9/8–10/5	10/6–10/31
1949	3/26–4/19	4/20–5/13	5/14–6/6	6/7–6/30	7/1–7/25	7/26–8/19
1950	5/5–5/31	6/1–6/26	6/27–7/21	7/22–8/15	8/16–9/9	9/10–10/3
1951	2/25–3/21	3/22–4/15	4/16–5/10	5/11–6/6	6/7–7/7	7/8–11/9

Libra	Scorpio	Sagittarius	Capricorn	Aquarius	Pisces
10/6–10/29	10/30–11/22	11/23–12/16	12/17–12/31	1/1–4/5	4/6–5/6
11/10–12/8	12/9–12/31	1/1–1/7	1/8	1/9–2/1	2/2–2/26
9/5–9/28	1/1–1/3	1/4–1/28	1/29–2/22	2/23–3/17	3/18–4/11
	9/29–10/23	10/24–11/16	11/17–12/11	12/12–12/31	
10/20–11/12	11/13–12/6	12/7–12/30	12/31	1/1–1/5	1/6–2/2
8/10–9/6	9/7–10/11	10/12–11/21	1/1–1/23	1/24–2/16	2/17–3/12
	11/22–12/31				
9/20–10/13	1/1–1/3	1/4–2/6	2/7–3/4	3/5–3/31	4/1–4/25
	10/14–11/6	11/7–11/30	12/1–12/24	12/25–12/31	
11/2–11/25	11/26–12/20	12/21–12/31		1/1–1/18	1/19–2/11
8/21–9/14	9/15–10/10	1/1–1/13	1/14–2/6	2/7–3/2	3/3–3/26
		10/11–11/5	11/6–12/4	12/5–12/31	
10/5–10/28	10/29–11/21	11/22–12/15	12/16–12/31	1/1–4/5	4/6–5/5
11/9–12/7	12/8–12/31		1/1–1/7	1/8–1/31	2/1–2/25
9/5–9/27	1/1–1/2	1/3–1/27	1/28–2/21	2/22–3/16	3/17–4/10
	9/28–10/22	10/23–11/15	11/16–12/10	12/11–12/31	
10/19–11/11	11/12–12/5	12/6–12/29	12/30–12/31	1/1–1/5	1/6–2/1
8/9–9/6	9/7–10/13	10/14–11/14	1/1–1/22	1/23–2/15	2/16–3/11
	11/15–12/31				
9/20–10/13	1/1–1/3	1/4–2/5	2/6–3/4	3/5–3/30	3/31–4/24
	10/14–11/6	11/7–11/30	12/1–12/24	12/25–12/31	
11/1–11/25	11/26–12/19	12/20–12/31		1/1–1/18	1/19–2/11
8/21–9/14	9/15–10/9	1/1–1/12	1/13–2/5	2/6–3/1	3/2–3/26
		10/10–11/5	11/6–12/4	12/5–12/31	
10/4–10/27	10/28–11/20	11/21–12/14	12/15–12/31	1/1–4/5	4/6–5/5
11/9–12/7	12/8–12/31		1/1–1/7	1/8–1/31	2/1–2/24
9/3–9/27	1/1–1/2	1/3–1/27	1/28–2/20	2/21–3/16	3/17–4/9
	9/28–10/21	10/22–11/15	11/16–12/10	12/11–12/31	
10/19–11/11	11/12–12/5	12/6–12/29	12/30–12/31	1/1–1/4	1/5–2/1
8/9–9/6	9/7–10/15	10/16–11/7	1/1–1/21	1/22–2/14	2/15–3/10
	11/8–12/31				
9/19–10/12	1/1–1/4	1/5–2/5	2/6–3/4	3/5–3/29	3/30–4/24
	10/13–11/5	11/6–11/29	11/30–12/23	12/24–12/31	
11/1–11/25	11/26–12/19	12/20–12/31		1/1–1/17	1/18–2/10
8/20–9/14	9/15–10/9	1/1–1/12	1/13–2/5	2/6–3/1	3/2–3/25
		10/10–11/5	11/6–12/5	12/6–12/31	
10/4–10/27	10/28–11/20	11/21–12/13	12/14–12/31	1/1–4/5	4/6–5/4
11/10–12/7	12/8–12/31		1/1–1/7	1/8–1/31	2/1–2/24

VENUS SIGNS 1901–2003

	Aries	Taurus	Gemini	Cancer	Leo	Virgo
1952	4/10–5/4	5/5–5/28	5/29–6/21	6/22–7/16	7/17–8/9	8/10–9/3
1953	2/2–3/3	3/4–3/31	7/8–8/3	8/4–8/29	8/30–9/24	9/25–10/18
	4/1–6/5	6/6–7/7				
1954	3/12–4/4	4/5–4/28	4/29–5/23	5/24–6/17	6/18–7/13	7/14–8/8
1955	4/25–5/19	5/20–6/13	6/14–7/7	7/8–8/1	8/2–8/25	8/26–9/18
1956	2/12–3/7	3/8–4/4	4/5–5/7	5/8–6/23	9/9–10/5	10/6–10/31
			6/24–8/4	8/5–9/8		
1957	3/26–4/19	4/20–5/13	5/14–6/6	6/7–7/1	7/2–7/26	7/27–8/19
1958	5/6–5/31	6/1–6/26	6/27–7/22	7/23–8/15	8/16–9/9	9/10–10/3
1959	2/25–3/20	3/21–4/14	4/15–5/10	5/11–6/6	6/7–7/8	7/9–9/20
					9/21–9/24	9/25–11/9
1960	4/10–5/3	5/4–5/28	5/29–6/21	6/22–7/15	7/16–8/9	8/10–9/2
1961	2/3–6/5	6/6–7/7	7/8–8/3	8/4–8/29	8/30–9/23	9/24–10/17
1962	3/11–4/3	4/4–4/28	4/29–5/22	5/23–6/17	6/18–7/12	7/13–8/8
1963	4/24–5/18	5/19–6/12	6/13–7/7	7/8–7/31	8/1–8/25	8/26–9/18
1964	2/11–3/7	3/8–4/4	4/5–5/9	5/10–6/17	9/9–10/5	10/6–10/31
			6/18–8/5	8/6–9/8		
1965	3/26–4/18	4/19–5/12	5/13–6/6	6/7–6/30	7/1–7/25	7/26–8/19
1966	5/6–6/31	6/1–6/26	6/27–7/21	7/22–8/15	8/16–9/8	9/9–10/2
1967	2/24–3/20	3/21–4/14	4/15–5/10	5/11–6/6	6/7–7/8	7/9–9/9
					9/10–10/1	10/2–11/9
1968	4/9–5/3	5/4–5/27	5/28–6/20	6/21–7/15	7/16–8/8	8/9–9/2
1969	2/3–6/6	6/7–7/6	7/7–8/3	8/4–8/28	8/29–9/22	9/23–10/17
1970	3/11–4/3	4/4–4/27	4/28–5/22	5/23–6/16	6/17–7/12	7/13–8/8
1971	4/24–5/18	5/19–6/12	6/13–7/6	7/7–7/31	8/1–8/24	8/25–9/17
1972	2/11–3/7	3/8–4/3	4/4–5/10	5/11–6/11		
			6/12–8/6	8/7–9/8	9/9–10/5	10/6–10/30
1973	3/25–4/18	4/18–5/12	5/13–6/5	6/6–6/29	7/1–7/25	7/26–8/19
1974						
	5/5–5/31	6/1–6/25	6/26–7/21	7/22–8/14	8/15–9/8	9/9–10/2
1975	2/24–3/20	3/21–4/13	4/14–5/9	5/10–6/6	6/7–7/9	7/10–9/2
					9/3–10/4	10/5–11/9

Libra	Scorpio	Sagittarius	Capricorn	Aquarius	Pisces
9/4–9/27	1/1–1/2	1/3–1/27	1/28–2/20	2/21–3/16	3/17–4/9
	9/28–10/21	10/22–11/15	11/16–12/10	12/11–12/31	
10/19–11/11	11/12–12/5	12/6–12/29	12/30–12/31	1/1–1/5	1/6–2/1
8/9–9/6	9/7–10/22	10/23–10/27	1/1–1/22	1/23–2/15	2/16–3/11
	10/28–12/31				
9/19–10/13	1/1–1/6	1/7–2/5	2/6–3/4	3/5–3/30	3/31–4/24
	10/14–11/5	11/6–11/30	12/1–12/24	12/25–12/31	
11/1–11/25	11/26–12/19	12/20–12/31		1/1–1/17	1/18–2/11
8/20–9/14	9/15–10/9	1/1–1/12	1/13–2/5	2/6–3/1	3/2–3/25
		10/10–11/5	11/6–12/6	12/7–12/31	
10/4–10/27	10/28–11/20	11/21–12/14	12/15–12/31	1/1–4/6	4/7–5/5
11/10–12/7	12/8–12/31		1/1–1/7	1/8–1/31	2/1–2/24
9/3–9/26	1/1–1/2	1/3–1/27	1/28–2/20	2/21–3/15	3/16–4/9
	9/27–10/21	10/22–11/15	11/16–12/10	12/11–12/31	
10/18–11/11	11/12–12/4	12/5–12/28	12/29–12/31	1/1–1/5	1/6–2/2
8/9–9/6	9/7–12/31		1/1–1/21	1/22–2/14	2/15–3/10
9/19–10/12	1/1–1/6	1/7–2/5	2/6–3/4	3/5–3/29	3/30–4/23
	10/13–11/5	11/6–11/29	11/30–12/23	12/24–12/31	
11/1–11/24	11/25–12/19	12/20–12/31		1/1–1/16	1/17–2/10
8/20–9/13	9/14–10/9	1/1–1/12	1/13–2/5	2/6–3/1	3/2–3/25
		10/10–11/5	11/6–12/7	12/8–12/31	
10/3–10/26	10/27–11/19	11/20–12/13	2/7–2/25	1/1–2/6	4/7–5/5
			12/14–12/31	2/26–4/6	
11/10–12/7	12/8–12/31		1/1–1/6	1/7–1/30	1/31–2/23
9/3–9/26	1/1	1/2–1/26	1/27–2/20	2/21–3/15	3/16–4/8
	9/27–10/21	10/22–11/14	11/15–12/9	12/10–12/31	
10/18–11/10	11/11–12/4	12/5–12/28	12/29–12/31	1/1–1/4	1/5–2/2
8/9–9/7	9/8–12/31		1/1–1/21	1/22–2/14	2/15–3/10
9/18–10/11	1/1–1/7	1/8–2/5	2/6–3/4	3/5–3/29	3/30–4/23
	10/12–11/5	11/6–11/29	11/30–12/23	12/24–12/31	
	11/25–12/18	12/19–12/31		1/1–1/16	1/17–2/10
10/31–11/24					
8/20–9/13	9/14–10/8	1/1–1/12	1/13–2/4	2/5–2/28	3/1–3/24
		10/9–11/5	11/6–12/7	12/8–12/31	
			1/30–2/28	1/1–1/29	
10/3–10/26	10/27–11/19	11/20–12/13	12/14–12/31	3/1–4/6	4/7–5/4
			1/1–1/6	1/7–1/30	1/31–2/23
11/10–12/7	12/8–12/31				

VENUS SIGNS 1901–2003

	Aries	Taurus	Gemini	Cancer	Leo	Virgo
1976	4/8–5/2	5/2–5/27	5/27–6/20	6/20–7/14	7/14–8/8	8/8–9/1
1977	2/2–6/6	6/6–7/6	7/6–8/2	8/2–8/28	8/28–9/22	9/22–10/17
1978	3/9–4/2	4/2–4/27	4/27–5/22	5/22–6/16	6/16–7/12	7/12–8/6
1979	4/23–5/18	5/18–6/11	6/11–7/6	7/6–7/30	7/30–8/24	8/24–9/17
1980	2/9–3/6	3/6–4/3	4/3–5/12	5/12–6/5	9/7–10/4	10/4–10/30
			6/5–8/6	8/6–9/7		
1981	3/24–4/17	4/17–5/11	5/11–6/5	6/5–6/29	6/29–7/24	7/24–8/18
1982	5/4–5/30	5/30–6/25	6/25–7/20	7/20–8/14	8/14–9/7	9/7–10/2
1983	2/22–3/19	3/19–4/13	4/13–5/9	5/9–6/6	6/6–7/10	7/10–8/27
					8/27–10/5	10/5–11/9
1984	4/7–5/2	5/2–5/26	5/26–6/20	6/20–7/14	7/14–8/7	8/7–9/1
1985	2/2–6/6	6/7–7/6	7/6–8/2	8/2–8/28	8/28–9/22	9/22–10/16
1986	3/9–4/2	4/2–4/26	4/26–5/21	5/21–6/15	6/15–7/11	7/11–8/7
1987	4/22–5/17	5/17–6/11	6/11–7/5	7/5–7/30	7/30–8/23	8/23–9/16
1988	2/9–3/6	3/6–4/3	4/3–5/17	5/17–5/27	9/7–10/4	10/4–10/29
			5/27–8/6	8/28–9/22	9/22–10/16	
1989	3/23–4/16	4/16–5/11	5/11–6/4	6/4–6/29	6/29–7/24	7/24–8/18
1990	5/4–5/30	5/30–6/25	6/25–7/20	7/20–8/13	8/13–9/7	9/7–10/1
1991	2/22–3/18	3/18–4/13	4/13–5/9	5/9–6/6	6/6–7/11	7/11–8/21
					8/21–10/6	10/6–11/9
1992	4/7–5/1	5/1–5/26	5/26–6/19	6/19–7/13	7/13–8/7	8/7–8/31
1993	2/2–6/6	6/6–7/6	7/6–8/1	8/1–8/27	8/27–9/21	9/21–10/16
1994	3/8–4/1	4/1–4/26	4/26–5/21	5/21–6/15	6/15–7/11	7/11–8/7
1995	4/22–5/16	5/16–6/10	6/10–7/5	7/5–7/29	7/29–8/23	8/23–9/16
1996	2/9–3/6	3/6–4/3	4/3–8/7	8/7–9/7	9/7–10/4	10/4–10/29
1997	3/23–4/16	4/16–5/10	5/10–6/4	6/4–6/28	6/28–7/23	7/23–8/17
1998	5/3–5/29	5/29–6/24	6/24–7/19	7/19–8/13	8/13–9/6	9/6–9/30
1999	2/21–3/18	3/18–4/12	4/12–5/8	5/8–6/5	6/5–7/12	7/12–8/15
					8/15–10/7	10/7–11/9
2000	4/6–5/1	5/1–5/25	5/25–6/13	6/13–7/13	7/13–8/6	8/6–8/31
2001	2/2–6/6	6/6–7/5	7/5–8/1	8/1–8/26	8/26–9/20	9/20–10/15
2002	3/7–4/1	4/1–4/25	4/25–5/20	5/20–6/14	6/14–7/10	7/10–8/7
2003	4/21–5/16	5/16–6/9	6/9–7/4	7/4–7/29	7/29–8/22	8/22–9/15

Libra	Scorpio	Sagittarius	Capricorn	Aquarius	Pisces
9/1–9/26	9/26–10/20	1/1–1/26	1/26–2/19	2/19–3/15	3/15–4/8
		10/20–11/14	11/14–12/8	12/9–1/4	
10/17–11/10	11/10–12/4	12/4–12/27	12/27–1/20/78		1/4–2/2
8/6–9/7	9/7–1/7			1/20–2/13	2/13–3/9
9/17–10/11	10/11–11/4	1/7–2/5	2/5–3/3	3/3–3/29	3/29–4/23
		11/4–11/28	11/28–12/22	12/22–1/16/80	
10/30–11/24	11/24–12/18	12/18–1/11/81			1/16–2/9
8/18–9/12	9/12–10/9	10/9–11/5	1/11–2/4	2/4–2/28	2/28–3/24
			11/5–12/8	12/8–1/23/82	
10/2–10/26	10/26–11/18	11/18–12/12	1/23–3/2	3/2–4/6	4/6–5/4
			12/12–1/5/83		
11/9–12/6	12/6–1/1/84			1/5–1/29	1/29–2/22
9/1–9/25	9/25–10/20	1/1–1/25	1/25–2/19	2/19–3/14	3/14–4/7
		10/20–11/13	11/13–12/9	12/10–1/4	
10/16–11/9	11/9–12/3	12/3–12/27	12/28–1/19		1/4–2/2
8/7–9/7	9/7–1/7			1/20–2/13	2/13–3/9
9/16–10/10	10/10–11/3	1/7–2/5	2/5–3/3	3/3–3/28	3/28–4/22
		11/3–11/28	11/28–12/22	12/22–1/15	
10/29–11/23	11/23–12/17	12/17–1/10			1/15–2/9
8/18–9/12	9/12–10/8	10/8–11/5	1/10–2/3	2/3–2/27	2/27–3/23
			11/5–12/10	12/10–1/16/90	
10/1–10/25	10/25–11/18	11/18–12/12	1/16–3/3	3/3–4/6	4/6–5/4
			12/12–1/5		
11/9–12/6	12/6–12/31	12/31–1/25/92		1/5–1/29	1/29–2/22
8/31–9/25	9/25–10/19	10/19–11/13	1/25–2/18	2/18–3/13	3/13–4/7
			11/13–12/8	12/8–1/3/93	
10/16–11/9	11/9–12/2	12/2–12/26	12/26–1/19		1/3–2/2
8/7–9/7	9/7–1/7			1/19–2/12	2/12–3/8
9/16–10/10	10/10–11/13	1/7–2/4	2/4–3/2	3/2–3/28	3/28–4/22
		11/3–11/27	11/27–12/21	12/21–1/15	
10/29–11/23	11/23–12/17	12/17–1/10/97			1/15–2/9
8/17–9/12	9/12–10/8	10/8–11/5	1/10–2/3	2/3–2/27	2/27–3/23
			11/5–12/12	12/12–1/9	
9/30–10/24	10/24–11/17	11/17–12/11	1/9–3/4	3/4–4/6	4/6–5/3
11/9–12/5	12/5–12/31	12/31–1/24		1/4–1/28	1/28–2/21
8/31–9/24	9/24–10/19	10/19–11/13	1/24–2/18	2/18–3/12	3/13–4/6
			11/13–12/8	12/8	
10/15–11/8	11/8–12/2	12/2–12/26	12/26/01–1/18/02	12/8/00–1/3/01	1/3–2/2
8/7–9/7	9/7–1/7/03		12/26/01–1/18	1/18–2/11	2/11–3/7
9/15–10/9	10/9–11/2	1/7–2/4	2/4–3/2	3/2–3/27	3/27–4/21
		11/2–11/26	11/26–12/21	12/21–1/14/04	

How to Use the Mars, Jupiter, and Saturn Tables

Find the year of your birth on the left side of each column. The dates when the planet entered each sign are listed on the right side of each column. (Signs are abbreviated to three letters.) Your birthday should fall on or between each date listed, and your planetary placement should correspond to the earlier sign of that period.

MARS SIGNS 1901–2003

Year	Month	Day	Sign		Year	Month	Day	Sign
1901	MAR	1	Leo		1905	JAN	13	Scp
	MAY	11	Vir			AUG	21	Sag
	JUL	13	Lib			OCT	8	Cap
	AUG	31	Scp			NOV	18	Aqu
	OCT	14	Sag			DEC	27	Pic
	NOV	24	Cap		1906	FEB	4	Ari
1902	JAN	1	Aqu			MAR	17	Tau
	FEB	8	Pic			APR	28	Gem
	MAR	19	Ari			JUN	11	Can
	APR	27	Tau			JUL	27	Leo
	JUN	7	Gem			SEP	12	Vir
	JUL	20	Can			OCT	30	Lib
	SEP	4	Leo			DEC	17	Scp
	OCT	23	Vir		1907	FEB	5	Sag
	DEC	20	Lib			APR	1	Cap
1903	APR	19	Vir			OCT	13	Aqu
	MAY	30	Lib			NOV	29	Pic
	AUG	6	Scp		1908	JAN	11	Ari
	SEP	22	Sag			FEB	23	Tau
	NOV	3	Cap			APR	7	Gem
	DEC	12	Aqu			MAY	22	Can
1904	JAN	19	Pic			JUL	8	Leo
	FEB	27	Ari			AUG	24	Vir
	APR	6	Tau			OCT	10	Lib
	MAY	18	Gem			NOV	25	Scp
	JUN	30	Can		1909	JAN	10	Sag
	AUG	15	Leo			FEB	24	Cap
	OCT	1	Vir			APR	9	Aqu
	NOV	20	Lib			MAY	25	Pic

	JUL	21	Ari	AUG	19	Can
	SEP	26	Pic	OCT	7	Leo
	NOV	20	Ari	1916 MAY	28	Vir
1910	JAN	23	Tau	JUL	23	Lib
	MAR	14	Gem	SEP	8	Scp
	MAY	1	Can	OCT	22	Sag
	JUN	19	Leo	DEC	1	Cap
	AUG	6	Vir	1917 JAN	9	Aqu
	SEP	22	Lib	FEB	16	Pic
	NOV	6	Scp	MAR	26	Ari
	DEC	20	Sag	MAY	4	Tau
1911	JAN	31	Cap	JUN	14	Gem
	MAR	14	Aqu	JUL	28	Can
	APR	23	Pic	SEP	12	Leo
	JUN	2	Ari	NOV	2	Vir
	JUL	15	Tau	1918 JAN	11	Lib
	SEP	5	Gem	FEB	25	Vir
	NOV	30	Tau	JUN	23	Lib
1912	JAN	30	Gem	AUG	17	Scp
	APR	5	Can	OCT	1	Sag
	MAY	28	Leo	NOV	11	Cap
	JUL	17	Vir	DEC	20	Aqu
	SEP	2	Lib	1919 JAN	27	Pic
	OCT	18	Scp	MAR	6	Ari
	NOV	30	Sag	APR	15	Tau
1913	JAN	10	Cap	MAY	26	Gem
	FEB	19	Aqu	JUL	8	Can
	MAR	30	Pic	AUG	23	Leo
	MAY	8	Ari	OCT	10	Vir
	JUN	17	Tau	NOV	30	Lib
	JUL	29	Gem	1920 JAN	31	Scp
	SEP	15	Can	APR	23	Lib
1914	MAY	1	Leo	JUL	10	Scp
	JUN	26	Vir	SEP	4	Sag
	AUG	14	Lib	OCT	18	Cap
	SEP	29	Scp	NOV	27	Aqu
	NOV	11	Sag	1921 JAN	5	Pic
	DEC	22	Cap	FEB	13	Ari
1915	JAN	30	Aqu	MAR	25	Tau
	MAR	9	Pic	MAY	6	Gem
	APR	16	Ari	JUN	18	Can
	MAY	26	Tau	AUG	3	Leo
	JUL	6	Gem	SEP	19	Vir

	NOV	6	Lib		APR	7	Pic
	DEC	26	Scp		MAY	16	Ari
1922	FEB	18	Sag		JUN	26	Tau
	SEP	13	Cap		AUG	9	Gem
	OCT	30	Aqu		OCT	3	Can
	DEC	11	Pic		DEC	20	Gem
1923	JAN	21	Ari	1929	MAR	10	Can
	MAR	4	Tau		MAY	13	Leo
	APR	16	Gem		JUL	4	Vir
	MAY	30	Can		AUG	21	Lib
	JUL	16	Leo		OCT	6	Scp
	SEP	1	Vir		NOV	18	Sag
	OCT	18	Lib		DEC	29	Cap
	DEC	4	Scp	1930	FEB	6	Aqu
1924	JAN	19	Sag		MAR	17	Pic
	MAR	6	Cap		APR	24	Ari
	APR	24	Aqu		JUN	3	Tau
	JUN	24	Pic		JUL	14	Gem
	AUG	24	Aqu		AUG	28	Can
	OCT	19	Pic		OCT	20	Leo
	DEC	19	Ari	1931	FEB	16	Can
1925	FEB	5	Tau		MAR	30	Leo
	MAR	24	Gem		JUN	10	Vir
	MAY	9	Can		AUG	1	Lib
	JUN	26	Leo		SEP	17	Scp
	AUG	12	Vir		OCT	30	Sag
	SEP	28	Lib		DEC	10	Cap
	NOV	13	Scp	1932	JAN	18	Aqu
	DEC	28	Sag		FEB	25	Pic
1926	FEB	9	Cap		APR	3	Ari
	MAR	23	Aqu		MAY	12	Tau
	MAY	3	Pic		JUN	22	Gem
	JUN	15	Ari		AUG	4	Can
	AUG	1	Tau		SEP	20	Leo
1927	FEB	22	Gem		NOV	13	Vir
	APR	17	Can	1933	JUL	6	Lib
	JUN	6	Leo		AUG	26	Scp
	JUL	25	Vir		OCT	9	Sag
	SEP	10	Lib		NOV	19	Cap
	OCT	26	Scp		DEC	28	Aqu
	DEC	8	Sag	1934	FEB	4	Pic
1928	JAN	19	Cap		MAR	14	Ari
	FEB	28	Aqu		APR	22	Tau

	JUN	2	Gem		AUG	19	Vir
	JUL	15	Can		OCT	5	Lib
	AUG	30	Leo		NOV	20	Scp
	OCT	18	Vir	1941	JAN	4	Sag
	DEC	11	Lib		FEB	17	Cap
1935	JUL	29	Scp		APR	2	Aqu
	SEP	16	Sag		MAY	16	Pic
	OCT	28	Cap		JUL	2	Ari
	DEC	7	Aqu	1942	JAN	11	Tau
1936	JAN	14	Pic		MAR	7	Gem
	FEB	22	Ari		APR	26	Can
	APR	1	Tau		JUN	14	Leo
	MAY	13	Gem		AUG	1	Vir
	JUN	25	Can		SEP	17	Lib
	AUG	10	Leo		NOV	1	Scp
	SEP	26	Vir		DEC	15	Sag
	NOV	14	Lib	1943	JAN	26	Cap
1937	JAN	5	Scp		MAR	8	Aqu
	MAR	13	Sag		APR	17	Pic
	MAY	14	Scp		MAY	27	Ari
	AUG	8	Sag		JUL	7	Tau
	SEP	30	Cap		AUG	23	Gem
	NOV	11	Aqu	1944	MAR	28	Can
	DEC	21	Pic		MAY	22	Leo
1938	JAN	30	Ari		JUL	12	Vir
	MAR	12	Tau		AUG	29	Lib
	APR	23	Gem		OCT	13	Scp
	JUN	7	Can		NOV	25	Sag
	JUL	22	Leo	1945	JAN	5	Cap
	SEP	7	Vir		FEB	14	Aqu
	OCT	25	Lib		MAR	25	Pic
	DEC	11	Scp		MAY	2	Ari
1939	JAN	29	Sag		JUN	11	Tau
	MAR	21	Cap		JUL	23	Gem
	MAY	25	Aqu		SEP	7	Can
	JUL	21	Cap		NOV	11	Leo
	SEP	24	Aqu		DEC	26	Can
	NOV	19	Pic	1946	APR	22	Leo
1940	JAN	4	Ari		JUN	20	Vir
	FEB	17	Tau		AUG	9	Lib
	APR	1	Gem		SEP	24	Scp
	MAY	17	Can		NOV	6	Sag
	JUL	3	Leo		DEC	17	Cap

1947	JAN	25	Aqu		MAR	20	Tau
	MAR	4	Pic		MAY	1	Gem
	APR	11	Ari		JUN	14	Can
	MAY	21	Tau		JUL	29	Leo
	JUL	1	Gem		SEP	14	Vir
	AUG	13	Can		NOV	1	Lib
	OCT	1	Leo		DEC	20	Scp
	DEC	1	Vir	1954	FEB	9	Sag
1948	FEB	12	Leo		APR	12	Cap
	MAY	18	Vir		JUL	3	Sag
	JUL	17	Lib		AUG	24	Cap
	SEP	3	Scp		OCT	21	Aqu
	OCT	17	Sag		DEC	4	Pic
	NOV	26	Cap	1955	JAN	15	Ari
1949	JAN	4	Aqu		FEB	26	Tau
	FEB	11	Pic		APR	10	Gem
	MAR	21	Ari		MAY	26	Can
	APR	30	Tau		JUL	11	Leo
	JUN	10	Gem		AUG	27	Vir
	JUL	23	Can		OCT	13	Lib
	SEP	7	Leo		NOV	29	Scp
	OCT	27	Vir	1956	JAN	14	Sag
	DEC	26	Lib		FEB	28	Cap
1950	MAR	28	Vir		APR	14	Aqu
	JUN	11	Lib		JUN	3	Pic
	AUG	10	Scp		DEC	6	Ari
	SEP	25	Sag	1957	JAN	28	Tau
	NOV	6	Cap		MAR	17	Gem
	DEC	15	Aqu		MAY	4	Can
1951	JAN	22	Pic		JUN	21	Leo
	MAR	1	Ari		AUG	8	Vir
	APR	10	Tau		SEP	24	Lib
	MAY	21	Gem		NOV	8	Scp
	JUL	3	Can		DEC	23	Sag
	AUG	18	Leo	1958	FEB	3	Cap
	OCT	5	Vir		MAR	17	Aqu
	NOV	24	Lib		APR	27	Pic
1952	JAN	20	Scp		JUN	7	Ari
	AUG	27	Sag		JUL	21	Tau
	OCT	12	Cap		SEP	21	Gem
	NOV	21	Aqu		OCT	29	Tau
	DEC	30	Pic	1959	FEB	10	Gem
1953	FEB	8	Ari		APR	10	Can

	JUN	1	Leo		NOV	14	Cap
	JUL	20	Vir		DEC	23	Aqu
	SEP	5	Lib	1966	JAN	30	Pic
	OCT	21	Scp		MAR	9	Ari
	DEC	3	Sag		APR	17	Tau
1960	JAN	14	Cap		MAY	28	Gem
	FEB	23	Aqu		JUL	11	Can
	APR	2	Pic		AUG	25	Leo
	MAY	11	Ari		OCT	12	Vir
	JUN	20	Tau		DEC	4	Lib
	AUG	2	Gem	1967	FEB	12	Scp
	SEP	21	Can		MAR	31	Lib
1961	FEB	5	Gem		JUL	19	Scp
	FEB	7	Can		SEP	10	Sag
	MAY	6	Leo		OCT	23	Cap
	JUN	28	Vir		DEC	1	Aqu
	AUG	17	Lib	1968	JAN	9	Pic
	OCT	1	Scp		FEB	17	Ari
	NOV	13	Sag		MAR	27	Tau
	DEC	24	Cap		MAY	8	Gem
1962	FEB	1	Aqu		JUN	21	Can
	MAR	12	Pic		AUG	5	Leo
	APR	19	Ari		SEP	21	Vir
	MAY	28	Tau		NOV	9	Lib
	JUL	9	Gem		DEC	29	Scp
	AUG	22	Can	1969	FEB	25	Sag
	OCT	11	Leo		SEP	21	Cap
1963	JUN	3	Vir		NOV	4	Aqu
	JUL	27	Lib		DEC	15	Pic
	SEP	12	Scp	1970	JAN	24	Ari
	OCT	25	Sag		MAR	7	Tau
	DEC	5	Cap		APR	18	Gem
1964	JAN	13	Aqu		JUN	2	Can
	FEB	20	Pic		JUL	18	Leo
	MAR	29	Ari		SEP	3	Vir
	MAY	7	Tau		OCT	20	Lib
	JUN	17	Gem		DEC	6	Scp
	JUL	30	Can	1971	JAN	23	Sag
	SEP	15	Leo		MAR	12	Cap
	NOV	6	Vir		MAY	3	Aqu
1965	JUN	29	Lib		NOV	6	Pic
	AUG	20	Scp		DEC	26	Ari
	OCT	4	Sag	1972	FEB	10	Tau

	MAR	27	Gem	1978	JAN	26	Can
	MAY	12	Can		APR	10	Leo
	JUN	28	Leo		JUN	14	Vir
	AUG	15	Vir		AUG	4	Lib
	SEP	30	Lib		SEP	19	Scp
	NOV	15	Scp		NOV	2	Sag
	DEC	30	Sag		DEC	12	Cap
1973	FEB	12	Cap	1979	JAN	20	Aqu
	MAR	26	Aqu		FEB	27	Pic
	MAY	8	Pic		APR	7	Ari
	JUN	20	Ari		MAY	16	Tau
	AUG	12	Tau		JUN	26	Gem
	OCT	29	Ari		AUG	8	Can
	DEC	24	Tau		SEP	24	Leo
1974	FEB	27	Gem		NOV	19	Vir
	APR	20	Can	1980	MAR	11	Leo
	JUN	9	Leo		MAY	4	Vir
	JUL	27	Vir		JUL	10	Lib
	SEP	12	Lib		AUG	29	Scp
	OCT	28	Scp		OCT	12	Sag
	DEC	10	Sag		NOV	22	Cap
1975	JAN	21	Cap		DEC	30	Aqu
	MAR	3	Aqu	1981	FEB	6	Pic
	APR	11	Pic		MAR	17	Ari
	MAY	21	Ari		APR	25	Tau
	JUL	1	Tau		JUN	5	Gem
	AUG	14	Gem		JUL	18	Can
	OCT	17	Can		SEP	2	Leo
	NOV	25	Gem		OCT	21	Vir
1976	MAR	18	Can		DEC	16	Lib
	MAY	16	Leo	1982	AUG	3	Scp
	JUL	6	Vir		SEP	20	Sag
	AUG	24	Lib		OCT	31	Cap
	OCT	8	Scp		DEC	10	Aqu
	NOV	20	Sag	1983	JAN	17	Pic
1977	JAN	1	Cap		FEB	25	Ari
	FEB	9	Aqu		APR	5	Tau
	MAR	20	Pic		MAY	16	Gem
	APR	27	Ari		JUN	29	Can
	JUN	6	Tau		AUG	13	Leo
	JUL	17	Gem		SEP	30	Vir
	SEP	1	Can		NOV	18	Lib
	OCT	26	Leo	1984	JAN	11	Scp

	AUG	17	Sag		JUL	12	Tau
	OCT	5	Cap		AUG	31	Gem
	NOV	15	Aqu		DEC	14	Tau
	DEC	25	Pic	1991	JAN	21	Gem
1985	FEB	2	Ari		APR	3	Can
	MAR	15	Tau		MAY	26	Leo
	APR	26	Gem		JUL	15	Vir
	JUN	9	Can		SEP	1	Lib
	JUL	25	Leo		OCT	16	Scp
	SEP	10	Vir		NOV	29	Sag
	OCT	27	Lib	1992	JAN	9	Cap
	DEC	14	Scp		FEB	18	Aqu
1986	FEB	2	Sag		MAR	28	Pic
	MAR	28	Cap		MAY	5	Ari
	OCT	9	Aqu		JUN	14	Tau
	NOV	26	Pic		JUL	26	Gem
1987	JAN	8	Ari		SEP	12	Can
	FEB	20	Tau	1993	APR	27	Leo
	APR	5	Gem		JUN	23	Vir
	MAY	21	Can		AUG	12	Lib
	JUL	6	Leo		SEP	27	Scp
	AUG	22	Vir		NOV	9	Sag
	OCT	8	Lib		DEC	20	Cap
	NOV	24	Scp	1994	JAN	28	Aqu
1988	JAN	8	Sag		MAR	7	Pic
	FEB	22	Cap		APR	14	Ari
	APR	6	Aqu		MAY	23	Tau
	MAY	22	Pic		JUL	3	Gem
	JUL	13	Ari		AUG	16	Can
	OCT	23	Pic		OCT	4	Leo
	NOV	1	Ari		DEC	12	Vir
1989	JAN	19	Tau	1995	JAN	22	Leo
	MAR	11	Gem		MAY	25	Vir
	APR	29	Can		JUL	21	Lib
	JUN	16	Leo		SEP	7	Scp
	AUG	3	Vir		OCT	20	Sag
	SEP	19	Lib		NOV	30	Cap
	NOV	4	Scp	1996	JAN	8	Aqu
	DEC	18	Sag		FEB	15	Pic
1990	JAN	29	Cap		MAR	24	Ari
	MAR	11	Aqu		MAY	2	Tau
	APR	20	Pic		JUN	12	Gem
	MAY	31	Ari		JUL	25	Can

	SEP	9	Leo		MAR	23	Tau
	OCT	30	Vir		MAY	3	Gem
1997	JAN	3	Lib		JUN	16	Can
	MAR	8	Vir		AUG	1	Leo
	JUN	19	Lib		SEP	17	Vir
	AUG	14	Scp		NOV	4	Lib
	SEP	28	Sag		DEC	23	Scp
	NOV	9	Cap	2001	FEB	14	Sag
	DEC	18	Aqu		SEP	8	Cap
1998	JAN	25	Pic		OCT	27	Aqu
	MAR	4	Ari		DEC	8	Pic
	APR	13	Tau	2002	JAN	18	Ari
	MAY	24	Gem		MAR	1	Tau
	JUL	6	Can		APR	13	Gem
	AUG	20	Leo		MAY	28	Can
	OCT	7	Vir		JUL	13	Leo
	NOV	27	Lib		AUG	29	Vir
1999	JAN	26	Scp		OCT	15	Lib
	MAY	5	Lib		DEC	1	Scp
	JUL	5	Scp	2003	JAN	17	Sag
	SEP	2	Sag		MAR	4	Cap
	OCT	17	Cap		APR	21	Aqu
	NOV	26	Aqu		JUN	17	Pic
2000	JAN	4	Pic		DEC	16	Ari
	FEB	12	Ari				

JUPITER SIGNS 1901–2003

1901	JAN	19	Cap	1909	OCT	11	Lib
1902	FEB	6	Aqu	1910	NOV	11	Scp
1903	FEB	20	Pic	1911	DEC	10	Sag
1904	MAR	1	Ari	1913	JAN	2	Cap
	AUG	8	Tau	1914	JAN	21	Aqu
	AUG	31	Ari	1915	FEB	4	Pic
1905	MAR	7	Tau	1916	FEB	12	Ari
	JUL	21	Gem		JUN	26	Tau
	DEC	4	Tau		OCT	26	Ari
1906	MAR	9	Gem	1917	FEB	12	Tau
	JUL	30	Can		JUN	29	Gem
1907	AUG	18	Leo	1918	JUL	13	Can
1908	SEP	12	Vir	1919	AUG	2	Leo

1920	AUG	27	Vir
1921	SEP	25	Lib
1922	OCT	26	Scp
1923	NOV	24	Sag
1924	DEC	18	Cap
1926	JAN	6	Aqu
1927	JAN	18	Pic
	JUN	6	Ari
	SEP	11	Pic
1928	JAN	23	Ari
	JUN	4	Tau
1929	JUN	12	Gem
1930	JUN	26	Can
1931	JUL	17	Leo
1932	AUG	11	Vir
1933	SEP	10	Lib
1934	OCT	11	Scp
1935	NOV	9	Sag
1936	DEC	2	Cap
1937	DEC	20	Aqu
1938	MAY	14	Pic
	JUL	30	Aqu
	DEC	29	Pic
1939	MAY	11	Ari
	OCT	30	Pic
	DEC	20	Ari
1940	MAY	16	Tau
1941	MAY	26	Gem
1942	JUN	10	Can
1943	JUN	30	Leo
1944	JUL	26	Vir
1945	AUG	25	Lib
1946	SEP	25	Scp
1947	OCT	24	Sag
1948	NOV	15	Cap
1949	APR	12	Aqu
	JUN	27	Cap
	NOV	30	Aqu
1950	APR	15	Pic
	SEP	15	Aqu
	DEC	1	Pic

1951	APR	21	Ari
1952	APR	28	Tau
1953	MAY	9	Gem
1954	MAY	24	Can
1955	JUN	13	Leo
	NOV	17	Vir
1956	JAN	18	Leo
	JUL	7	Vir
	DEC	13	Lib
1957	FEB	19	Vir
	AUG	7	Lib
1958	JAN	13	Scp
	MAR	20	Lib
	SEP	7	Scp
1959	FEB	10	Sag
	APR	24	Scp
	OCT	5	Sag
1960	MAR	1	Cap
	JUN	10	Sag
	OCT	26	Cap
1961	MAR	15	Aqu
	AUG	12	Cap
	NOV	4	Aqu
1962	MAR	25	Pic
1963	APR	4	Ari
1964	APR	12	Tau
1965	APR	22	Gem
	SEP	21	Can
	NOV	17	Gem
1966	MAY	5	Can
	SEP	27	Leo
1967	JAN	16	Can
	MAY	23	Leo
	OCT	19	Vir
1968	FEB	27	Leo
	JUN	15	Vir
	NOV	15	Lib
1969	MAR	30	Vir
	JUL	15	Lib
	DEC	16	Scp
1970	APR	30	Lib

	AUG	15	Scp	1985	FEB	6	Aqu
1971	JAN	14	Sag	1986	FEB	20	Pic
	JUN	5	Scp	1987	MAR	2	Ari
	SEP	11	Sag	1988	MAR	8	Tau
1972	FEB	6	Cap		JUL	22	Gem
	JUL	24	Sag		NOV	30	Tau
	SEP	25	Cap	1989	MAR	11	Gem
1973	FEB	23	Aqu		JUL	30	Can
1974	MAR	8	Pic	1990	AUG	18	Leo
1975	MAR	18	Ari	1991	SEP	12	Vir
1976	MAR	26	Tau	1992	OCT	10	Lib
	AUG	23	Gem	1993	NOV	10	Scp
	OCT	16	Tau	1994	DEC	9	Sag
1977	APR	3	Gem	1996	JAN	3	Cap
	AUG	20	Can	1997	JAN	21	Aqu
	DEC	30	Gem	1998	FEB	4	Pic
1978	APR	12	Can	1999	FEB	13	Ari
	SEP	5	Leo		JUN	28	Tau
1979	FEB	28	Can		OCT	23	Ari
	APR	20	Leo	2000	FEB	14	Tau
	SEP	29	Vir		JUN	30	Gem
1980	OCT	27	Lib	2001	JUL	14	Can
1981	NOV	27	Scp	2002	AUG	1	Leo
1982	DEC	26	Sag	2003	AUG	27	VIR
1984	JAN	19	Cap				

SATURN SIGNS 1903–2003

1903	JAN	19	Aqu		DEC	7	Gem
1905	APR	13	Pic	1915	MAY	11	Can
	AUG	17	Aqu	1916	OCT	17	Leo
1906	JAN	8	Pic		DEC	7	Can
1908	MAR	19	Ari	1917	JUN	24	Leo
1910	MAY	17	Tau	1919	AUG	12	Vir
	DEC	14	Ari	1921	OCT	7	Lib
1911	JAN	20	Tau	1923	DEC	20	Scp
1912	JUL	7	Gem	1924	APR	6	Lib
	NOV	30	Tau		SEP	13	Scp
1913	MAR	26	Gem	1926	DEC	2	Sag
1914	AUG	24	Can	1929	MAR	15	Cap

Year	Mon	Day	Sign		Year	Mon	Day	Sign
	MAY	5	Sag		1971	JUN	18	Gem
	NOV	30	Cap		1972	JAN	10	Tau
1932	FEB	24	Aqu			FEB	21	Gem
	AUG	13	Cap		1973	AUG	1	Can
	NOV	20	Aqu		1974	JAN	7	Gem
1935	FEB	14	Pic			APR	18	Can
1937	APR	25	Ari		1975	SEP	17	Leo
	OCT	18	Pic		1976	JAN	14	Can
1938	JAN	14	Ari			JUN	5	Leo
1939	JUL	6	Tau		1977	NOV	17	Vir
	SEP	22	Ari		1978	JAN	5	Leo
1940	MAR	20	Tau			JUL	26	Vir
1942	MAY	8	Gem		1980	SEP	21	Lib
1944	JUN	20	Can		1982	NOV	29	Scp
1946	AUG	2	Leo		1983	MAY	6	Lib
1948	SEP	19	Vir			AUG	24	Scp
1949	APR	3	Leo		1985	NOV	17	Sag
	MAY	29	Vir		1988	FEB	13	Cap
1950	NOV	20	Lib			JUN	10	Sag
1951	MAR	7	Vir			NOV	12	Cap
	AUG	13	Lib		1991	FEB	6	Aqu
1953	OCT	22	Scp		1993	MAY	21	Pic
1956	JAN	12	Sag			JUN	30	Aqu
	MAY	14	Scp		1994	JAN	28	Pic
	OCT	10	Sag		1996	APR	7	Ari
1959	JAN	5	Cap		1998	JUN	9	Tau
1962	JAN	3	Aqu			OCT	25	Ari
1964	MAR	24	Pic		1999	MAR	1	Tau
	SEP	16	Aqu		2000	AUG	10	Gem
	DEC	16	Pic			OCT	16	Tau
1967	MAR	3	Ari		2001	APR	21	Gem
1969	APR	29	Tau		2003	JUN	3	Can

CHAPTER 5

Astrology's Graphics: How to Read Those Fascinating Symbols on Your Chart

When you see an astrology chart for the first time, you'll be looking at a strange foreign language of pictographs, little symbols that look as ancient as cave drawings. These symbols or *glyphs,* as they are called, are used by astrologers worldwide and by computer astrology programs. So, if you want to read a horoscope chart or use one of the popular astrology programs on your PC, you must learn the glyphs.

Besides enabling you to read a horoscope chart, each glyph contains clues to the meaning of the signs and the planets. Since there are only twelve signs and ten planets (not counting a few asteroids and other space creatures some astrologers use), it's a lot easier than learning to read a foreign language.

Here's a code cracker for the glyphs, beginning with the glyphs for the planets. To those who already know their glyphs, don't just skim over the chapter. These familiar graphics have hidden meanings you will discover!

The Glyphs for the Planets

The glyphs for the planets are easy to learn. They're simple combinations of the most basic visual elements: the circle, the semicircle or arc, and the cross. However, each component of a glyph has a special meaning in relation to the other parts of the symbol.

The circle, which has no beginning or end, is one of the oldest symbols of spirit or spiritual forces. All of the early diagrams of the heavens—spiritual territory—are shown in circular form. The never-ending line of the circle is the perfect symbol for eternity. The semicircle or arc is an incomplete circle, symbolizing the receptive, finite soul, which contains spiritual potential in the curving line.

The vertical line of the cross symbolizes movement from heaven to earth. The horizontal line describes temporal movement, here and now, in time and space. Combined in a cross, the vertical and horizontal planes symbolize manifestation in the material world.

The Sun Glyph ☉

The sun is always shown by this powerful solar symbol, a circle with a point in the center. The center point is you, your spiritual center, and the symbol represents your infinite personality incarnating (the point) into the finite cycles of birth and death.

The sun has been represented by a circle or disk since ancient Egyptian times when the solar disk represented the Sun God, Ra. Some archaeologists believe the great stone circles found in England were centers of sun worship. This particular version of the symbol was brought into common use in the sixteenth century after German occultist and scholar Cornelius Agrippa (1486–1535) wrote a book called *Die Occulta Philosophia,* which became accepted as the authority in its field. Agrippa collected many medieval astrological and magical symbols in this book, which have been used by astrologers since then.

The Moon Glyph ☽

The moon glyph is the most recognizable symbol on a chart, a left-facing arc stylized into the crescent moon. As part of a circle, the arc symbolizes the potential fulfillment of the entire circle, the life force that is still incomplete. Therefore, it is the ideal representation of the reactive, receptive, emotional nature of the moon.

The Mercury Glyph ☿

Mercury contains all three elemental symbols: the crescent, the circle, and the cross in vertical order. This is the "Venus with a hat" glyph (compare with the symbol of Venus). With another stretch of the imagination, can't you see the winged cap of Mercury the messenger? Think of the upturned crescent as antennae that tune in and transmit messages from the sun, reminding you that Mercury is the way you communicate, the way your mind works. The upturned arc is receiving energy into the spirit or solar circle, which will later be translated into action on the material plane, symbolized by the cross. All the elements are equally sized because Mercury is neutral; it doesn't play favorites! This planet symbolizes objective, detached, unemotional thinking.

The Venus Glyph ♀

Here the relationship is between two components: the circle of spirit and the cross of matter. Spirit is elevated over matter, pulling it upward. Venus asks, "What is beautiful? What do you like best? What do you love to have done to you?" Consequently, Venus determines both your ideal of beauty and what feels good sensually. It governs your own allure and power to attract, as well as what attracts and pleases you.

The Mars Glyph ♂

In this glyph, the cross of matter is stylized into an arrowhead pointed up and outward, propelled by the circle of spirit. With a little imagination, you can visualize it as the shield and spear of Mars, the ancient god of war. You can deduce that Mars embodies your spiritual energy projected into the outer world. It's your assertiveness, your initiative, your aggressive drive, what you like to do to others, your temper. If you know someone's Mars, you know whether they'll blow up when angry or do a slow burn. Your task is to use your outgoing Mars energy wisely and well.

The Jupiter Glyph ♃

Jupiter is the basic cross of matter, with a large stylized crescent perched on the left side of the horizontal, temporal plane. You might think of the crescent as an open hand, because one meaning of Jupiter is "luck," what's handed to you. You don't have to work for what you get from Jupiter; it comes to you, if you're open to it.

The Jupiter glyph might also remind you of a jumbo jet plane, with a huge tail fin, about to take off. This is the planet of travel, mental and spiritual, of expanding your horizons via new ideas, new spiritual dimensions, and new places. Jupiter embodies the optimism and enthusiasm of the traveler about to embark on an exciting adventure.

The Saturn Glyph ♄

Flip Jupiter over, and you've got Saturn. This might not be immediately apparent because Saturn is usually stylized into an "h" form like the one shown here. The principle it expresses is the opposite of Jupiter's expansive tendencies. Saturn pulls you back to earth: the receptive arc is pushed down underneath the cross of matter. Before there are any rewards or expansion, the duties and obligations of the material world must be considered. Saturn says, "Stop, wait, finish your chores before you take off!"

Saturn's glyph also resembles the sickle of old "Father Time." Saturn was first known as Chronos, the Greek god of time, for time brings all matter to an end. When it was the most distant planet (before the discovery of Uranus), Saturn was believed to be the place where time stopped. After the soul departed from earth, it journeyed back to the outer reaches of the universe and finally stopped at Saturn, or at "the end of time."

The Uranus Glyph ♅

The glyph for Uranus is often stylized to form a capital "H" after Sir William Herschel who discovered the planet. But the more esoteric version curves the two pillars of the

H into crescent antennae, or "ears," like satellite disks receiving signals from space. These are perched on the horizontal material line of the cross of matter and pushed from below by the circle of the spirit. To many sci-fi fans, Uranus looks like an orbiting satellite.

Uranus channels the highest energy of all, the white electrical light of the universal spiritual force that holds the cosmos together. This pure electrical energy is gathered from all over the universe. Because Uranian energy doesn't follow any ordinary celestial drumbeat, it can't be controlled or predicted (which is also true of those who are strongly influenced by this eccentric planet). In the symbol, this energy is manifested through the balance of polarities (the two opposite arms of the glyph) like the two polarized wires of a light bulb.

The Neptune Glyph Ψ

Neptune's glyph is usually stylized to look like a trident, the weapon of the Roman god Neptune. However, on a more esoteric level, it shows the large upturned crescent of the soul pierced through by the cross of matter. Neptune nails down, or materializes, soul energy, bringing impulses from the soul level into manifestation. That is why Neptune is associated with imagination or "imagining in," making an image of the soul. Neptune works through feeling, sensitivity, and mystical capacity to bring the divine into the earthly realm.

The Pluto Glyph ♀

Pluto is written two ways. One is a composite of the letters "PL," the first two letters of the word Pluto and coincidentally the initials of Percival Lowell, one of the planet's discoverers. The other, more esoteric symbol is a small circle above a large open crescent that surmounts the cross of matter. This depicts Pluto's power to regenerate. Imagine a new little spirit emerging from the sheltering cup of the soul. Pluto rules the forces of life and death. After this planet has passed a sensitive point in your chart, you are transformed, reborn in some way.

Sci-fi fans might visualize this glyph as a small satellite (the circle) being launched. It was shortly after Pluto's discovery that we learned how to harness the nuclear forces that made space exploration possible. Pluto rules the transformative power of atomic energy, which totally changed our lives and from which there is no turning back.

The Glyphs for the Signs

On an astrological chart, the glyph for the sign will appear after that of the planet. For example, when you see the moon glyph followed first by a number and then by another glyph representing the sign, this means that the moon was passing over a certain degree of that astrological sign at the time of the chart. On the dividing lines between the houses on your chart, you'll find the symbol for the sign that rules the house.

Because sun sign symbols do not contain the same basic geometric components of the planetary glyphs, we must look elsewhere for clues to their meanings. Many have been passed down from ancient Egyptian and Chaldean civilizations with few modifications. Others have been adapted over the centuries. In deciphering many of the glyphs, you'll often find that the symbols reveal a dual nature of the sign, which is not always apparent in the usual sun sign descriptions. For instance, the Gemini glyph is similar to the Roman numeral for two, and reveals this sign's longing to discover a twin soul. The Cancer glyph may be interpreted as resembling either the nurturing breasts or the self-protective claws of a crab, both symbols associated with the contrasting qualities of this sign. Libra's glyph embodies the duality of the spirit balanced with material reality. The Sagittarius glyph shows that the aspirant must also carry along the earthly animal nature in his quest. The Capricorn sea goat is another symbol with dual emphasis. The goat climbs high, yet is always pulled back by the deep waters of the unconscious. Aquarius embodies the double waves of mental detachment, balanced by the desire for connection with others in a friendly way. Finally, the two fishes of Pisces, which are forever tied together, show the duality of the soul and the spirit that must be reconciled.

The Aries Glyph ♈

Since the symbol for Aries is the Ram, this glyph is obviously associated with a ram's horns, which characterize one aspect of the Aries personality—an aggressive, me-first, leaping-headfirst attitude. But the symbol can be interpreted in other ways as well. Some astrologers liken it to a fountain of energy, which Aries people also embody. The first sign of the zodiac bursts on the scene eagerly, ready to go. Another analogy is to the eyebrows and nose of the human head, which Aries rules, and the thinking power that is initiated in the brain.

One theory of this symbol links it to the Egyptian god Amun, represented by a ram in ancient times. As Amun-Ra, this god was believed to embody the creator of the universe, the leader of all the other gods. This relates easily to the position of Aries as the leader (or first sign) of the zodiac, which begins at the spring equinox, a time of the year when nature is renewed.

The Taurus Glyph ♉

This is another easy glyph to draw and identify. It takes little imagination to decipher the bull's head with long curving horns. Like its symbol the Bull, the archetypal Taurus is slow to anger but ferocious when provoked, as well as stubborn, steady, and sensual. Another association is the larynx (and thyroid) of the throat area (ruled by Taurus) and the eustachian tubes running up to the ears, which coincides with the relationship of Taurus to the voice, song, and music. Many famous singers, musicians, and composers have prominent Taurus influences.

Many ancient religions involved a bull as the central figure in fertility rites or initiations, usually symbolizing the victory of man over his animal nature. Another possible origin is in the sacred bull of Egypt, who embodied the incarnate form of Osiris, god of death and resurrection. In early Christian imagery, the Taurus Bull represented St. Luke.

The Gemini Glyph ♊

The standard glyph immediately calls to mind the Roman numeral for two (II) and the Twins symbol, as it is called, for Gemini. In almost all drawings and images used for this sign, the relationship between two persons is emphasized. Usually one twin will be touching the other, which signifies communication, human contact, the desire to share.

The top line of the Gemini glyph indicates mental communication, while the bottom line indicates shared physical space.

The most famous Gemini legend is that of the twin sons, Castor and Pollux, one of whom had a mortal father while the other was the son of Zeus, king of the gods. When it came time for the mortal twin to die, his grief-stricken brother pleaded with Zeus, who agreed to let them spend half the year on earth in mortal form and half in immortal life, with the gods on Mt. Olympus. This reflects a basic duality of humankind, which possesses an immortal soul yet is also subject to the limits of mortality.

The Cancer Glyph ♋

Two convenient images relate to the Cancer glyph. It is easiest to decode the curving claws of the Cancer symbol, the Crab. Like the crab, Cancer's element is water. This sensitive sign also has a hard protective shell to protect its tender interior. The crab must be wily to escape predators, scampering sideways and hiding under rocks. The crab also responds to the cycles of the moon, as do all shellfish. The other image is that of two female breasts, which Cancer rules, showing that this is a sign that nurtures and protects others as well as itself.

In ancient Egypt, Cancer was also represented by the scarab beetle, a symbol of regeneration and eternal life.

The Leo Glyph ♌

Notice that the Leo glyph seems to be an extension of Cancer's glyph, with a significant difference. In the Cancer glyph, the lines curve inward protectively. The Leo glyph expresses energy outwardly. And there is no duality in the symbol, the Lion, or in Leo, the sign.

Lions have belonged to the sign of Leo since earliest times. It is not difficult to imagine the king of beasts with his sweeping mane and curling tail from this glyph. The upward sweep of the glyph easily describes the positive energy of Leo: the flourishing tail, their flamboyant qualities. Another analogy, perhaps a stretch of the imagination, is that of a heart leaping up with joy and enthusiasm, also very typical of Leo, which also rules the heart. In early Christian imagery, the Leo Lion represented St. Mark.

The Virgo Glyph ♍

You can read much into this mysterious glyph. For instance, it could represent the initials of "Mary Virgin," or a young woman holding a staff of wheat, or stylized female genitalia, all common interpretations. The "M" shape might also remind you that Virgo is ruled by Mercury. The cross beneath the symbol reveals the grounded, practical nature of this earth sign.

The earliest zodiacs link Virgo with the Egyptian goddess Isis who gave birth to the god Horus, after her husband Osiris had been killed, in the archetype of a miraculous conception. There are many ancient statues of Isis nursing her baby son, which are reminiscent of medieval Virgin and Child motifs. This sign has also been associated with the image of the Holy Grail, when the Virgo symbol was substituted with a chalice.

The Libra Glyph ♎

It is not difficult to read the standard image for Libra, the Scales, into this glyph. There is another meaning, however, that is equally relevant: the setting sun as it descends over the horizon. Libra's natural position on the zodiac wheel is the descendant, or sunset position (as the Aries natural position is the ascendant, or rising sign). Both images relate to Libra's personality. Libra is always weighing pros and cons for a balanced decision. In the sunset image, the sun (male) hovers over the horizontal earth (female) before setting. Libra is the space between these lines, harmonizing yin and yang, spiritual and material, male and female, ideal and real worlds. The glyph has also been linked to the kidneys, which are ruled by Libra.

The Scorpio Glyph ♏

With its barbed tail, this glyph is easy to identify as the Scorpion for the sign of Scorpio. It also represents the male sexual parts, over which the sign rules. From the arrowhead, you can draw the conclusion that Mars was once its ruler. Some earlier Egyptian glyphs for Scorpio represent it as an erect serpent, so the Serpent is an alternate symbol.

Another symbol for Scorpio, which is not identifiable in this glyph, is the Eagle. Scorpios can go to extremes, either soaring like the eagle or self-destructing like the scorpion. In early Christian imagery, which often used zodiacal symbols, the Scorpio Eagle was chosen to symbolize the intense apostle St. John the Evangelist.

The Sagittarius Glyph ♐

This glyph is one of the easiest to spot and draw: an upward pointing arrow lifting up a cross. The arrow is pointing skyward, while the cross represents the four elements of the material world, which the arrow must convey. Elevating materiality into spirituality is an important Sagittarius quality, which explains why this sign is associated with higher learning, religion, philosophy, travel—the aspiring professions. Sagittarius can also send barbed arrows of frankness in the pursuit of truth, so the Archer symbol for Sagittarius is apt. (Sagittarius is also the sign of the supersalesman.)

Sagittarius is symbolically represented by the centaur, a mythological creature who is half man, half horse, aiming his arrow toward the skies. Though Sagittarius is motivated by spiritual aspiration, it also must balance the powerful appetites of the animal nature. The centaur Chiron, a figure in Greek mythology, became a wise teacher who, after many adventures and world travels, was killed by a poisoned arrow.

The Capricorn Glyph ♑

One of the most difficult symbols to draw, this glyph may take some practice. It is a representation of the sea goat: a mythical animal that is a goat with a curving fish's tail. The goat part of Capricorn wants to leave the waters of the emotions and climb to the elevated areas of life. But the fish tail is the unconscious, the deep chaotic psychic level that draws the goat back. Capricorn is often trying to escape the deep, feeling part of life by submerging himself in work, steadily ascending to the top. To some people, the glyph represents a seated figure with a bent knee, a reminder that Capricorn governs the knee area of the body.

An interesting aspect of this glyph is the contrast of the sharp pointed horns—which represent the penetrating, shrewd, conscious side of Capricorn—with the swishing tail—which represents its serpentine, unconscious, emotional force. One Capricorn legend, which dates from Roman times, tells of the earthy fertility god, Pan, who tried to save himself from uncontrollable sexual desires by jumping into the Nile. His upper body then turned into a goat, while the lower part became a fish. Later, Jupiter gave him a safe haven in the skies, as a constellation.

The Aquarius Glyph ♒

This ancient water symbol can be traced back to an Egyptian hieroglyph representing streams of life force. Symbolized by the Water Bearer, Aquarius is distributor of the waters of life—the magic liquid of regeneration. The two waves can also be linked to the positive and negative charges of the electrical energy that Aquarius rules, a sort of universal wavelength. Aquarius is tuned in intuitively to higher forces via this electrical force. The duality of the glyph could also refer to the dual nature of Aquarius, a sign that runs hot and cold and that is friendly but also detached in the mental world of air signs.

In Greek legends, Aquarius is represented by Ganymede, who was carried to heaven by an eagle in order to become the cup bearer of Zeus and to supervise the annual flooding of the Nile. The sign later became associated with aviation and notions of flight.

The Pisces Glyph)(

Here is an abstraction of the familiar image of Pisces, two Fishes swimming in opposite directions yet bound together by a cord. The Fishes represent the spirit—which yearns for the freedom of heaven—and the soul—which remains attached to the desires of the temporal world. During life on earth, the spirit and the soul are bound together. When they complement each other, instead of pulling in opposite directions, they facilitate the Pisces creativity. The ancient version of this glyph, taken from the Egyptians, had no connecting line, which was added in the fourteenth century.

In another interpretation, it is said that the left fish indicates the direction of involution or the beginning of a cycle, while the right fish signifies the direction of evolution, the way to completion of a cycle. It's an appropriate grand finale for Pisces, the last sign of the zodiac.

CHAPTER 6

Astrology on the Internet

If you're online, you'll have no trouble finding astrology sites. Astrology is everywhere on the Internet, and a popular feature on most of the big websites. However, if you're curious to see a copy of your chart (or someone else's), want to study astrology in depth, or chat with another astrology fan then you'll need a guided tour!

There you'll find a whole new world of astrology waiting for a click of your mouse. Thousands of astrological sites offer you everything from chart services to chat rooms to individual readings. Even better, you'll find *free* software, *free* charts, *free* articles to download. You can virtually get an education in astrology from your computer screen, share your insights with new astrology-minded pals in a chat room or on a mailing list, then later meet them in person at one of the hundreds of conferences around the world.

The following sites were chosen for general interest from the vast number of astrology-oriented places on the net. Many have their own selection of links to other sites for further exploration. One caveat: Though these sites were selected with longevity in mind, the Internet is a volatile place where sites can disappear or change without notice. Therefore, some of our sites may have changed addresses, names, or content by the time this book is published.

Free Charts

Astrolabe Software at *http://www.alabe.com* distributes some of the most creative and user-friendly programs now available; Solar Fire is a favorite of top astrologers. Visitors to the site are greeted with a chart of the time you log on. You can get your chart calculated, with a free mini-interpretation e-mailed to you.

For an instant chart, surf to *http://www.astro.ch* and check into Astrodienst, an international site that has long been one of the best astrology sites on the Internet. Its world atlas will give you the accurate longitude and latitude of your birthplace for setting up your horoscope. Then you can print out your chart in a range of easy-to-read formats. One handy feature for beginners: The planetary placement is listed in words alongside the chart (a real help for those who haven't yet learned to read the astrology glyphs).

There are many other attractions at this site, such as a list of your astro-twins (famous people born on your birth-date). The site even sorts the "twins" to feature those who also have your identical rising sign. You can then click on their names and get an instant chart of your famous sign-mates.

Planning a vacation or relocation? First check an astro-map at Astro-click Travel, another clever feature on the Astrodienst site. On the interactive chart that appears, you can view your astrological chart projected on a map of the earth. The lines on the chart that track each of the planets indicate what type of experience you might expect at that location. Click on a line, and up pops an explanation. So click before you travel!

Free Software

Software manufacturers on the Web are generous with free downloads of demo versions of their software. You may then calculate charts using their data. Before you invest serious money in astrology software, you can see how the program works for your needs. You can preview Astrolabe Software programs favored by many professional astrologers at *http://www.alabe.com*. Check out the latest demo of Solar Fire, one of the most user-friendly astrology programs available—you'll be impressed.

Matrix Software, another source of terrific astrology software, also offers free demo disks. Address: *http:www.astrologysoftware.com*

A Free Fully Functional Astrology Program

Walter Pullen's amazingly complete Astrolog program is offered absolutely free at the site. Address: *http://www.magitech.com/~cruiser1/astrolog.htm*

Astrolog is an ultrasophisticated program with all the features of much more expensive programs. It comes in versions for all formats—DOS, Windows, MAC, UNIX—and has some cool features such as a revolving globe and a constellation map. A "must" for those who want to get involved with astrology without paying big bucks for a professional-caliber program. Or for those who want to add Astrolog's unique features to their astrology software library. This program has it all!

Another Free Program!

Surf to *http://www.astroscan.ca* for a free program called Astroscan. Stunning graphics and ease of use make this a winner. Astroscan has a fun list of celebrity charts you can call up with a few clicks.

A Super Shareware Program

Check out Halloran Software's site at *http://www.halloran.com*. There are several levels of Windows astrology software from which to choose. The Astrology for Windows shareware program is available in unregistered demo form as a free download and in registered form for $26.50 (at this writing). The calculations in this program may be all that an astrology hobbyist needs. The price for the full-service program is certainly reasonable.

Free Oracle Readings

There are many diversions at the Matrix site; you may consult the stars, the I Ching, the runes, and the tarot. Here's where to connect with news groups and online discussions. Their almanac helps you schedule the best day to sign on the dotted line, ask for a raise, or plant your rosebush. Address: *http://thenewage.com*

Online Astrology Course

Schedule a long visit to *http://www.panplanet.com* where you will find the Canopus Academy of Astrology, a site loaded with goodies. For the experienced astrologer, there is a collection of articles from top astrologers. They've done the work for you when it comes to picking the best astrology links on the Web, so be sure to check out those bestowed with the Canopus Award of Excellence.

Astrologer Linda Reid, an accomplished astrology teacher and author, offers a complete online curriculum for all levels of astrology study plus individual tutoring. To get your feet wet, Linda is offering an excellent beginners' course at this site, a terrific way to get off and running in astrology.

Top Astrologers Comment on Current Events

The StarIQ site is home to many top astrologers, who comment on the latest news as well as submit articles. Visit this site for an astrological take on the headlines, and be sure to read the articles from some of the best minds in astrology. Address: *http://www.StarIQ.com*

Visit an Astro-Mall

For lighter entertainment, go to Astronet, *http://www.astrology.com/astronet*, for the Internet's equivalent of an astrology mall. Astronet offers interactive fun for everyone. At this writing, there's a special area for teenage astrology fans, advice to the lovelorn, plus a grab bag of horoscopes, a shopping area for books, reports, and software as well as links to all the popular fashion magazine astrology columns.

Swoon.com is another mall-like site aimed at dating, mating, and relating. It has fun features to spark up your love life and plenty of advice for lovers. Address: *http://www.swoon.com*

Find an Astrologer Here

The A.F.A. Website

This is the interesting website of the prestigious American Federation of Astrologers. The A.F.A. has a directory of astrologers restricted to those who meet their stringent requirements. Check out their correspondence course if you would like to study astrology in depth. Address: *http://www.astrologers.com*

The NCGR Website

The website of the National Council for Geocosmic Research (NCGR), a leading astrology organization that places great emphasis on education, has a list of accredited astrologers nationwide on their site. Address: *http://www.geocosmic.org*

Tools Every Astrologer Needs Are Online

Internet Atlas

Find the geographic longitude and latitude and the correct time zone for any city worldwide. You'll need this information to calculate a chart. Address: *http:/www.astro.ch/atlas*

The Exact Time Anywhere in the World

A fun site with fascinating graphics that give you the exact time anywhere in the world. Click on the world map, and the correct time and zone for that place light up. Address: *http://www.timeticker.com*

Check the Weather Forecast

More accurate than your local TV forecast is the Weathersage, who uses astrology to predict snowstorms and hurricanes. Get your long-range forecast at this super site. Address: *http//www.weathersage.com*

Celebrate the Queen's Birthday

A great jumping off place for an astrology tour of the Internet, this site has a veritable Burke's Peerage of royal birthdays. There's a good selection of articles; tools such as a U.S. and World Atlas; information on conferences, software, tapes, and groups. The links at this site will send you off in the right direction. Information about the latest Palm Pilot astrology software is also available here. Adress: *http://www.zodiacal.com*

Get a View of the Night Sky

Visit *http://www.skyviewzone.com* for a look at the evening's constellations. It is also an excellent place to preview and order the sophisticated Kepler astrology software.

Astrology Worldwide

Interested in astrology in Europe? Deborah Houlding, one of the U.K.'s top astrologers, has gathered some of the finest European talent on this super website, as well as a comprehensive list of links and conferences. Tour the world of astrology here. Address: *http://astrology-world.com*

Astrology Alive

Barbara Schermer has one of the most innovative and holistic approaches to astrology. She was one of the first astrologers to go online, so there's always a "cutting edge" to this site and a great list of links. Barbara is always on top of what's happening now in astrology. Address: *http:// www.astrologyalive.com*

National Council for Geocosmic Research (NCGR)

A key stop on any astrological tour of the Net. Here's where you can find local chapters in your area, get information on the NCGR testing and certification programs, get a conference schedule. There is a list of certified astrologers for those who want readings. Order lecture tapes from their nationwide conferences, or get complete lists of conference topics to study at home. Good links to resources. Address: *http://www.geocosmic.org*

Where to Find Charts of the Famous

When the news is breaking, you can bet Lois Rodden will be the first to get accurate birthdays of the headline-makers, and put up their charts on her website: *http:// www.astrodatabank.com*. Rodden's meticulous research is astrology's most reliable source for data of the famous and infamous. Her website specializes in birthdays and charts of current newsmakers, political figures, and international celebrities. You can also participate in an analysis of the charts and see what other astrologers have to say about them. The AstroDatabank program, which you can purchase at the site, provides thousands of birthdays sorted into categories. It's an excellent research tool.

Here is another site with birthdays and charts of famous and infamous people: *http://www.astropro.com*

Go to *http://www.imdb.com* for a comprehensive list of

film celebrities including bios, plus lists of famous couples from today and yesteryear. Look under "biographies."

Yet another good source for celebrity birthdates is the humorous Metamaze site: *http://www.metamaze.com/bdays*. You can find some interesting offbeat newsmakers here.

For Astrology Books

National Clearinghouse for Astrology Books

A wide selection of books on all aspects of astrology, from the basics to advanced, is available at this online bookstore. Also, many hard-to-find and recycled books. Address: *http://www.astroamerica.com*

The following addresses also have a good selection of astrology books for sale, some of which are unique to the site.

http://www.panplanet.com
http://thenewage.com
http://www.astrocom.com

Browse the huge astrology list of online bookstore Amazon.com at *http://www.amazon.com*.

Astrology Tapes for At-Home Study

You can study at home with world-famous astrologers via audiocassette recordings from Pegasus Tapes. There's an extensive selection taped from conferences, classes, lectures, and seminars. An especially good source for astrologers who emphasize psychological and mythological themes. Address: *http://www.pegasustape.com*

For History and Mythology Buffs

Be sure to visit the astrology section of this gorgeous site, dedicated to the history and mythology of many traditions.

One of the most beautifully designed sites we've seen. Address: *http://www.elore.com*

The leading authority on the history of astrology, Robert Hand, has an excellent site that features his cutting-edge research. See what one of astrology's great teachers has to offer. Address: *http://www.robhand.com*

The Project Hindsight group of scholarly astrologers is devoted to restoring the astrology of the Hellenistic period, the primary source for all later Western astrology. There are fascinating articles for astrology fans on this site. Address: *http://www.projecthindsight.com*

C.U.R.A. is a European site for historical researchers. Lots of information, especially if you speak French or Spanish. Address: *http://cura.free.fr*

Readers interested in mythology should also check out *http://pantheon.org/mythical* for stories of gods and goddesses.

Astrology Magazine

The Mountain Astrologer

A favorite magazine of astrology fans, *The Mountain Astrologer* has an interesting website featuring the latest news from an astrological point of view, plus feature articles from the magazine. Address: *http://www.mountainastrologer.com*

Financial Astrology

Find out how financial astrologers play the market. Here are hot picks, newsletters, specialized financial astrology software, and mutual funds run by astrology seers. Go to *www.afund.com* or *www.alphee.com* for tips and forecasts from two top financial astrologers.

CHAPTER 7

The Sydney Omarr Yellow Pages

If you've caught the "astrology bug," you'll want to expand your knowledge and connect with other astrology fans. Here are the resources you need to find the right astrology software for your computer, to meet other astrology fans, to study advanced techniques, or to buy books and tapes. You'll find the latest products and services available, as well as astrology organizations that hold meetings and conferences in your area.

Whether you'd like to know more about such specialties as financial astrology or techniques for timing events, or if you'd prefer the psychological or mythological approach, you'll meet the top astrologers at conferences sponsored by the National Council for Geocosmic Research. NCGR is dedicated to providing quality education, bringing astrologers and astrology fans together at conferences, and promoting fellowship. Their course structure provides a systematized study of the many facets of astrology.

You can explore astrology via your computer no matter what your level of expertise. Even if you are using an older model, there are still calculation and interpretation programs available. They may not have all the bells and whistles or the exciting graphics, but they'll get the job done!

Newcomers to astrology should learn some of the basics, including the glyphs, before you invest in a computer program. Use Chapter 5 in this book to help you learn the symbols easily; then you'll be able to read the charts without consulting the "help" section of your software every time. Several programs such as Astrolabe's Solar Fire have pop-up definitions to help you decipher the meanings of planets and aspects. Just click your mouse on a glyph or an icon on the screen, and a window with an instant definition appears.

You don't have to spend a fortune to get a perfectly adequate astrology program. In fact, if you are connected to the Internet, you can download one free. Astrology software is available at all price levels, from a sophisticated free application like Astrolog, which you can download from the website, to inexpensive programs for under $100 such as Winstar Express, to the more expensive astrology programs such as Winstar Plus, Solar Fire, or Io (for the MAC), which are used by serious students and professionals. Before you make an investment, it's a good idea to download a sample, which is usually available on the company's website, or to order a demo disk.

If you're baffled by the variety of software available, most of the companies on our list will be happy to help you find the right application for your needs.

Students of astrology who live in out-of-the-way places or are unable to fit classes into your schedule have several options. There are online courses offered at astrology websites, such as *www.panplanet.com*, the NCGR and A.F.A. websites. Some astrology teachers will send you a series of audiotapes, or you can order audiotaped seminars of recent conferences. Other teachers offer correspondence courses that use their workbooks or computer printouts.

Nationwide Astrology Organizations and Conferences

Contact these organizations for information on conferences, workshops, local meetings, conference tapes, referrals.

National Council for Geocosmic Research (NCGR)

Educational workshops, tapes, conferences, and a directory of professional astrologers are available from this nationwide organization devoted to promoting astrological education. For a $35 annual membership fee, you get their excellent publications and newsletters, plus the opportunity to network with other astrology buffs at local chapter events (there are chapters in 20 states).

For general information about NCGR, contact:

NCGR
P.O. Box 38866
Los Angeles, CA 90038
Website: http://www.geocosmic.org/

American Federation of Astrologers (A.F.A.)

This is one of the oldest astrological organizations in the United States, established 1938. They offer conferences, conventions, and a thorough correspondence course. If you are looking for a reading, the website will refer you to an accredited A.F.A. astrologer.

A.F.A.
P.O. Box 22040
Tempe, AZ 85285-2040
Phone: (888) 301-7630 or (480) 838-1751
Fax: (480) 838-8293
Website: http://www.astrologers.com

Association for Astrological Networking (A.F.A.N.)

Did you know that astrologers are still being harassed for practicing astrology? A.F.A.N. provides support and legal information, and works toward improving the public image of astrology. A.F.A.N.'s network of local astrologers links with the international astrological community. Here are the people who will go to bat for astrology when it is attacked in the media. Everyone who cares about astrology should join!

A.F.A.N.
8306 Wilshire Blvd.
PMB 537
Beverly Hills, CA 90211
Phone: (800) 578-2326
E-mail: info@afan.org
Website: http://www.afan.org

Astrology Conferences on Tape

Would you like to hear top astrology lectures on tape? Pegasus has a wonderful selection of tapes from conferences, featuring world-famous astrologers.

Pegasus Tapes
P.O. Box 419
Santa Ysabel, CA 92070

International Society for Astrology Research (ISAR)

For lectures, workshops, seminars. An international organization of professional astrologers dedicated to encouraging the highest standards of quality in the field of astrology with an emphasis on research.

ISAR
P.O. Box 38613
Los Angeles, CA 90038
Website: http://www.isarastrology.com
Phone: (800) 924-4747 or (510) 222-9436
Fax: (510) 222–2202

Astrology Software

Astrolabe

One of the top astrology software resources. Check out the latest version of their powerful Solar Fire software for

Windows. It's a breeze to use and will grow with your increasing knowledge of astrology to the most sophisticated levels. This company also markets a variety of programs for all levels of expertise and a wide selection of computer-generated astrology readings. A good resource for innovative software as well as applications for older computers.

Astrolabe
Box 1750-R
Brewster, MA 02631
Phone: (800) 843-6682
Website: http://www.alabe.com

Matrix Software

A wide variety of software in all price ranges, demo disks, student and advanced level, lots of interesting readings. Check out Winstar Express, a powerful but reasonably priced program suitable for all skill levels.

Matrix Software
407 N. State Street
Big Rapids, MI 49307
Phone: (800) 416-3924
Website: http://www.astrologysoftware.com

Astro Communications Services (ACS)

Books, software for MAC and IBM compatibles, individual charts, and telephone readings are offered by this California company. Find technical astrology materials here such as The American Ephemeris and PC atlases. ACS will calculate and send charts to you, a valuable service if you do not have a computer.

ACS Publications
5521 Ruffin Road
San Diego, CA 92123
Phone: (800) 888-9983

Fax: (858) 492-9917
Website: http://www.astrocom.com

Air Software

Here you'll find powerful, creative astrology software, like Star Trax 2000. For beginners, check out Father Time, which finds your best days. Check out Nostradamus, which answers all your questions. Financial astrology programs for stock market traders are a specialty.

Air Software
115 Caya Avenue
West Hartford, CT 06110
Phone: (800) 659-1247
Website: http://www.alphee.com

Time Cycles Research: For MAC Users

Here's where MAC users can find astrology software that's as sophisticated as it gets. If you have a MAC, you'll love their beautiful graphic IO Series programs.

Time Cycles Research
375 Willets Avenue
Waterford, CT 06385
Fax: (860) 442-0625
Website: http://www.timecycles.com

Astrology Magazines

In addition to articles by top astrologers, most have listings of astrology conferences, events, and local happenings.

American Astrology
Dept. 4
P.O. Box 2021
Marion, OH 43306-8121

Dell Horoscope
P.O. Box 54097
Boulder, CO 80322-4097

The Mountain Astrologer
P.O. Box 970
Cedar Ridge, CA 95924
Website: http://www.mountainastrologer.com

Astrology College

An accredited college dedicated to astrology is here at last!
Check out the Kepler College listed below.

Kepler College of Astrological Arts and Sciences

A degree-granting college, which is also a center of astrology, has long been the dream of the astrological community and is a giant step forward in providing credibility to the profession.

Therefore, the opening of Kepler College in 2000 was a historical event for astrology. It is the only college in the western hemisphere authorized to issue B.A. and M.A. degrees in Astrological Studies. The entire curriculum is based on astrology.

For more information, contact:

Kepler College of Astrological Arts and Sciences
4630 200th Street SW
Suite P
Lynnwood, WA 98036
Voice: (425) 673-4292
Fax: (425) 673-4983
Website: http://www.kepler.edu

CHAPTER 8

Consulting a Cosmic Counselor: What a Personal Reading Can Do for You

Could it be time for an astrology reading? An important date is coming up, perhaps a wedding or the start of a new business, and you're wondering if an astrologically picked date could influence the outcome. You've fallen in love and must know if it will last forever. Your partnership is not going well, and you're not sure if you can continue to work together. You're in a downslide when problems seem insurmountable. Or you simply want to have your chart interpreted by an expert. There are so many options for readings that sorting through them can be a daunting task. Besides individual one-on-one readings with a professional astrologer, there are telephone readings, Internet readings, tapes, computer-generated reports, and celebrity-sponsored readings. Here's what to look for and some cautionary notes.

Done by a qualified astrologer, the personal reading can be an empowering experience if you want to reach your full potential, size up a lover or business situation, or find out what the future has in store. There are astrologers who are specialists in certain areas such as finance or medical astrology. And, unfortunately, there are many questionable practitioners who range from streetwise gypsy fortune-tellers to unscrupulous scam artists. The following basic guidelines can help you sort out your options to find the reading that's right for you.

What Information an Astrologer Needs

Nothing compares to a one-on-one consultation with a professional astrologer who has analyzed thousands of charts and can pinpoint the potential in yours. During your reading, you can get your specific questions answered. For instance, how to get along better with your mate or co-worker. There are many astrologers who now combine their skills with training in psychology and are well-suited to help you examine your alternatives.

To give you an accurate reading, an astrologer needs certain information from you: the date, time, and place where you were born. (A horoscope can be cast about anyone or anything that has a specific time and place.) Most astrologers will then enter this information into a computer, which will calculate a chart in seconds. From the resulting chart, the astrologer will do an interpretation.

If you don't know your exact birth time, you can usually locate it at the Bureau of Vital Statistics at the city hall or county seat of the state where you were born. If you still have no success in getting your time of birth, some astrologers can estimate an approximate birth time by using past events in your life to determine the chart. This technique is called *rectification*.

Choose an Astrologer with Care

Choose your astrologer with the same care as any trusted adviser such as a doctor, lawyer, or banker. Unfortunately, anyone can claim to be an astrologer—to date, there is no licensing of astrologers or universally established professional criteria. However, there are nationwide organizations of serious, committed astrologers that can help you in your search.

Good places to start your investigation are organizations such as the American Federation of Astrologers (A.F.A.) or the National Council for Geocosmic Research (NCGR), which offer a program of study and certification. If you live near a major city, there is sure to be an active NCGR chapter or astrology club in your area; many are listed in astrology magazines available at your local newsstand. In response to many requests for referrals, the NCGR has compiled a directory of professional astrologers, which includes a glossary of terms and an explanation of specialties within the astrological field. Contact the NCGR headquarters (see Chapter 6 and Chapter 7 in this book) for information.

Warning Signals

As a potentially lucrative freelance business, astrology has always attracted self-styled experts who may not have the knowledge or the counseling experience to give a helpful reading. These astrologers can range from the well-meaning amateur to the charlatan or street-corner gypsy who has for many years given astrology a bad name. Be very wary of astrologers who claim to have occult powers or who make pretentious claims of celebrated clients or miraculous achievements. You can often tell from the initial phone conversation if the astrologer is legitimate. He or she should ask for your birthday time and place, then conduct the conversation in a professional manner. Any astrologer who gives a reading based only on your sun sign is highly suspect.

When you arrive at the reading, the astrologer should be prepared. The consultation should be conducted in a private, quiet place. The astrologer should be interested in your problems of the moment. A good reading involves feedback on your part. So if the reading is not relating to your concerns, you should let the astrologer know. You should feel free to ask questions and get clarifications of technical terms. The more you actively participate, rather than expecting the astrologer to carry the reading or come forth with oracular predictions, the more meaningful your experience will be. An astrologer should help you validate your current experience and be frank about possible negative happenings, but also suggest a positive course of action.

In their approach to a reading, some astrologers may be more literal, others more intuitive. Those who have had counseling training may take a more psychological approach. Though some astrologers may seem to have an almost psychic ability, extrasensory perception or any other parapsychological talent is not essential. A very accurate picture can be drawn from the data in your horoscope chart.

An astrologer may do several charts for each client, including one for the time of birth and a "progressed chart," showing the evolution from birth to the present time. According to your individual needs, there are many other possibilities, such as a chart for a different location if you are contemplating a change of place. Relationships between any two people, things, or events can be interpreted with a chart that compares one partner's horoscope with the other's. A composite chart, which uses the midpoint between planets in two individual charts to describe the relationship, is another commonly used device.

An astrologer will be particularly interested in transits, those times when cycling planets activate the planets or sensitive points in your birth chart. These indicate important events in your life.

Many astrologers offer tape-recorded readings, another option to consider, especially if the astrologer you choose lives at a distance. In this case, you'll be mailed a taped reading based on your birth chart. This type of reading is more personal than a computer printout and can give you valuable insights, though it is not equivalent to a live dialogue with the astrologer when you can discuss your specific interests and issues of the moment.

What to Expect from a Telephone Reading

Telephone readings come in two varieties: a dial-in taped reading, usually recorded in advance by an astrologer, or a live consultation with an "astrologer" on the other end of the line. The taped readings are general daily or weekly forecasts, applied to all members of your sign and charged by the minute. The quality depends on the astrologer. One caution: Be aware that these readings can run up quite a telephone bill, especially if you get into the habit of calling every day. Be sure that you are aware of the per-minute cost of each call beforehand.

Live telephone readings also vary with the expertise of the astrologer. Ideally, the astrologer at the other end of the line enters your birth data into a computer, which then quickly calculates your chart. This chart will be referred to during the consultation. The advantage of a live telephone reading is that your individual chart is used and you can ask about a specific problem. However, before you invest in any reading, be sure that your astrologer is qualified and that you fully understand in advance how much you will be charged. There should be no unpleasant financial surprises later.

About Computer-Generated Reports

Companies that offer computer programs (such as ACS, Matrix, Astrolabe) also offer a variety of computer-generated horoscope readings. These can be quite comprehensive, offering a beautiful printout of the chart plus many pages of detailed information about each planet and aspect of the chart. You can then study it at your convenience. Of course, the interpretations will be general, since there is no personal input from you, and may not cover your immediate concerns. Since computer-generated horoscopes are much lower in cost than live consultations, you might consider them as either a supplement or a preparation for an eventual live reading. You'll then be more familiar with your chart and able to plan specific questions in advance. They also make a terrific gift for astrology fans. (There are several companies, listed in Chapters 6 and 7, that offer computerized readings prepared by reputable astrologers.)

Whichever option you decide to pursue, may your reading be an empowering one!

CHAPTER 9

What You Need to Know About Your Rising Sign

At the moment you were born, announcing your arrival in the world with a lusty cry, your horoscope was determined by the astrological sign passing over the eastern horizon. This sign is known as either your *rising sign* or your *ascendant.* What makes a horoscope "yours" is this rising sign. Other babies born later or earlier on the same day, in the same hospital, will have most planets in the same signs as you do. Most of your classmates in elementary school will have several planets in the same signs as your planets, especially the slow-moving planets (Uranus, Neptune, Pluto) and very possibly Jupiter and Saturn, which usually spend a year or more in each sign. But the moment you were born, in a specific place, is yours alone.

The degree of the sign on the horizon is important because it determines the signs that will influence the houses of your chart. As the earth turns on its axis every 24 hours, so does the horoscope change with the rotation. Every four minutes a new degree of the 360-degree zodiac passes over the horizon, and every two hours a new sign will rise. If you have read the description of the "houses" in Chapter 3 of this book, you'll know that the houses are twelve stationary divisions of the horoscope, which represent areas of life. The sign moving over the boundary (cusp) of each house describes that area of life. Sagittarius on the cusp of the second house, for instance, means you will deal with money in a Sagittarius way.

The rising sign marks the border of the first house, which represents your first presentation to the world, your physical body, how you come across to others. Once the rising

132

sign is established, it becomes possible to analyze a chart accurately because the astrologer knows in which house or area of life the planets will operate. For instance, if Mars is in Gemini and your rising sign is Taurus, then Mars will most likely be active in the second house, the house of finances, of your chart. If you were born later in the day and your rising sign is Virgo, then Mars will be positioned at the top of your chart, energizing your tenth house, the house of career.

Many astrologers insist on knowing the exact time of a client's birth before they will analyze a chart. The more exact your birth time, the more accurately an astrologer can position the planets in your chart. This is important because if you were born when the midportion of a sign was rotating over the horizon and a key planet, let's say Saturn, was in the early degrees of that sign, then it would already be over the horizon, located in the twelfth house rather than the first. So the interpretation of your horoscope would be quite different: You would not have the serious Saturn influence in the way you come across to others, which would be the case if you were born an hour earlier. If a planet is near the ascendant, sometimes even a few minutes can make a big difference.

Your rising sign has an important relationship with your sun sign. Some will complement the sun sign; others hide it under a totally different mask, as if playing an entirely different role, making it difficult to guess the person's sun sign from outer appearances. This may be the reason why you might not look or act like your sun sign's archetype. For example, a Leo with a conservative Capricorn ascendant would come across as much more serious than a Leo with a fiery Aries or Sagittarius ascendant. The exception is when the sun sign is reinforced by other planets. Then, with other planets on its side, the sun may assert its personality much more strongly, overcoming the image of a contradictory rising sign. As another example, a Leo with Venus and Jupiter also in Leo might counteract the conservative image of the Capricorn ascendant given in the first example. However, in most cases, the ascendant is the ingredient most strongly reflected in the first impression you make.

Rising signs change every two hours with the earth's rotation. Those born early in the morning when the sun was on the horizon will be most likely to project the image of their sun sign. These people are often called a "double Aries" or a "double Virgo" because the same sun sign and ascendant reinforce each other.

Look up your rising sign from the chart at the end of this chapter. Since rising signs change every two hours, it is important to know your birth time as close to the minute as possible. Even a few minutes' difference could change the rising sign and therefore the setup of your chart. If you are unsure about the exact time, but know within a few hours, check the following descriptions to see which is most like the personality you project.

Aries Rising: Fiery Emotions

You are the most aggressive version of your sun sign, with boundless energy that can be used productively if it's channeled in the right direction. Watch a tendency to overreact emotionally and blow your top. You come across as openly competitive, a positive asset in business or sports. Be on guard against impatience, which could lead to head injuries. Your walk and bearing could have the telltale head forward Aries posture. You may wear more bright colors, especially red, than others of your sign. You may also have a tendency to drive your car faster.

Taurus Rising: The Earth Mother

You'll exude a protective nurturing quality, even if you're male, which draws those in need of TLC and support. You're slow-moving, with a beautiful (or distinctive) speaking or singing voice that can be especially soothing or melodious. You probably surround yourself with comfort, good food, luxurious surroundings, and other sensual pleasures. You prefer welcoming others into your home to gadding about. You may have a talent for business, especially in trading, appraising, and real estate. A Taurus ascendant gives a well-padded or curvaceous physique that gains weight easily. Women with this ascendant are naturally sexy in a bodacious way.

Gemini Rising: Expressive Talents

You're naturally sociable, with lighter, more ethereal mannerisms than others of your sign, especially if you're female. You love to communicate with people, and express your ideas and feelings easily. You may have a talent for writing or public speaking. You may thrive on a constantly changing scenario with a varied cast of characters, though you may be far more sympathetic and caring than you project. You will probably travel widely, changing partners and jobs several times (or juggle two at once). Physically, you should cultivate a calm, tranquil atmosphere because your nerves are quite sensitive.

Cancer Rising: Sensitive Antennae

Like billionaire Bill Gates, you are naturally acquisitive, possessive, private, a moneymaker. You easily pick up others' needs and feelings—a great gift in business, the arts, and personal relationships. But you must guard against overreacting or taking things too personally, especially during full moon periods. Find creative outlets for your natural nurturing gifts, such as helping the less fortunate, particularly children. Your insights would be helpful in psychology. Your desire to feed and care for others would be useful in the restaurant, hotel, or child-care industries. You may be especially fond of wearing romantic old clothes, collecting antiques, and, of course, dining on exquisite food. Since your body may retain fluids, pay attention to your diet. To relax, escape to places near water.

Leo Rising: The Scene Player

You may come across as more poised than you really feel. However, you play it to the hilt, projecting a proud royal presence. A Leo ascendant gives you a natural flair for drama, like Marilyn Monroe. You'll also project a much more outgoing, optimistic, sunny personality than others of your sign. You take care to please your public by always projecting your best star quality, probably tossing a luxuriant mane of hair or sporting a striking hairstyle. Females often dazzle with spectacular jewelry. Since you may have a strong parental nature, you could well be the regal family matriarch or patriarch.

Virgo Rising: Cool and Calculating

Virgo rising masks your inner nature with a practical, analytical outer image. You seem neat, orderly, more particular than others of your sign. Others in your life may feel they must live up to your high standards. Though at times you may be openly critical, this masks a well-meaning desire to have only the best for loved ones. Your sharp eye for details could be used in the financial world, or your literary skills could draw you to teaching or publishing. The healing arts, health care, and service-oriented professions attract many with a Virgo ascendant. Like Madonna, you're likely to take good care of yourself, with great attention to health, diet, and exercise. Physically, you may have a very sensitive digestive system.

Libra Rising: The Charmer

Libra rising makes you appear as a charmer, more of a social, public person than others of your sign. Your private life will extend beyond your home and family to include an active social life. You may tend to avoid confrontations in relationships, preferring to smooth the way or negotiate diplomatically, rather than give in to an emotional reaction. Because you are interested in all aspects of a situation, you may be slow to reach decisions. Physically, you'll have good proportions and pleasing symmetry. You're likely to have pleasing, if not beautiful, facial features. You move gracefully, and you have a winning smile and good taste in your clothes and home decor. Legal, diplomatic, or public relations professions could draw your interest. Men with Libra rising, like Bill Clinton and John F. Kennedy, have charming smiles and an easy social manner that charms the ladies.

Scorpio Rising: Magnetic Power

Even when you're in the public eye, like Jacqueline Onassis, you never lose your intriguing air of mystery and sense of underlying power. You can be a master manipulator, always in control and moving comfortably in the world of power. Your physical impression comes across as intense. Many of you have remarkable eyes, with a direct, penetrating gaze. But you'll never reveal your private agenda, and you tend to keep your true feelings under wraps (watch a tendency toward paranoia). You may have an interesting romantic history with secret love affairs. Many of you heighten your air of mystery by wearing black. You're happiest near water and should provide yourself with a seaside retreat.

Sagittarius Rising: The Wanderer

You travel with this ascendant. You may also be a more outdoor, sportive type, with an athletic, casual, outgoing air. Your moods are camouflaged with cheerful optimism or a philosophical attitude. Though you don't hesitate to speak your mind, you can also laugh at your troubles or crack a joke more easily than others of your sign, like Candice Bergen who is best known for her comedy role as the outspoken "Murphy Brown." A Sagittarius ascendant can also draw you to the field of higher education or to spiritual life. You'll seem to have less attachment to things and people, and may travel widely. Your strong, fast legs are a physical bonus.

Capricorn Rising: Serious Business

This rising sign makes you come across as serious, goal-oriented, disciplined, and careful with cash. You are not one of the zodiac's big spenders, though you might splurge occasionally on items with good investment value. You're the traditional, conservative type in dress and environment, and you might come across as quite formal and business-like. You'll function well in a structured or corporate environment where you can climb to the top. (You are always aware of who's the boss.) In your personal life, you could be a loner or a single parent who is "father and mother" to your children. Like Paul Newman, you're likely to prefer a quiet private life to living in the spotlight.

Aquarius Rising: One of a Kind

You come across as less concerned about what others think and could even be a bit eccentric. Your appearance is sure to be unique and memorable. You're more at ease with groups of people than others in your sign, and you may be attracted to public life. Your appearance may be unique, either unconventional or unimportant to you. Those of you whose sun is in a water sign (Cancer, Scorpio, Pisces) may exercise your nurturing qualities with a large group, an extended family, or a day-care or community center. Audrey Hepburn and Princess Diana, who had this rising sign, were known for their unique charisma and work on behalf of worthy causes.

Pisces Rising: Romantic Roles

Your creative, nurturing talents are heightened and so is your ability to project emotional drama. And your dreamy eyes and poetic air bring out the protective instinct in others. You could be attracted to the arts, especially theater, dance, film, and photography, or to psychology, spiritual practice, and charity work. You are happiest when you are using your creative ability to help others, like Robert Redford has done. Since you are vulnerable to mood swings, it is especially important for you to find interesting, creative work where you can express your talents and boost your self-esteem. Accentuate the positive. Be wary of escapist tendencies, particularly involving alcohol or drugs to which you are supersensitive.

RISING SIGNS—A.M. BIRTHS

	1 AM	2 AM	3 AM	4 AM	5 AM	6 AM	7 AM	8 AM	9 AM	10 AM	11 AM	12 NOON
Jan 1	Lib	Sc	Sc	Sc	Sag	Sag	Cap	Cap	Aq	Aq	Pis	Ar
Jan 9	Lib	Sc	Sc	Sag	Sag	Sag	Cap	Cap	Aq	Pis	Ar	Tau
Jan 17	Sc	Sc	Sc	Sag	Sag	Cap	Cap	Aq	Aq	Pis	Ar	Tau
Jan 25	Sc	Sc	Sag	Sag	Sag	Cap	Cap	Aq	Pis	Ar	Tau	Tau
Feb 2	Sc	Sc	Sag	Sag	Cap	Cap	Aq	Pis	Pis	Ar	Tau	Gem
Feb 10	Sc	Sag	Sag	Sag	Cap	Cap	Aq	Pis	Ar	Tau	Tau	Gem
Feb 18	Sc	Sag	Sag	Cap	Cap	Aq	Pis	Pis	Ar	Tau	Gem	Gem
Feb 26	Sag	Sag	Sag	Cap	Aq	Aq	Pis	Ar	Tau	Tau	Gem	Gem
Mar 6	Sag	Sag	Cap	Cap	Aq	Pis	Pis	Ar	Tau	Gem	Gem	Can
Mar 14	Sag	Cap	Cap	Aq	Aq	Pis	Ar	Tau	Tau	Gem	Gem	Can
Mar 22	Sag	Cap	Cap	Aq	Pis	Ar	Ar	Tau	Gem	Gem	Can	Can
Mar 30	Cap	Cap	Aq	Pis	Pis	Ar	Tau	Tau	Gem	Can	Can	Can
Apr 7	Cap	Cap	Aq	Pis	Ar	Ar	Tau	Gem	Gem	Can	Can	Leo
Apr 14	Cap	Aq	Aq	Pis	Ar	Tau	Tau	Gem	Gem	Can	Can	Leo
Apr 22	Cap	Aq	Pis	Ar	Ar	Tau	Gem	Gem	Gem	Can	Leo	Leo
Apr 30	Aq	Aq	Pis	Ar	Tau	Tau	Gem	Can	Can	Can	Leo	Leo
May 8	Aq	Pis	Ar	Ar	Tau	Gem	Gem	Can	Can	Leo	Leo	Leo
May 16	Aq	Pis	Ar	Tau	Gem	Gem	Can	Can	Can	Leo	Leo	Vir
May 24	Pis	Ar	Ar	Tau	Gem	Gem	Can	Can	Leo	Leo	Leo	Vir
June 1	Pis	Ar	Tau	Gem	Gem	Can	Can	Can	Leo	Leo	Vir	Vir
June 9	Ar	Ar	Tau	Gem	Gem	Can	Can	Leo	Leo	Leo	Vir	Vir
June 17	Ar	Tau	Gem	Gem	Can	Can	Can	Leo	Leo	Vir	Vir	Vir
June 25	Tau	Tau	Gem	Gem	Can	Can	Leo	Leo	Leo	Vir	Vir	Lib
July 3	Tau	Gem	Gem	Can	Can	Can	Leo	Leo	Vir	Vir	Vir	Lib
July 11	Tau	Gem	Gem	Can	Can	Leo	Leo	Leo	Vir	Vir	Lib	Lib
July 18	Gem	Gem	Can	Can	Can	Leo	Leo	Vir	Vir	Vir	Lib	Lib
July 26	Gem	Gem	Can	Can	Leo	Leo	Vir	Vir	Vir	Lib	Lib	Lib
Aug 3	Gem	Can	Can	Can	Leo	Leo	Vir	Vir	Vir	Lib	Lib	Sc
Aug 11	Gem	Can	Can	Leo	Leo	Leo	Vir	Vir	Vir	Lib	Lib	Sc
Aug 18	Can	Can	Can	Leo	Leo	Vir	Vir	Vir	Lib	Lib	Sc	Sc
Aug 27	Can	Can	Leo	Leo	Leo	Vir	Vir	Lib	Lib	Lib	Sc	Sc
Sept 4	Can	Can	Leo	Leo	Leo	Vir	Vir	Vir	Lib	Lib	Sc	Sc
Sept 12	Can	Leo	Leo	Leo	Vir	Vir	Lib	Lib	Lib	Sc	Sc	Sag
Sept 20	Leo	Leo	Leo	Vir	Vir	Vir	Lib	Lib	Sc	Sc	Sc	Sag
Sept 28	Leo	Leo	Leo	Vir	Vir	Lib	Lib	Lib	Sc	Sc	Sag	Sag
Oct 6	Leo	Leo	Vir	Vir	Vir	Lib	Lib	Sc	Sc	Sc	Sag	Sag
Oct 14	Leo	Vir	Vir	Vir	Lib	Lib	Lib	Sc	Sc	Sag	Sag	Cap
Oct 22	Leo	Vir	Vir	Lib	Lib	Lib	Sc	Sc	Sc	Sag	Sag	Cap
Oct 30	Vir	Vir	Vir	Lib	Lib	Sc	Sc	Sc	Sag	Sag	Cap	Cap
Nov 7	Vir	Vir	Lib	Lib	Lib	Sc	Sc	Sc	Sag	Sag	Cap	Cap
Nov 15	Vir	Vir	Lib	Lib	Sc	Sc	Sc	Sag	Sag	Cap	Cap	Aq
Nov 23	Vir	Lib	Lib	Lib	Sc	Sc	Sag	Sag	Sag	Cap	Cap	Aq
Dec 1	Vir	Lib	Lib	Sc	Sc	Sc	Sag	Sag	Cap	Cap	Aq	Aq
Dec 9	Lib	Lib	Lib	Sc	Sc	Sag	Sag	Sag	Cap	Cap	Aq	Pis
Dec 18	Lib	Lib	Sc	Sc	Sc	Sag	Sag	Cap	Cap	Aq	Aq	Pis
Dec 28	Lib	Lib	Sc	Sc	Sag	Sag	Sag	Cap	Aq	Aq	Pis	Ar

RISING SIGNS—P.M. BIRTHS

	1 PM	2 PM	3 PM	4 PM	5 PM	6 PM	7 PM	8 PM	9 PM	10 PM	11 PM	12 MIDNIGHT
Jan 1	Tau	Gem	Gem	Can	Can	Can	Leo	Leo	Vir	Vir	Vir	Lib
Jan 9	Tau	Gem	Gem	Can	Can	Leo	Leo	Leo	Vir	Vir	Vir	Lib
Jan 17	Gem	Gem	Can	Can	Can	Leo	Leo	Vir	Vir	Vir	Lib	Lib
Jan 25	Gem	Gem	Can	Can	Leo	Leo	Leo	Vir	Vir	Lib	Lib	Lib
Feb 2	Gem	Can	Can	Can	Leo	Leo	Vir	Vir	Vir	Lib	Lib	Sc
Feb 10	Gem	Can	Can	Leo	Leo	Leo	Vir	Vir	Lib	Lib	Lib	Sc
Feb 18	Can	Can	Can	Leo	Leo	Vir	Vir	Vir	Lib	Lib	Sc	Sc
Feb 26	Can	Can	Leo	Leo	Leo	Vir	Vir	Lib	Lib	Lib	Sc	Sc
Mar 6	Can	Leo	Leo	Leo	Vir	Vir	Vir	Lib	Lib	Sc	Sc	Sc
Mar 14	Can	Leo	Leo	Vir	Vir	Vir	Lib	Lib	Lib	Sc	Sc	Sag
Mar 22	Leo	Leo	Leo	Vir	Vir	Lib	Lib	Lib	Sc	Sc	Sc	Sag
Mar 30	Leo	Leo	Vir	Vir	Vir	Lib	Lib	Sc	Sc	Sc	Sag	Sag
Apr 7	Leo	Leo	Vir	Vir	Lib	Lib	Lib	Sc	Sc	Sc	Sag	Sag
Apr 14	Leo	Vir	Vir	Vir	Lib	Lib	Sc	Sc	Sc	Sag	Sag	Cap
Apr 22	Leo	Vir	Vir	Lib	Lib	Lib	Sc	Sc	Sc	Sag	Sag	Cap
Apr 30	Vir	Vir	Vir	Lib	Lib	Sc	Sc	Sc	Sag	Sag	Cap	Cap
May 8	Vir	Vir	Lib	Lib	Lib	Sc	Sc	Sag	Sag	Sag	Cap	Cap
May 16	Vir	Vir	Lib	Lib	Sc	Sc	Sc	Sag	Sag	Cap	Cap	Aq
May 24	Vir	Lib	Lib	Lib	Sc	Sc	Sag	Sag	Sag	Cap	Cap	Aq
June 1	Vir	Lib	Lib	Sc	Sc	Sc	Sag	Sag	Cap	Cap	Aq	Aq
June 9	Lib	Lib	Lib	Sc	Sc	Sag	Sag	Sag	Cap	Cap	Aq	Pis
June 17	Lib	Lib	Sc	Sc	Sc	Sag	Sag	Cap	Cap	Aq	Aq	Pis
June 25	Lib	Lib	Sc	Sc	Sag	Sag	Sag	Cap	Cap	Aq	Pis	Ar
July 3	Lib	Sc	Sc	Sc	Sag	Sag	Cap	Cap	Aq	Aq	Pis	Ar
July 11	Lib	Sc	Sc	Sag	Sag	Sag	Cap	Cap	Aq	Pis	Ar	Tau
July 18	Sc	Sc	Sc	Sag	Sag	Cap	Cap	Aq	Aq	Pis	Ar	Tau
July 26	Sc	Sc	Sag	Sag	Sag	Cap	Cap	Aq	Pis	Ar	Tau	Tau
Aug 3	Sc	Sc	Sag	Sag	Cap	Cap	Aq	Aq	Pis	Ar	Tau	Gem
Aug 11	Sc	Sag	Sag	Sag	Cap	Cap	Aq	Pis	Ar	Tau	Tau	Gem
Aug 18	Sc	Sag	Sag	Cap	Cap	Aq	Pis	Pis	Ar	Tau	Gem	Gem
Aug 27	Sag	Sag	Sag	Cap	Cap	Aq	Pis	Ar	Tau	Tau	Gem	Gem
Sept 4	Sag	Sag	Cap	Cap	Aq	Pis	Pis	Ar	Tau	Gem	Gem	Can
Sept 12	Sag	Sag	Cap	Aq	Aq	Pis	Ar	Tau	Tau	Gem	Gem	Can
Sept 20	Sag	Cap	Cap	Aq	Pis	Pis	Ar	Tau	Gem	Gem	Can	Can
Sept 28	Cap	Cap	Aq	Aq	Pis	Ar	Tau	Tau	Gem	Gem	Can	Can
Oct 6	Cap	Cap	Aq	Pis	Ar	Ar	Tau	Gem	Gem	Can	Can	Leo
Oct 14	Cap	Aq	Aq	Pis	Ar	Tau	Tau	Gem	Gem	Can	Can	Leo
Oct 22	Cap	Aq	Pis	Ar	Ar	Tau	Gem	Gem	Can	Can	Leo	Leo
Oct 30	Aq	Aq	Pis	Ar	Tau	Tau	Gem	Can	Can	Can	Leo	Leo
Nov 7	Aq	Aq	Pis	Ar	Tau	Tau	Gem	Can	Can	Can	Leo	Leo
Nov 15	Aq	Pis	Ar	Tau	Gem	Gem	Can	Can	Can	Leo	Leo	Vir
Nov 23	Pis	Ar	Ar	Tau	Gem	Gem	Can	Can	Leo	Leo	Leo	Vir
Dec 1	Pis	Ar	Tau	Gem	Gem	Can	Can	Can	Leo	Leo	Vir	Vir
Dec 9	Ar	Tau	Tau	Gem	Gem	Can	Can	Leo	Leo	Leo	Vir	Vir
Dec 18	Ar	Tau	Gem	Gem	Can	Can	Can	Leo	Leo	Vir	Vir	Vir
Dec 28	Tau	Tau	Gem	Gem	Can	Can	Leo	Leo	Vir	Vir	Vir	Lib

CHAPTER 10

Parenting by the Stars

During 2003, the lucky and expansive planet Jupiter travels through Leo, the sign of children, then moves into Virgo, the sign of caregiving. It's the ideal time to look at what astrology has to say about parenting. By illuminating your child's basic nature, astrology can help you decide which kind of care will develop positive attributes and fulfill the individual needs of each sun sign.

If you are planning a family, you might be considering timing the birth of your child to complement the other family sun signs. However, there is also the theory that each child will come at a time that will be right for what he or she is meant to accomplish. In other words, if you were hoping for a Libra child and he or she arrives during Virgo, that Virgo energy may be just what is needed to stimulate or complement your family. Remember, there are many astrological elements besides the sun sign that indicate strong family ties. Usually each child will share a particular planetary placement, an emphasis on a particular sign or house, or a certain chart configuration with the parents and other family members. Often there is a significant planetary angle that will define the parent–child relationship, such as family sun signs that form a T-square or a triangle.

One important thing you can do is to be sure the exact moment of birth is recorded. (There are many jokes about the astrologer–mother who goes into labor with a stopwatch!) This will be essential in calculating an accurate astrological chart, if you should wish to have one drawn up in the future.

The following descriptions can be applied to the sun or moon sign (if known) of a child. The sun sign will describe basic personality, and the moon sign indicates the child's emotional needs. It wouldn't hurt to read Pisces as well, with Mars and Uranus in Pisces for much of this year, since many children born in 2003 will have a strong Pisces emphasis.

The Aries Child

Baby Aries is quite a handful! This energetic child will walk—and run—as soon as possible, and perform daring feats of exploration. Caregivers should be vigilant. Little Aries seems to know no fear, and is especially vulnerable to head injuries. Many Aries children, in their rush to get on with life, seem hyperactive; they are easily frustrated when they can't get their own way. Violent temper tantrums and dramatic physical displays are par for the course with this child.

The very young Aries should be monitored carefully, since they are prone to take risks and may injure themselves. Aries love to take things apart and may break toys easily. But with encouragement, the child will develop formidable coordination. Aries bossy tendencies should be molded into leadership qualities rather than bullying techniques. Otherwise, the "me-first" Aries will have many clashes with other strong-willed youngsters. Encourage this child to take out aggressions and frustrations in active, competitive sports, where they usually excel. When young Aries learns to focus energies long enough to master a subject and learns consideration for others, the indomitable Aries spirit will rise to the head of the class.

The Caregiver for Aries

Since this child is usually vocal in expressing needs, you'll have little guesswork. Your key emphasis is to help this child control his or her temper, develop self-discipline, and respect authority. You may find yourself breaking up quite a few arguments. Be vigilant, but give this child plenty of space. Encourage young Aries to express overflowing energy in constructive physical activity and to develop leadership skills. It is important to emphasize manners and consideration for others, which will help willful Aries get along socially with playmates.

The Taurus Child

This is a cuddly, affectionate child who eagerly explores the world of the senses, especially the sense of taste and touch. The Taurus child can be a big eater and will put on weight easily if not encouraged to exercise. Since this child likes comfort and gravitates to beauty, try coaxing little Taurus to exercise to music. Or take him or her outdoors on hikes or long walks in a local park or woodland. Though Taurus may be a slow learner, this sign has an excellent retentive memory and generally masters a subject thoroughly. Taurus is interested in results and will see each project patiently through to completion, continuing long after others have given up.

Choose Taurus toys carefully to help develop innate talents. Construction toys, such as blocks or erector sets, appeal to their love of building. Paints or crayons develop their sense of color. Many Taurus have musical talent and love to sing, which is apparent at a young age. Little Taurus will usually want a pet or two, and a few plants of his or her own. Give little Taurus a mini-garden and watch the natural green thumb develop. This child has a strong sense of acquisition and an early grasp of material value. After filling a piggy bank, Taurus graduates to a savings account—before other children have even started to learn the value of money.

The Caregiver for Taurus

Be affectionate, demonstrative, and generous with hugs and cuddles. Teach little Taurus to share possessions and to give as well as to accumulate. Be patient. Any pushing will bring out the Taurus stubborn side, and Taurus has a will that won't be budged. Introduce changes and new things gradually, for Taurus adapts best when well prepared.

The Gemini Child

Little Gemini will talk as soon as possible, filling the air with questions and chatter. This is a friendly child who enjoys social contact, seems to require company, and adapts quickly to different surroundings. Geminis have quick minds that easily grasp the use of words, books, and telephones, and will probably learn to talk and read at an earlier age than most.

Though they are fast learners, Gemini may have a short attention span, darting from subject to subject. Projects and games that help focus the mind could be used to help them concentrate. Musical instruments, typewriters, and computers help older Gemini children combine mental with manual dexterity. Geminis should be encouraged to finish what they start before they go on to another project. Otherwise, they can become jack-of-all trade types who have trouble completing anything they do. Their disposition is usually cheerful and witty, making these children popular with their peers and delightful company at home.

The Caregiver for Gemini

Gemini needs good communication, discussion, and sharing. This is a verbal child who enjoys talking things over and who grasps ideas easily. Avoid isolation or too much solitude. Give this child a variety of toys to suit the need for diversity. Alternate different kinds of activity. Teach little Gemini to follow projects through to completion.

The Cancer Child

This emotional, sensitive child is especially influenced by patterns set in early life. Young Cancers cling to their first memories as well as their childhood possessions. They thrive in calm emotional waters, with a loving, protective mother, and usually remain close to her (even if their relationship with her was difficult) throughout their lives. Divorce, death—anything that disturbs the safe family unit—is devastating to Cancers, who may need extra support and reassurance during a family crisis.

They sometimes need a firm hand to push the positive, creative side of their personality and to discourage them from getting swept away by emotional moods or resorting to emotional manipulation to get their way. If this child is praised and encouraged to find creative expression, Cancers will be able to express their positive side consistently on a firm, secure foundation.

The Caregiver for Cancer

Pour on praise and encouragement, and tone down criticism. The calmer the home atmosphere, the better. This child may need more time with Mother than other children, so be sure that the primary caregiver is warm, motherly, and supportive.

The Leo Child

Leo children love the limelight and will plot to get the lion's share of attention. These children assert themselves with flair and drama, and can behave like tiny tyrants to get their way. But in general they have a sunny, positive disposition, and are rarely subject to blue moods. At school, they're the type that is voted most popular, head cheerleader, homecoming queen. Leo is sure to be noticed for personality, if not for stunning looks or academic work; the homely Leo will be a class clown; the unhappy Leo can be the class bully.

Above all, a Leo child cannot tolerate being ignored for long. Drama or performing arts classes, sports, and school politics are healthy ways for Leo to be a star. But Leos must learn to take lesser roles occasionally, or they will have some painful put-downs in store. Usually, Leo popularity is well earned; they are hard workers who try to measure up to their own high standards—and usually succeed.

The Caregiver for Leo

Warmth, affection, praise, and attention are key words for Leo's parents and caregivers. Choose an open, warm, positive person to care for Leo, rather than a strict disciplinarian. Give Leo plenty of playmates, a fun atmosphere. Lonely Leos will resort to dramatic scenes to capture center stage. Encourage their natural leadership ability. Cheer on their outside activities. Develop their performing talents. It is important to teach them to channel their "show-off" tendencies in creative ways so they learn to share the spotlight.

The Virgo Child

The young Virgo can be a quiet, serious child, with a quick, intelligent mind. Early on, little Virgo shows far more attention to detail and concern with small things than other children. Little Virgo has a built-in sense of order and a fascination of how things work. It is important for these children to have a place of their own, which they can order as they wish and where they can read or busy themselves with crafts and hobbies.

This child's personality can be very sensitive. Little Virgo may get "hyper" and overreact to seemingly small irritations, which can take the form of stomach upsets or delicate digestive systems. But this child will flourish where there is mental stimulation and a sense of order. Virgos thrive in school, especially in writing or language skills, and seem truly happy when buried in books. Chances are, young Virgo will learn to read ahead of classmates. Hobbies that involve detail work or that develop fine craftsmanship are especially suited to young Virgos.

The Caregiver for Virgo

Though they might not show it, Virgo children need demonstrations of affection and support to shore up sensitive self-esteem. Coach the shy child in social and athletic skills. Perfecting a sport or dance routine can engross young Virgos and give them healthy exercise. (It is often difficult to get these children to exercise.) Young Virgos may be quite demanding of themselves and others, so encourage them to lighten up and to be more accepting of imperfections.

The Libra Child

The Libra child learns early about the power of charm and good looks. This is often a very physically appealing child with an enchanting dimpled smile, who is naturally sociable and enjoys the company of both children and adults. It is a rare Libra child who is a discipline problem. But when their behavior is unacceptable, they respond better to calm discussion than displays of emotion, especially if the discussion revolves around fairness. Because young Libras without a strong direction tend to drift with the mood of the group, these children should be encouraged to develop their unique talents and powers of discrimination so they can later stand on their own.

In school, this child is usually popular and will often have to choose between social invitations and studies. In the teen years, social pressures mount as the young Libra begins to look for a partner. This is the sign of "best friends," so Libra's choice of companions can have a strong effect on his or her future direction. Beautiful Libra girls may be tempted to go steady or have an unwise early marriage. Chances are, both sexes will fall in and out of love several times in their search for the ideal partner.

The Caregiver for Libra

Naturally cooperative, Libras are usually quite easy to supervise. These children relate well to others and usually enjoy playing with other children. Or they'll share activities with a companion or special friend. Develop their creative talents and artistic hobbies. Give them an attractive harmonious atmosphere to live in, letting them choose the colors and decor of their room.

The Scorpio Child

The Scorpio child may seem quiet and shy on the surface, but will surprise others with intensity of feelings and force of willpower. Scorpio children are single-minded when they want something and intensely passionate about whatever they do. One of a caregiver's tasks is to teach this child to balance activities and emotions, yet at the same time to make the most of their great concentration and intense commitment.

Since young Scorpios do not show their depth of feelings easily, parents will have to learn to read almost imperceptible signs that troubles are brewing beneath the surface. Both Scorpio boys and girls enjoy games of power and control on or off the playground. She may take an early interest in the opposite sex, masquerading as a tomboy, while he may be intensely competitive and something of a loner. When their powerful energies are directed into work, sports, or challenging studies, Scorpio is a superachiever thoroughly focused on a goal. With trusted friends, young Scorpio is devoted and caring—the proverbial friend "through thick and thin," loyal for life.

The Caregiver for Scorpio

Scorpio children need a great deal of affection and guidance in expressing their sensitive feelings. It is especially important not to violate their trust (these children can instantly detect what's going on behind closed doors), invade their privacy (allow them secret places to stash special belongings), or read their diary. A creative caregiver can help channel one of this child's greatest assets—the intense Scorpio drive—into constructive areas that will assure approval and success.

The Sagittarius Child

This restless, athletic child will be out of the playpen and off on explorative adventures as soon as possible. Little Sagittarius is remarkably well coordinated, attempting daredevil feats on any wheeled vehicle from scooters to skateboards. These natural athletes need little encouragement to channel their energies into sports. Their cheerful friendly dispositions earn them popularity in school. Once they have found a subject where their talent and imagination can soar, they will do well academically. They love animals, especially horses, and will be sure to have a pet or two, if not a home zoo. When they are old enough to take care of themselves, they'll clamor to be off on adventures of their own, away from home if possible.

This is a child who loves to travel, will not get homesick at summer camp, and may sign up to be a foreign exchange student or spend summers abroad. Outdoor adventure appeals to little Sagittarius, especially if it involves an active sport, such as skiing, cycling, or mountain climbing. Give them enough space and encouragement, and their fiery spirit will propel them to achieve high goals.

The Caregiver for Sagittarius

This independent child needs plenty of room to move around—no fenced-in playpens. Take the young Sagittarius on your travels, letting him or her explore new places. This is a great game player, full of laughs and fun. Be enthusiastic. Encourage Sagittarius to aim high and follow through, to take responsibility for their actions.

The Capricorn Child

This purposeful goal-oriented child will work to capacity if he or she feels this will bring results. They're not ones who enjoy work for its own sake—there must be an end in sight. Authority figures can do much to motivate this child. But once set on an upward path, young Capricorn will mobilize his or her energy and talent and will work harder, and with more perseverance, than any other sign. Capricorn has built-in self-discipline that can achieve remarkable results, even if lacking the flashy personality, quick brainpower, or penetrating insight of others. Once involved, young Capricorn will stick to a task until it is mastered. This child also knows how to use others to advantage, and may well become the team captain or class president.

A wise parent will set realistic goals for the Capricorn child, paving the way for the early thrill of achievement. Youngsters should be encouraged to express their caring, feeling side to others, as well as their natural aptitude for leadership. Capricorn children may be especially fond of grandparents and older relatives, and will enjoy spending time with them and learning from them. It is not uncommon for young Capricorns to have an older mentor or teacher who guides them. With their great respect for authority, Capricorn children will take this influence very much to heart.

The Caregiver for Capricorn

Capricorn responds well to a structured environment with clear boundaries and rules. Reward early achievements, helping young Capricorn aim high and set realistic goals. Give them small responsibilities early (they can handle it) and much praise. Teach them generosity with their siblings and playmates. Encourage Capricorn to nurture younger friends and pets. Help them relate to their peer group in a noncompetitive way.

The Aquarius Child

The Aquarius child has an innovative, well-focused mind that often streaks so far ahead of peers that this child seems like an "oddball." Routine studies never hold the restless youngster for long; he or she will look for another, more experimental place to try out their ideas and to develop their inventions. Life is a laboratory to the inquiring Aquarius mind.

School politics, sports, science, and the arts offer scope for this child's talents. But if there is no room for expression within approved social limits, Aquarius is sure to rebel. Questioning institutions and religions comes naturally, so these children may find an outlet elsewhere, becoming "rebels with a cause." It is better not to force this child to conform. Instead, channel forward-thinking young minds into constructive group activities.

The Caregiver for Aquarius

Play up whatever is unique about Aquarius children; never criticize them for being nonconformists. Encourage independence, originality, and inventiveness. Give them a safe place to explore and experiment. When disciplining Aquarius, appeal to reason and concern for the good of the group, rather than enforcing rigid rules.

The Pisces Child

Give young Pisces praise, applause, and a gentle but firm push in the right direction. Lovable Pisces children may be abundantly talented. But they may be hesitant to express themselves because they are quite sensitive and easily hurt. It is a parent's challenge to help them gain self-esteem and self-confidence. However, this same sensitivity makes them trusted friends who'll have many confidants as they develop socially. It also endows many Pisces with spectacular creative talent.

Pisces adores drama and theatrics of all sorts. Encourage them to channel their creativity into art forms rather than indulging in emotional dramas. As they develop their creative ideas, they may need more solitude than other children. But though daydreaming can be creative, it is important that these natural dreamers not dwell too long in the world of fantasy. Teach them practical coping skills for the real world. Since Pisces are sensitive physically, parents should help them build strong bodies with proper diet and regular exercise. Young Pisces may gravitate to individual sports, such as swimming, sailing, and skiing, rather than to team sports. Or they may prefer artistic physical activities like dance or ice skating.

Born "givers," these children are often drawn to the underdog (they fall quickly for sob stories) and attract those who might take advantage of their empathic nature. Teach them to choose friends wisely and to set boundaries in relationships, to protect their emotional vulnerability—invaluable lessons in later life.

The Caregiver for Pisces

Since Pisces children react strongly to their emotional and physical environment, give them a harmonious, rational atmosphere to balance their sensitive feelings. Establish clear emotional boundaries to give Pisces secure footing. Build up their confidence by praising their natural creative talent. Because Pisces children need to integrate their world of fantasy with the realities of life, emphasize the need to develop order, clarity, and discrimination.

CHAPTER 11

Let Astrology Point the Way to Financial Opportunity

Coming up is a year of changes, the logical time to revamp your finances. Like many tyrants, kings, and tycoons, you, too, can benefit from astrology's insights in predicting current growth trends. (The legendary tycoon J. P. Morgan is rumored to have consulted an astrologer.) So find out where your best opportunities lie and what stage of the wheel of success you'll be passing through this year, then make savvy decisions to play the market or stay on the sidelines. Using the trends in this chapter, you can formulate your strategy for building wealth in any kind of market during 2003.

Think Out of the Box

When the planet Uranus changes signs, as it does in 2003, it's time to think out of the box and tune your antennae to the future. As Uranus moves into Pisces, all things relating to Pisces will become major issues for the next seven years. While Uranus was in Aquarius, the sign of high technology, it sent the stocks of dot coms and Internet start-ups soaring. Now watch what it does for Pisces businesses. Scientific medicine should have spectacular success. Look for new advances in pharmaceuticals, especially antibiotics (inspired by bioterrorism), in embryonic research, and in genetics. Hospitals should become more focused on treating each person as an individual, perhaps based on a personal genetic profile. There should be terrific investment opportunities in these areas.

Our huge appetite for oil (petroleum is associated with Pisces) has caused international crises and conflicts, and may remain one of America's most vulnerable points. This year, expect major changes in our energy policy and consumption. Redesigned fuel-efficient or electrical cars are possibilities. Offshore oil exploration and development of oceanic energy reserves may be accelerated, as well as development of hydroelectric power companies, as we tap oceans and rivers for power sources. Look for investment opportunities in power-saving devices of all kinds.

Pisces is associated with all things aquatic, of course. Fish farms, water purifying systems, swimming pools, ocean studies, shipping, sea plants as food, ocean exploration, submarine travel, and naval supplies are investment possibilities.

Creative areas have historically done well, as Uranus in Pisces stimulates avant-garde artists. New music, computer-generated art and entertainment, and the dance world (especially ballet) should thrive. Other Pisces areas include film, footwear, cosmetics, podiatry, fountains, gases, dance, alcohol and other intoxicants, any business involving fantasy and creativity, religion-oriented businesses, yoga and other spiritual practices, retreats, charities, and any institutions that help the underdog.

The Jupiter Factor

Good fortune and big money are always associated with Jupiter, which embodies the principle of expansion. Jupiter has a twelve-year cycle, staying in each sign for approximately one year. When Jupiter enters a sign, the fields influenced by that sign seem new and profitable, and they usually provide excellent investment opportunities. Areas of speculation governed by the sign Jupiter is passing through will have the hottest market potential—they're the ones that currently arouse excitement and enthusiasm.

During 2003, Jupiter transits two signs. It completes its

trip through Leo on August 27, then enters Virgo. The areas each sign influences should have expansive opportunities. Readers with strong fire sign (Leo, Aries, Sagittarius) influences in their horoscope should have many growth opportunities during the first half of the year. Those born in earth signs (Virgo, Capricorn, Taurus) should take advantage of Jupiter's beneficial rays starting in September.

On the downside, Aquarius may feel out of sync and need to focus on relationships rather than a personal agenda until Jupiter changes signs in September.

Jupiter-Favored Growth Areas

Look to areas favored by Leo until August 27: games, places of amusement, show business, theater, entertainers, jewelry, showy floral arrangements, gold and the gold coin business, golf, loan companies, oranges, the Pacific Ocean area, all pleasurable and luxurious things, high fashion, sporting events and arenas, gambling casinos, the Sun Belt.

Starting in September, watch these efficient Virgo-related areas: organizers, accountants, administrators, haute cuisine, public health, the medical and health industry, medicinal herbs, grain production, education, the service business, sanitation, sewing and tailoring, personal trainers, health clubs. All that is health-promoting, detail-oriented, and educational gets a big boost from Virgo.

In Your Personal Life

Find the house where Jupiter in Leo and Jupiter in Virgo will fall in your chart to indicate where you'll have the most expansive potential this year. Just look up your rising sign from the chart in this book (pp. 140–141) and check the following list. (Those who know their exact birth time and place, and who have access to the Internet, can get an accurate chart online from one of the sources recommended in the Internet chapter in this book.)

ARIES RISING: A CREATIVE BONANZA
For anyone involved in creative fields, this is bonanza time—the inspiration flows! Put some fun into your life and

help others to do so for profit. Your best ideas will come when you play at your job (don't they always?), finding more creative ways to get the work done. The only danger here is too much fun—you may be more interested in pleasure than profit. Love affairs, fun times, and recreation can impose on work time. You may find it difficult to stick to any routines. Since this placement also rules children, you may find yourself involved with them in some way—or you may become a parent.

TAURUS RISING: LUCK BEGINS AT HOME
Your success potential is tied to your domestic life. This is often a time of moving or relocating, as you try to arrange your personal lifestyle for the next twelve years. This is the time to establish your personal space, strengthen family ties, and give yourself a solid base of operations. You can now create the much-needed balance between your private life and the outside world that will shore you up for the next twelve years. Aim for greater family harmony and inner strength. Opportunities to invest in real estate could be winners.

GEMINI RISING: COMMUNICATIONS
You will overflow with ideas, so record them for future reference. Write up a storm! Sign up for a course that interests you—it could pay off in the future. Your social life is buzzing, as the phone rings off the hook. Make new business contacts in your local area. You may also find a lucky financial venture that involves your friends or siblings. In the fall, home life takes priority. This is the time to redecorate, renovate, expand, or buy a new home.

CANCER RISING: INCREASE YOUR SECURITY
Be a saver, not a spender, this year. Now is the time to use those contacts you made last year to consolidate your financial security. You may find that your cash flow increases, as there is generally more money available for big splurges. Watch this tendency! It might be a better idea to use this time of opportunity to protect yourself with backup

157

funds for a more secure future. This is a time to develop good money management habits!

LEO RISING: THE IMAGE THAT SELLS

For most of the year, you hold the luckiest cards. With Jupiter energizing your ascendant, you look like a winner without even trying. Use this time to kick off the next twelve-year cycle in the most advantageous way. Circulate among influential people, make personal contacts, sell yourself. Push yourself out in the public eye, even if you're the shy type. This is the time to be your most social self! One cautionary note: Jupiter means expansion—and this position rules your physical body—so watch your diet. You'll tend to put on weight easily. The latter half of the year, focus on making a budget and savings plan that you can live with. If you've been caught up in an extravagant lifestyle, do a reality check.

VIRGO RISING: WARM-UP FOR THE BIG TIME

You've come to the end of a twelve-year Jupiter cycle, and in September will start another cycle. Use the first half of the year to review what you've learned in the last twelve years, to experiment with new ventures. Proceed slowly, as you will be bringing many matters that have occupied you over the past dozen years to a close. It's also a good time to get centered spiritually, to line up your ducks in a row, so you'll be ready to seize the moment when opportunities arise in September with Jupiter in Virgo. Then go for it in October when you'll hold the best cards in the deck.

LIBRA RISING: THE BIG LEAGUE

Jupiter brings you group connections this year. Others will be looking to you for inspiration. Since you can now win the support of the movers and shakers in your field and are ready to lead the pack, put some of the ideas formulated in previous cycles into action. This is the time when you make the team, come to the aid of your party, or find a new audience for your talents. In the fall, you may be ready for some solitude! This is a good time to rest, regroup, do some solitary creative work, or fund-raise for your favorite hospital or charity.

SCORPIO RISING: BUILD YOUR PRESTIGE

It's a great time to promote yourself, be highly visible, and build up your professional image. This cycle favors public activities rather than domestic life. It's a great time to deal with VIPs and top brass. You should be feeling superconfident, and it will show. You may be starting a new career or making a stronger commitment to the one you're in. Follow up with social contacts, and exercise your leadership skill in the fall.

SAGITTARIUS RISING: AIM HIGH

This is the ideal time to get higher education, develop your philosophy of life, and formulate new directions for the future. Aim high, look at the big overall picture. Publish your book, get a college or graduate degree, travel abroad. Expand your mind and horizons. Take a calculated risk. You may feel like changing your life around and trying something completely new. The ideas you get early in the year and the interesting people you meet will enhance your reputation and career.

CAPRICORN RISING: WATCH THE CASH FLOW

You'll have opportunities to use credit and to deal with banks, loan companies, and the IRS. Be very careful with your credit cards during this period. There could be a strong temptation to overextend. You may find others more than willing to lend you money at high interest. If you're a risk taker, you may have to keep a strict eye on expenditures—Jupiter encourages gambling! You might also find yourself managing money for others and getting involved in joint ventures.

AQUARIUS RISING: MAKING COMMITMENTS

Commitments can be fortunate for you this year. Many people marry at this time. However, this is not a good time for solo ventures. You are best off working in tandem and letting your partner share the spotlight. You may have to submerge your own agenda for a while in order to take full advantage of this period. So think "togetherness." You can use others to your advantage, but don't try to take over. Since this is the area of open enemies, you could learn much about your adversaries and gain the advantage in the future.

PISCES RISING: DETAILS, DETAILS
This is the time when you may seem bogged down in details, in learning the operation of the company from the ground up, or in taking care of the mundane aspects that make a business operate efficiently. But remember, it is only through creating a smooth working operation that fortunes can be made in the long haul. You have only to read the financial section of your newspaper to see how many promising companies get swept away by poor management. This is also an excellent time to take care of yourself. Set up a diet and exercise regime. Get your body in good shape.

CHAPTER 12

The Astro-Dating Game

Be a love magnet by using the secrets of astrological seduction.

Do you know the turn-on color for Aries? Would you take a Cancer to a family dinner? Would playing hard to get make a Taurus pursue you? If you're looking for love, you'll want to make the best first impression possible to get your romance off to the right start. So what do you wear?

Look no further than astrology to give you the stellar secrets to attracting, pleasing, and pampering potential partners. In your sun sign chapters in this book you can evaluate your compatibility with every other sign. Then it's time to cast your bait in the right direction. Here's how to play the Astro-Dating game with every sign: where to meet one, where to go, and what to do.

Aries

WHERE TO MEET ONE:
Aries are impulsive, action-ready types who love the newest, hottest places. Keep up on the latest happenings in your town, the hip restaurants, sports events, competitions. You'll find Aries where the action is. When you get together, keep an upbeat, enthusiastic, positive attitude. No complaining, heavy emotions, or talk about previous relationships, please! Don't be too easy to get—this is one sign that enjoys pursuit.

WHERE TO GO:
Your Ram is an activist, so don't plan a cozy evening at home unless Aries is doing the cooking or watching the

tennis matches. Think adventure, excitement, fast action. Keep Aries moving. The newest dance club, a sports event, games of all kinds are good. Try races, adventure sports, spicy foods, the newest "scene," a live music event, a hike together, a workout, a bike trip, the wildest rides at your local amusement park. Be a doer!

WHAT TO WEAR:
Light Aries fires with red—if not a whole outfit, just a touch somewhere interesting. Wear one of the newest trends (if it looks good on you). Wear a hat to attract Aries attention. By all means, be up-to-date fashionwise. Be sure whatever shoes you wear can take lots of action, since you'll be on the go! Nothing turns a Ram off more than a date with sore feet!

Taurus

WHERE TO MEET ONE:
Meet Taurus where there's money to be made or handled: a stock broker's office, a bank, an investment adviser, a real estate office, a store. Scout the local real estate for sales in your area. A pet shop, dog run, zoo, or animal training school could lure animal lovers. Gardening stores, home improvement stores, art galleries, music stores, concerts, food emporiums, restaurants, and parks are other Taurus hangouts. Warning: This is a possessive sign, so if Taurus likes you, playing hard to get could be a signal that you're not interested.

WHERE TO GO:
Think rich and delicious. Taurus loves luxury, comfort, beauty, so let that be your clue. Pick a sensual environment. If you're inviting Taurus home, be sure to stock your refrigerator and be sure the place looks good and smells good. If you're wining and dining, scope out your Bull's food preferences and head for the poshest restaurant in town. If you're a super chef, then do a culinary tour de force for

Taurus, and be sure there are plenty of seconds. Finish with the richest dessert you can find, or have some delicious ice cream on hand. If you can't afford to wine and dine, then find the cafe with the best desserts and go after dinner. You can't go wrong with music, but find out what Taurus likes first. Other earthy attractions: picnics at a beautiful country setting, Shakespeare plays (he was a Taurus). Taurus is touchy-feely, so a dual massage could set the stage for seduction.

WHAT TO WEAR:
Most Taurus prefer classic, elegant, conservative clothes in beautiful sensual fabrics. There is the odd Taurus who wants you to look like a "babe" and goes for heavy-handed sex appeal. But if you're thinking long term, wear something soft and feminine (if you're female) in a fabric that begs to be touched, like cashmere. Taurus women like the rich look, so, if you're a man, dress like a tycoon or like you're about to become one.

Gemini

WHERE TO MEET ONE:
Keep up with the latest news and hit the hot spots. Geminis are on a constant search for mental stimulation, so they're sure to be at the most interesting place in town. A bookstore, a lecture by a famous person, the opening of a restaurant, the local newspaper office, the newest movie. A party, wedding, or other social event draws sociable Geminis. Don't be possessive with Gemini—this sign loves to flirt and will interpret jealousy as insecurity, a real downer.

WHERE TO GO:
Choose a place that appeals to Gemini mental interests and love of variety. Have several alternatives if Gemini gets bored or restless with your first choice. Pick a venue that promotes good conversation and has stimulating people nearby. Gemini is curious about other people. So if there

are different cultures living in your town, unusual places, even if a bit oddball, plan an evening of exploration. Variety is spice to Gemini. So expect to share your dinner, or opt for a buffet or a cuisine where dishes are shared by everybody. A party followed by a lecture followed by a buffet dinner would be perfect. Gemini enjoys scenes with a constant flow of attractive people. A museum, a hot cafe or coffee bar, an exercise class, or a walk in an unexplored neighborhood would be fun. Be spontaneous. Don't hesitate to scrap your plans and try something else if the place you choose doesn't live up to expectations.

WHAT TO WEAR:
Gemini has an eye for style and will appreciate anything unique or unusual you wear. You can be as high fashion as you want with this sign. Just don't look boring. Since Gemini is attracted to beautiful hands, be sure your nails are manicured and wear a lovely ring.

Cancer

WHERE TO MEET ONE:
Food, family, shelter, and water are your key words for Cancer. Head for the shore, take boating or sailing lessons. Vacation at a resort with sailing or a fabulous beach. A gourmet restaurant or food store, a cooking class, a family reunion, an art or music venue, the local Home Depot, a housewarming party, a cookout at the beach are all places you might meet a Cancer. Take a course in photography or interior design (Cancers are talented at both).

WHERE TO GO:
Cancers are born romantics, highly emotional and sensitive. Usually, they're domestic and love to cook, so a terrific restaurant or an evening at home cooking together would go over well. Pull out your best dishes, candles, wine, and music for this home-loving sign. If you're going out, seafood is sure to be a hit. Rent a romantic movie, attend a

concert, go sailing or swimming—anything near water will be appreciated. Cancers are family-oriented, so don't be afraid to include them in your family celebrations. Encourage their creativity by taking a course together in cooking, photography, interior design, or home maintenance.

WHAT TO WEAR:
If you're a woman, wear something soft and clingy that shows off your curvaceous bosom; a nice chest is a big plus with Cancer. Classy couture looks are also winners (many top designers and fashion icons are Cancer). Cancers are sensitive to color coordination, so you're better off wearing subtle blues, greens, or neutrals that blend together. Think Armani. Jarring brights or oddball styles are a no-no.

Leo

WHERE TO MEET ONE:
Head for the Leo lairs: public life, politics, show business, big business, major social events, prestige restaurants, country clubs, gambling casinos, sporting events. Your Leo enjoys the spotlight. Join an amateur theater group or acting class. Canvass for your local political club. Shop at the priciest clothing and jewelry stores. Polish up your dancing technique, and shine with Leo on the dance floor. Parties are Leo magnets, so dress to the nines and socialize. Your attitude should be upbeat, positive, and adoring. Leo loves compliments—in quantity!

WHERE TO GO:
Show off your Leo—this is not a sign that prefers quiet evenings at home. Invite Leo to a local charity ball, a top sporting event, a big party. Take Leo out on the town, but make sure to go first-class. Leos love dressing up to the nines and consorting with local celebrities. Throw a party of your own and ask Leo to be cohost or hostess. Then invite the most attractive people you know. Cultural events, the theater, rock concerts, opera, nightclubs are Leo terri-

tory. Give Leo the royal treatment, and they'll return the favor. Theater is always a Leo favorite. Make it an upbeat show, such as a musical, with beautiful costumes.

WHAT TO WEAR:
Male or female, be sure your hair is looking its best—the Lion is always aware of manes. Wear your best designer duds, and Leo will love to show you off. But be sure you don't outshine your mate (difficult to do, with Leo).

Virgo

WHERE TO MEET ONE:
No-nonsense Virgo is discriminating and enjoys high-quality events, places with a purpose, educational or health-oriented activities. Health-oriented Virgos can be found doing volunteer work at hospitals, serving in health food stores, taking notes at nutritional lectures. Virgos like detailed crafts and can often be found perfecting their skills in crafts workshops. Bookstores and literary events appeal to bookish Virgos.

WHERE TO GO:
Put some thought into planning your Virgo date. Virgos are not especially spur-of-the-moment types. Aim for quality and mental stimulation rather than showmanship. Virgo is discriminating, so go somewhere that's the best in its class (not necessarily the most expensive). A picnic or hike in a beautiful outdoor setting, a cultural or literary event, a seminar or lecture with a notable speaker, an exhibit, a museum or a walking tour of a favorite neighborhood, a wine- or food-tasting event are appealing possibilities. Virgo is interested in health, so take a yoga class together. Be sure to tidy up your home if you're inviting Virgo over. Serve healthful food that is not too complicated but well prepared.

WHAT TO WEAR:
Clean, neat, and elegant are Virgo rules. Whatever your style, be it tailored or avant-garde, be sure it's clean and well pressed. Your grooming should be faultless. White is a special Virgo color, and what could give you a cleaner look! Remember Ingrid Bergman's white suit in *Casablanca* or Garbo's white evening gown.

Libra

WHERE TO MEET ONE:
Beauty-loving Libras are fond of all the arts and are one of the most social signs. Parties, gatherings, anywhere people meet and greet are where to find Libra. Fashion shows, art openings, charity events are likely Libra meeting places. Take a course in interior design or fashion design. Haunts of the legal profession might also turn up some Libras, lovers of fairness and justice. When you've met your Libra, keep it light and lively. Libras do not want to know about any heavy emotional baggage.

WHERE TO GO:
You're in luck. Libra likes to do things with a partner, and will be happy to accompany you shopping, hanging out, traveling, socializing. Libra adores fine dining in an elegant atmosphere. Let Libra revamp your wardrobe or give your home a makeover. Libra adores frequent, thoughtful gifts like flowers or the latest novel. Cultural events, art films, dual sports like tennis, kayaking, a bicycle built for two, dancing would be fun with Libra. Take a cooking or art course together.

WHAT TO WEAR:
Libra is the most fashion-conscious of all signs, so be sure to look your best. Pay particular attention to color harmony—clashing colors are a Libra turnoff. Choose pale, subtle shades, nothing glaring, with an interesting accessory or two. Wear a touch of pink, a favorite Libra color.

Scorpio

WHERE TO MEET ONE:
Scorpio, one of the zodiac's great water lovers, will often be found biking, hiking, or just hanging out by the shore or riverside. Scorpio is fascinated by power and the mysteries of life, so look for Scorpios in places where powerful, charismatic types gather. Dynamic sports, powerful racing machines, military or police hangouts, edgy musical venues are their ticket. A bookstore that specializes in murder mysteries could be a Scorpio lair. Ancient history or archaeology has great appeal to Scorpio, so investigate the local digs or fine antiques stores. A lecture by the latest guru or preacher with hypnotic appeal is sure to attract the more spiritual Scorpios. Keep your air of mystery around Scorpio—don't tell all or be too available. Let them try to figure you out.

WHERE TO GO:
Take Scorpio to a mystery play or thriller movie. A seafood restaurant is usually a winner. They may prefer to spend time alone with you, so choose a beautiful, secluded place where you can focus on each other. And don't bring your cell phone! A more casual date could be stargazing, a midnight walk along the beach, an afternoon sail, exploring the hidden places in your city. Sporting events with lots of intense action attract Scorpio, so get tickets to your local tournament.

WHAT TO WEAR:
Scorpio loves sexy black, especially black leather, whether it's buttery soft or biker tough. Touchy-feely fabrics like cashmere appeal. Show off your sexuality in a subtle way, unless you want Scorpio to take action immediately.

Sagittarius

WHERE TO MEET ONE:
Sporting events and tournaments attract Sagittarius. Gambling casinos and comedy clubs are also meccas for this

fun-loving sign. Join the hottest sports club, and wear bright, sharp workout wear. Learn a new sport, especially one that uses the legs like hiking, climbing, skiing. Tours to interesting and often remote places attract wandering Sagittarius. Keep your disposition sunny-side up with this sign. Brush up on a few good jokes. Be healthy, happy, and ready for adventure.

WHERE TO GO:
Make your date an active one: kayaking or canoeing on your local river or lake, playing tennis or golf, exploring a local park, training for a marathon together, biking your local hills. Sagittarius likes to laugh, so go to a comedy club, play silly games, go to a fair or carnival with wild rides. Sagittarius loves horses, so go to the local racetrack or go horseback riding. Any event involving animals is sure to be a hit: the zoo, the circus, a horse show or dog show.

WHAT TO WEAR:
Wear great-looking sportswear, especially if it shows off your legs. Sagittarius has lots of fashion flair, so go all out with designer duds if you're going out on the town. You can run wild with fashion—Sagittarius will love your adventurous spirit.

Capricorn

WHERE TO MEET ONE:
You're most likely to meet Capricorn on the job or where business people hang out. Join an investment club. Conservative environments attract Capricorns: country clubs, golf or tennis clubs, traditional resorts. Capricorns are strivers, so find them at stores where fine clothing is sold, at upper-range real estate offices (selling or buying property), auctions, or charity benefits. Mountain-climbing clubs or ski resorts are good bets for meeting a Mountain Goat (as the Goat is the symbol for Capricorn). Behave yourself with this sign—no outrageous behavior, please.

WHERE TO GO:
Think classic, all-American fun, nothing too unconventional. Capricorns appreciate quality, but not extravagance, so take them to a traditional restaurant rather than a flashy one. Don't swamp them with totally unfamiliar food. Capricorns enjoy outdoor activity: hiking in your local park, a round of golf, or a set of tennis together. Good seats at the theater, opera, or a rock concert would impress this sign. Capricorn takes romance seriously, so proceed in a slow, stately, and proper way. Observe all the formalities, and brush up on your manners.

WHAT TO WEAR:
Capricorn has an eye for quality, so wear that elegant vintage dress. Well-cut classic clothes appeal to most Capricorns. A few designer labels wouldn't hurt. Go for the ladylike look rather than overtly sexy. In other words, look like someone who could be introduced to Mother.

Aquarius

WHERE TO MEET ONE:
Aquarius can turn up anywhere there's something new, original, or political happening. A computer expo, a far-out rock concert, a political rally, a fund-raiser for an offbeat cause, a political protest, a radical lecture, a team sport, a lecture by a far-out new guru, a cutting-edge clothing store are possibilities. Aquarius likes groups and is sure to have plenty of buddies, so join the party! When you meet your dreamboat, don't be possessive. Although this sign is loaded with charisma and a magnet to the opposite sex, once they're interested in you, they tend to keep it platonic with others.

WHERE TO GO:
Think out of the box and try something offbeat. Don't be too romantic, too fast. Aquarius likes to be friends first. Aquarius loves doing things that are unconventional, new,

cutting edge. They love surprises, doing things spontaneously, so nothing should seem too "planned." Include a group of like-minded friends, people Aquarius might like to meet. Raise funds for a worthy cause together. Attend a lecture at your local New Age center. Meditate together. Canvass your neighborhood together for your favorite candidate.

WHAT TO WEAR:
Wear something original and memorable that sets you apart from the crowd. Try wearing electric blue, an Aquarius color. You don't have to be conventional with this sign. Just wear what is appropriate to the event, with a slight personal twist.

Pisces

WHERE TO MEET ONE:
Waterside places are the Pisces habitat. Try the local beach, marina, yacht club, surfer store, fish market, trout stream. Pisces rules illusion. Therefore, any place that has to do with show business, such as a drama or filmmaking course, should have a quota of this sign. In sports, find Pisces on the ice: skating and hockey are favorites. You'll find this sign at spiritual places such as yoga retreats or church socials. Charity work and hospital volunteering could net you one of the Fishes.

WHERE TO GO ON A DATE:
A film or play is the obvious choice. Choose a restaurant that has a definite mood. Pisces loves exotic food in a dramatic setting. Seafood restaurants, those with harbor or river views, are sure winners. A wine tasting, poetry reading, sunset sail, afternoon at the aquarium, picnic by the lake, dancing, ice skating, ice fishing are all good bets. Pisces loves fantasy, romance, mood-inducing settings with a touch of magic. Let your imagination roam free—the more theatrical the setting, the better.

WHAT TO WEAR:

To please the Pisces male, appeal to his fantasy. Chances are, it will be a touch exotic, soft, feminine, flowing. Show off your mermaid curves. Men of this sign, like Fabio, can be colorful and flamboyant like the heroes of a romance novel, so dress like a heroine.

The Scorpio Orbit—
Your Personality, Love
Connections, Family, Work,
and Style!

Are You True to Your Cosmic Calling?

What is a Scorpio like? The recipe for the Scorpio personality is derived from several ingredients. Your sign's *element:* water. The way Scorpio *operates:* fixed—a builder, a controller. Your sign's *polarity:* negative, feminine, yin. Your *planetary ruler:* Pluto, the planet of transformation. Your sign's *place* in the zodiac: eighth, in the place of sex and power. Put 'em all together, and you've got Scorpio.

Everything we say about Scorpio is extrapolated from the above recipe.

Some of you may say, "I'm not like the typical Scorpio at all!" Powerful planetary placements in other signs could make you appear more flamboyant, as, for example, the singer Bjork. The more Scorpio emphasis in your horoscope, the more you'll fit the descriptions in the following chapters.

CHAPTER 13

Scorpio Profiles

The Scorpio Man: Man of Mystery

You're that mysterious stranger with the cool facade few can penetrate. You don't need to flex muscles to show off your masculinity. Your penetrating eyes send the message to every woman.

If the truth be known, you're much more interested in issues of power and control. You're challenged by unsolved problems and mysteries of any kind. You're a natural detective who won't stop until he knows what makes things and people tick. In spite of your aloof manner, you're always aware of what is going on (especially of who is running the show), and you're remarkably perceptive about people's true motives.

Beneath your deliberately cool surface, you may be far less secure. One of the most sensitive signs of the zodiac, you keep your vulnerability a dark secret to seal yourself off from rejection. When you do fall for someone, nothing less than total possession will do. Scorpio feels he should own the woman he loves (though he's also able to enjoy pure sex for its own sake elsewhere). Yours is the most possessive sign, with no toleration for disloyalty.

You are single-minded in pursuit of what you want, be it a job, a prize, or a person. It was with good reason that Scorpio fashion designer Calvin Klein named his first fragrance "Obsession." Your great concentration, intensity, and stamina make you a formidable competitor. But your love of power can degenerate into manipulation, bullying, and even violence if you are frustrated. You harbor a grudge and seek revenge when injured. As Teddy Roosevelt said, "Speak softly, but carry a big stick."

In a Relationship

When Scorpio falls in love, you are so single-minded about the object of your affection that, if you lose that love for any reason, you are devastated. Often this is the one experience that can teach Scorpio about healthy detachment and the wisdom of getting to know someone slowly and gradually for longevity's sake.

After issues of power and control are settled within the relationship, you become a loyal and devoted mate. But first you may go through a period of testing in which you are not above using emotional manipulation to gain the upper hand. You need a partner who will provide rational balance and perspective when you go to extremes and who will help you look on the lighter, brighter side of life.

The Scorpio Woman: Intensely Attractive

Like your male counterpart, the mysterious, mesmerizing Scorpio woman hides intense emotions under a cool, controlled facade. But inside you are passionate, determined, and totally committed to everything you do. This makes you seem very stable and somewhat predictable. You're not one for surprises or spontaneous moves; there is usually a strategy behind every step you take. All your formidable energy is zeroed in on your goal. The Scorpio woman is rarely plagued by self-doubt. You know exactly where you are going and rarely waver from your path. Once committed, you remain loyal and dedicated, and you will patiently see your projects through to completion. Hillary Clinton embodies these typical Scorpio traits.

Scorpio is the "heaviest" sign of the zodiac, so let those who skim the surface of life be forewarned. You delve deep and demand total commitment—anything less is not worthwhile. Since you are extremely vulnerable beneath your cool controlled surface, you are deeply hurt by betrayal. When disappointed, you can strike back with lethal accuracy.

The good girl/bad girl extremes of Scorpio are reflected

in the sex-charged and power charged roles Scorpio actresses have played in recent years. Jodie Foster and Julia Roberts both gained fame playing sexually charged roles in *Taxi Driver, The Accused,* and *Pretty Woman.* Demi Moore raised eyebrows with the pregnant nude cover of *Vanity Fair* magazine. Meg Ryan astonished with her simulated orgasm in the film *When Harry Met Sally.* Scorpio singer k.d. lang won the cover of a national magazine when she declared herself a lesbian. Scorpios Jodie Foster and Goldie Hawn have braved the Hollywood establishment by producing and directing their own projects.

Unfortunately, Scorpio intensity frightens away many who are not ready to commit to a bond that reaches to the soul level. The Scorpio woman considers this kind of fright a weakness, and so she blocks out many potentially interesting relationships. It is only after a period of tempering that you learn tolerance for a more balanced and rational relationship—and learn to give your partner space to be his own person.

A Scorpio woman is not one to play around with or take lightly. Though you may seem very sweet and naive, you can quickly see through deception. An excellent detective, you sense immediately when something is hidden, yet you yourself are never completely open about your own motives. This secretiveness can cause suspicion and mistrust. Others wonder what is lurking beneath that unruffled surface.

Anger brings out your venomous side. Scorpio has a suspicious streak and often overreacts to imaginary slights. You tend to see things in black and white, and you go to extremes when you're upset. Then it is very difficult to coax you out of a black mood. You are more likely to get revenge than to forgive and forget.

In a Relationship

Much maligned as a femme fatale, the typical Scorpio is a one-man (at a time) woman, intensely loyal and devoted to your mate. Though you may experiment before settling down, as a Scorpio you are looking for total commitment.

After marriage, you're so completely involved with your husband that you can be devastated if the marriage fails. However, once committed, your intense involvement could backfire if you become overly demanding, possessive, and jealous. Then you will smother a more freedom-loving partner. You must learn not to give in to those negative suspicions, which can escalate into destructive paranoia.

You reach your full potential as a mate once you have learned to share yourself with your partner rather than try to control the relationship. On the plus side, as a Scorpio you will stay with your true mate after he earns your trust, even through the most difficult times, as Hillary Clinton demonstrated. You are someone he can count on to support him, no matter what the sacrifice. And, in the long run, you can transform his life for the better.

Scorpio in the Family

The Scorpio Parent

Scorpios are committed to everything they do, especially to being a good parent. Though you may not express your feelings openly, you are able to convey to your children a feeling of being deeply loved. It is this strong foundation of emotional security that gives your children confidence. Trust and loyalty are unspoken givens. You'll defend your children to the maximum, and you'll provide them with the ways and means to live up to your high hopes. But you are a strict parent who insists on control and discipline, which could create problems with an equally strong-willed child. You may have to learn lessons of flexibility and tolerance from your children. And you will also have to learn when to let go, to allow your children to follow their own interests in the outside world. However, your children always know you will be there for them, ready to provide a life raft in the roughest waters.

The Scorpio Stepparent

In marriage, Scorpios can be intensely possessive of a mate. It is especially important that you and your stepchildren get along before the marriage, and that you are sincerely willing to reach out to them. Otherwise, power struggles can develop. It would also help to discuss problems openly as they occur rather than let anger, hurt feelings, or misunderstandings build up. Be flexible enough to allow your mate time with the children, apart from you. Have some outside activities to help diffuse your energy, so it is not overly concentrated on the family.

The Scorpio Grandparent

Grandchildren can provide some of the most liberating, joyful experiences of your life. At last you can show your playful childlike side, with a fun-loving little playmate who demands nothing of you. You're free from the disciplining responsibilities of parenthood and the intense emotional commitment. You're no longer involved in power struggles or overworked, so you're free to spend happy times with the children. Grandchildren can also bring out the generosity in Scorpio, particularly when providing for their future security. You'll make a lasting impression on the youngest generation, and they'll make you feel born again!

CHAPTER 14

Scorpio Flair: Your Key to Looking and Living Well

Why is it you look better in black? Love mystery novels and thriller films? Crave seaside vacations? Gravitate to homes near the water? It could be you're responding to the call of Scorpio! Each sun sign resonates to certain colors, styles, and places, which are sure to be your favorites. Use the following guide to steer your style in the right direction. The advice on where-to-go, what-to-wear, and how to create your happiest place to live is based on the specific colors, surroundings, and attitudes that best suit your Scorpio personality type. You can't go wrong!

The Scorpio House Beautiful

It's either-or for Scorpio decor. Either you'll go all out for plenty of dark woods, rich tapestry colors, sensual sink-in upholstery, brocade walls, luxurious leather or suede coverings, and Oriental rugs. Or you'll pare down to the bare essentials (like Calvin Klein), going stark and minimal, almost monastic, and sticking to one or two colors, often black and white. The latter kind of Scorpio may ignore the surroundings entirely, focusing on another aspect of life. This kind of Scorpio might live in a virtually unfurnished apartment, simply because he or she is not involved enough to decorate. For those who do care, marine motifs, voluptuous nudes, and dramatic artifacts appeal to you. Or you may go for the Victorian look, with carved wood furniture. You'll pay special attention to the bedroom, perhaps pulling out all the stops with satin sheets, mirrored walls, and seductive lighting effects.

Scorpio Music

Scorpios love intense music, thundering symphonies, and dramatic operas with life-and-death themes. But Scorpios also love sexy tangos, sensual cello sounds, Paul Simon, Bonnie Raitt, Joni Mitchell. Mysterious New Age music has Scorpio appeal. More avant-garde Scorpios go for powerful heavy-metal sounds with a driving beat and undercurrent of danger. The black leather and biker paraphernalia side of the rock scene is pure Scorpio. Gospel music can also stir your soul. The new CD burners were made for Scorpios, as you love to control what you hear. Now you can make your own kind of music in whatever combination of sounds turns you on.

Scorpio Colors

Basic black and a deep, rich burgundy are traditional Scorpio colors. But some Scorpios, particularly if they are pale blondes, prefer off-white tones of neutrals. The deep blues of the sea also resonate with Scorpio.

Scorpio Fashion Guide

Scorpios make an unforgettable fashion statement, whatever personal style is chosen. Like other fixed signs, they usually stick to a trademark look: the sporty, classic style of Jodie Foster; the avant-garde trendiness of Chloe Sevigny and Bjork; the ultrafeminine gamine look of Winona Ryder. Many Scorpio women, like Lauren Hutton, prefer man-tailored styles. Scorpios love to wear black, particularly black velvet or black leather. Scorpio will use intense makeup, or none at all, to dramatize strong bone structure and mesmerizing eyes.

Indulge yourself in some sexy accessories like stiletto boots, lacy lingerie, and at least one vibrantly colored scarf—just to hint at your inner passionate nature.

Calvin Klein's fashion style is pure Scorpio, with its streamlined, uncluttered sexy look from head to toe. (Leave it to a Scorpio to put a woman in man-styled underwear and name a fragrance "Obsession.") Pauline Trigere is known for dramatic, elegant high fashion. Rae Kawaikubo of Comme des Garçons goes to the opposite extreme to make a severe avant-garde statement with stark, futuristic looks. For jewelry, the dramatic designs of Marina Schiano are scene-stealers.

The Healing Arts of Scorpio

Too much coffee? Too little sleep? Headaches slowing you down or allergies acting up? Scorpio's fast-paced, action-packed life can be stressful, so here are some ways to unwind and put the spring back into your step.

Scorpio is the sign of "all-or-nothing" extremes, which can take a toll on your health unless you temper your intensity with discipline and balance. Though your sign usually has a strong constitution that can literally rise from the ashes of extreme illness or misfortune, resist the temptation to take this for granted or sabotage your health with self-destructive habits. Try to curb excessive tendencies in any area of your life. Know when to quit and when to seek help—and don't hesitate to ask for help when you need it.

Your sign rules the regenerative and eliminative organs. Therefore, it follows that sexual activity can be a source of good or ill health for Scorpio. It is important to examine your attitudes about sex, to follow safe sexual practices, and to seek balance in sex—as in all other areas of your life.

Yo-yo dieting, with its extreme ups and downs, can be another Scorpio problem. Some Scorpios will go to great lengths to become thin, even resorting to surgical means such as television personality Roseanne's stomach-stapling operation. The radically thin Scorpio actress Calista Flock-hart has drawn worried criticism for her shrinking size. Rather than obsessing about food and diet, try to diffuse this energy into other areas of your life.

It's no accident that Scorpio's month coincides with football season, which reminds us that sports are a very healthy way to diffuse emotions. If you enjoy winter sports, be sure to prepare ahead of time for the ski slopes or the ice rinks. Be sure to warm up your muscles before you go all out. Water sports are a terrific outlet for Scorpio, so sign up for pool aerobics or competitive swimming. And be sure to treat yourself to a vacation at a spectacular tropical beach resort. Somehow, just being near a salt water environment can restore your equilibrium.

Scorpio Hip Hideaways and Hangouts

Sometimes you just have to get away from it all! Scorpios relax to the sound of the pounding surf. Find a beach that's away from the crowd, one that feels like yours alone, such as the deserted beaches of Martha's Vineyard, Baja California, or the Caribbean in off-season.

You will never go to a place because it's "in," at least not for a vacation. You prefer a place where there is a challenge or a mystical experience such as a difficult mountain to scale, great fishing or skiing, unexplored terrain, the ruins of an ancient civilization. Australia, Brazil, Morocco, Norway, and China are exotic Scorpio destinations that fill the bill. You'll enjoy exploring the classic treasures of Greece, Mexico, and Peru as well as the erotically decorated temples of India.

Scorpios can travel with minimum luggage and are usually expert packers. Invest in some leather carry-on bags so you can skip the baggage claim and avoid lost luggage. Combination locks should keep your possessions secure, though you might want to look into a hidden money belt or a waist packet to store your vital items. Take wearable waterproof containers to the beach to hold credit cards and cash. Scorpios who are truly concerned with security can find clothes hangers with secret compartments to store valuables. Hidden pockets or compartments of any kind are very much a Scorpio thing!

Credit cards are ruled by Scorpio. Before you go, be sure to check which cards are accepted and how much cash you'll need. Investigate travel insurance and any special travel deal provided by your credit card company.

CHAPTER 15

Scorpio Survival Skills on the Job

Scorpios are born survivors in the workplace. You usually know exactly what you want and will put in the necessary groundwork to prepare for a top position. You are capable of getting and keeping great responsibility, though others may underestimate your quiet demeanor, at first mistaking it for shyness.

Scorpio talents often work best within a structured organization rather than in a freelance situation. Large companies give you a wide scope and plenty of potential power. Higher-ups soon notice how you stay cool in a crisis and keep your job well under control. As the zodiac's super sleuth, you shine in detective, research, or troubleshooting spots. Concentration and focus help in life-or-death fields such as medicine and in high-pressure television spots where you'll be the steady anchor. (Pat Sajak, Jane Pauley, Morley Safer, Walter Cronkite, and Dick Cavett are good examples in broadcasting.) Handling other people's money can be trusted to Scorpio accountants, financial planners, investment bankers, and brokers. Your sharp perception works for you in psychology, psychotherapy, or the theater. Both the fashion world (Calvin Klein) and fine arts (Picasso) know your strong statements. Stay away from jobs that have a dead end, that are in risky fly-by-night businesses, or that require on-the-spot improvisation rather than steady discipline.

For examples of Scorpio survivors, you shouldn't go farther than Bill Gates of Microsoft or U.S. Senator Hillary Clinton. These Scorpios have weathered great storms and emerged with mega-success through shrewd career maneuvers and careful planning. Like most Scorpios in power positions, they have been able to transform the lives of others: Gates through his work combating disease in Africa, and Hillary through her job as New York's senator during the World Trade center crisis.

The Scorpio Boss

You hire your staff with a keen perception of everyone's needs and motives. You are totally in command of all that happens in your domain and will rarely hand over the reins, even temporarily. Since you do not trust easily, you may be hesitant to delegate and so take on too much responsibility yourself. Your suspiciousness could even degenerate into paranoia, where you think of others in black-and-white terms, either for you or against you. But you care intensely about your work and are generous with others who are equally dedicated. A winner of power games, you can be lethal with competition. However, you are extremely supportive of anyone who gives you the proper respect and loyalty.

Scorpio on a Team

Since you aim for total control of your job, you will always have a motive behind your moves. You like work where there is a challenge and a chance to wield power, whether it's a weapon, a big machine, or a company checkbook. Sometimes Scorpio will work overtime to make yourself indispensable, simply for the power of being so needed! You are always aware of what is happening in the office, of who's doing what to whom. You are particularly good at assessing the weak points of others (or of the organization), and using this to your advantage. When you're interested in your work, you have unbeatable stamina—tolerating working conditions and hours that would make others rebel! You are very steady and stable on the job, rarely getting sidetracked to another profession or seduced by another organization.

To Get Ahead Fast

Pick a job where there is a weakness you can correct or chaos you can order—and then take over! Play up your best characteristics:

- Cool control
- Stamina
- Perception
- Concentration
- Ability to handle pressure
- Steadiness
- Drive

CHAPTER 16

Scorpio Rich and Famous: And How They Got There!

There's no better way to learn about the pitfalls and prizes of your sign than to study the lives of your rich and famous sign-mates. For sure you'll find the intense Scorpio drive in Ted Turner and Bill Gates. The Scorpio magnetism is in Billy Graham and Hillary Clinton. Strong women of the silver screen like Vivien Leigh and Hedy Lamarr are archetypal Scorpio sirens. Scorpios who dance to their own tune: Whoopi Goldberg, k.d. lang, Bjork, Chloe Sevigny.

Astrology can tell you more about your sun sign heroes and heroines than tabloids or magazine articles. Like what really turns them on (check their Venus). Or what makes them rattled (scope their Saturn). Compare similarities and differences between the celebrities who embody the typical Scorpio sun sign traits and those who seem untypical. Then look up the influence of other planets in the horoscope of your favorites, using the charts in this book. It's a fun way to further your education in astrology.

Scorpio Celebrities

Sarah Bernhardt (10/23/1844)
Michael Crichton (10/23/42)
Kevin Kline (10/24/47)
Pat Sajak (10/26/46)
Hillary Clinton (10/26/47)
Jaclyn Smith (10/26/47)
John Cleese (10/27/39)

Tracy Nelson (10/25/63)
Pablo Picasso (10/25/1881)
Simon LeBon (10/27/58)
Marla Maples (10/27/63)
Evelyn Waugh (10/28/03)
Dennis Franz (10/28/44)
Annie Potts (10/28/52)
Bill Gates (10/28/55)
Julia Roberts (10/28/67)
Richard Dreyfuss (10/29/47)
Kate Jackson (10/29/48)
Winona Ryder (10/29/48)
Louis Malle (10/30/32)
Grace Slick (10/30/39)
Dale Evans (10/31/12)
Diedre Hall (10/31/49)
Jane Pauley (10/31/50)
Harry Hamlin (10/31/51)
Lyle Lovett (11/1/57)
Jenny McCarthy (11/1/72)
Daniel Boone (11/2/1754)
Stefanie Powers (11/2/42)
k.d. lang (11/2/61)
Charles Bronson (11/3/22)
Roseanne (11/3/52)
Kate Capshaw (11/3/53)
Pauline Trigere (11/4/12)
Yanni (11/4/22)
Sean "Puffy" Combs (11/4/69)
Matthew McConaughey (11/4/69)
Roy Rogers (11/5/12)
Ike Turner (11/5/31)
Sam Shepard (11/5/43)
Tatum O'Neal (11/5/63)
Mike Nichols (11/6/31)
Maria Shriver (11/6/55)
Ethan Hawke (11/6/70)
Billy Graham (11/7/18)
Bonnie Raitt (11/8/49)
Carl Sagan (11/9/34)
Richard Burton (11/10/25)

Roy Scheider (11/10/32)
Demi Moore (11/11/62)
Calista Flockhart (11/11/64)
Leonardo DiCaprio (11/11/74)
Grace Kelly (11/12/29)
Richard Mulligan (11/13/32)
Whoopi Goldberg (11/13/55)
Aaron Copland (11/14/1900)
Prince Charles (11/14/48)
Ed Asner (11/15/29)
Bo Derek (11/16/56)
Lauren Hutton (11/17/43)
Danny DeVito (11/17/44)
Linda Evans (11/18/42)
Ted Turner (11/19/38)
Ahmad Rashad (11/19/49)
Jodie Foster (11/19/62)
Sean Young (11/20/59)
Marlo Thomas (11/21/38)
Goldie Hawn (11/21/45)
Mariel Hemingway (11/21/61)
Nicolette Sheridan (11/21/63)
Bjork (11/21/59)

CHAPTER 17

Scorpio Connections: How You Get Along with Every Sign

Your intense Scorpio nature makes your choice of a partner especially important. Whether you're looking for a business partner or a life companion, this compatibility "cheat sheet" will help you understand each other's basic needs. Once you understand how your partner's sun sign is likely to view commitment and what each of you wants from a relationship, you'll be in a much better position to judge whether your cosmic combination has lasting potential.

Scorpio/Aries

WHAT WORKS:
One of the zodiac's challenging pairs, your Mars-ruled chemistry could ignite with frequent battles of the sexes. You both love a dare! Neither of you gives in, but you'll never bore each other (though you might wear each other out). Aries direct, uncomplicated forcefulness especially intrigues Scorpio, and you are caught off guard, for once.

WHAT DOESN'T:
You both could play so hard to get that you never really connect! Aries never quite trusts secretive Scorpio, while Scorpio intrigues and power plays can fizzle under direct Aries fire. You are both jealous and controlling, but this dynamic duo can work if you focus on high ideals and mutual respect.

Scorpio/Taurus

WHAT WORKS:
Many marriages happen when these opposites attract. Taurus has a calming effect on Scorpio innate paranoia. And Taurus responds to Scorpio intensity and fascinating air of mystery. Together, these signs have the perfect complement of sensuality and sexuality.

WHAT DOESN'T:
Problems of control are inevitable when you both want to run the show. Avoid long and bitter battles or silent stand-offs by drawing territorial lines from the start.

Scorpio/Gemini

WHAT WORKS:
You're a fascinating mystery to each other. Gemini is immune from Scorpio paranoia, laughs away dark moods, and matches wits in power games. Scorpio intensity, focus, and sexual magnetism draw scattered Gemini like a moth to a flame.

WHAT DOESN'T:
Scorpio can get "heavy," possessive, and jealous—intense feelings that Gemini doesn't take seriously. To make this one last, Gemini needs to treat Scorpio like the one and only, while Scorpio must use a light touch, and learn not to take Gemini flirtations to heart.

Scorpio/Cancer

WHAT WORKS:
Cancer actually enjoys Scorpio intensity and possessiveness—it shows how much they care! And, like Scorpio

Prince Charles and Cancer Camilla Parker Bowles (also Princess Diana, another Cancer), this pair cares deeply about those they love. Strong emotions are a great bond that can survive heavy storms.

WHAT DOESN'T:
Your Scorpio mysterious and melancholy moods can leave Cancer feeling isolated and insecure. And the more Cancer clings, the more Scorpio withdraws. Outside interests can lighten the mood—or provide a means of escape.

Scorpio/Leo

WHAT WORKS:
Scorpio innate power with Leo confidence and authority can make a fascinating high—profile combination like Leo Arnold Schwarzenegger and Scorpio Maria Shriver or Hillary and Bill Clinton. There is great mutual respect and loyalty here, as well as sexual dynamite. You two magnetic, unconquerable heroes offer each other enough challenges to keep the sparks flying.

WHAT DOESN'T:
Scorpio natural secretiveness and Leo openness could conflict, especially if Scorpio reveals a powerful will and need for control from under a deceptively quiet facade. And Leo is often surprised by the sheer intensity of your Scorpio drive and willpower. Though as a Scorpio you won't fight for the spotlight, you will often exercise control from behind the scenes. When these two intense, stubborn, demanding signs collide, it's a no-win situation.

Scorpio/Virgo

WHAT WORKS:
With Scorpio, Virgo encounters intense feelings too powerful to intellectualize or analyze. This could be a grand pas-

sion, especially when Scorpio is challenged to uncover the Virgo earthy, sensual side. Your penetrating minds are simpatico, and so is your dedication to meaningful work (here is a fellow healer). Virgo provides the stability and structure that keep Scorpio on the right track.

WHAT DOESN'T:
Virgo may cool off if Scorpio goes to extremes or plays manipulative games. Scorpio could find Virgo perfectionism irritating and the Virgo approach to sex too limited.

Scorpio/Libra

WHAT WORKS:
The interplay of Scorpio intensity and Libra objectivity makes an exciting cat-and-mouse game. Libra intellect and flair balance your powerful Scorpio charisma. Scorpio adds warmth and substance to the cool Libra demeanor.

WHAT DOESN'T:
Libra must learn to handle your sensitive Scorpio feelings with velvet gloves. When not taken seriously, Scorpio retaliates with a force that could send the Libra scales swinging way off balance. On the other hand, Scorpio must give Libra room to exercise his or her mental and social skills.

Scorpio/Scorpio

WHAT WORKS:
The list of legendary Scorpio-Scorpio couples reads like a historical who's who—Abigail and John Adams, Marie and Pierre Curie, Dale Evans and Roy Rogers. You'll match each other's intensity and commitment, knowing instinctively where to tread with caution.

WHAT DOESN'T:
Since you both like to be in control, power struggles are always on the menu. Share some of your secrets. Air your grievances immediately rather than letting them fester.

Scorpio/Sagittarius

WHAT WORKS:
Sagittarius sees an erotic adventure in Scorpio—and doesn't mind playing with fire. Scorpio is impressed with Sagittarius high ideals, energy, and competitive spirit. Sagittarius humor diffuses Scorpio intensity, while Scorpio provides the focus for Sagittarius to reach those goals.

WHAT DOESN'T
Scorpio sees through schemes and won't fall for a sales pitch unless it has substance. Sagittarius may object to your Scorpio drive for power rather than for higher goals. Sagittarius will flee from Scorpio possessiveness or heavy-handed controlling tactics.

Scorpio/Capricorn

WHAT WORKS:
Sexy Scorpio takes the Capricorn mind off business. Though you could get wrapped up in each other, you are also turned on by power and position. You'll join forces to scale the heights.

WHAT DOESN'T:
Capricorn has no patience for intrigue or hidden agendas. Scorpio will find this sign supremely focused on his or her own goals. Capricorn won't be easily diverted, even if this means leaving your Scorpio emotional needs—and ego—in the backseat.

Scorpio/Aquarius

WHAT WORKS:
Both of you respect each other's uncompromising position and mental focus. You will probably have an unconventional relationship—spiced up by sexual experimentation and the element of surprise.

WHAT DOESN'T:
Scorpio could feel that Aquarius is a loose cannon who is likely to sink the ship. Or both of these fixed signs could come to a stubborn stand-off. Aquarius tunes out Scorpio possessiveness. Scorpio looks elsewhere for intimacy and intensity.

Scorpio/Pisces

WHAT WORKS:
When these two signs click, nothing gets in their way. The Pisces desire to merge completely with a beloved is just the all-or-nothing message Scorpio has been waiting for. These two will play it to the hilt, often shedding previous spouses or bucking public opinion (like Liz Taylor and Richard Burton once did).

WHAT DOESN'T:
Both signs are possessive, yet neither likes to be possessed. Scorpio could easily mistake Pisces vulnerability for weakness—a big mistake. Both signs fuel each other's escapist tendencies when dark moods hit. Learning to merge without submerging one's identity is an important lesson for this couple.

CHAPTER 18

Astrological Outlook for Scorpio in 2003

During this year, you have much to do with Taurus, Leo, and another Scorpio. It will be necessary to make corrections, to revise material, to check measurements. Your work will be appreciated and, whether in domestic or professional areas, you'll be considered "essential."

During the first month, do some writing. Read, teach, and learn. It will be a very romantic January as well. Your morale is boosted by someone of the opposite sex who declares, "At times I can hardly keep my hands off you!" It would be wise not to believe everything you hear. Be analytical. Don't be satisfied merely to know something happened—find out why it happened.

During January, especially the first half, take special care in handling sharp objects. Mars, your co-ruling planet, will be in your sign of Scorpio until January 16th. Be careful also in the way you talk to employees. The tendency will be to act on impulse and possibly to speak out of turn.

During February the emphasis will be on structure and design as well as where you live and with whom. A domestic adjustment is necessary, which could involve a change of residence or marital status. You will be more aware of music, of your own voice, and of your ability to dance or march to your own tune.

In early June, Saturn will enter Cancer, your ninth house. This planetary position relates to advertising, publishing, travel, and greater recognition of spiritual values. During June, you make a fresh start and could fall "madly in love."

April and June will be your most memorable months.

Throughout the year, you will have luck with these numbers: 4, 6, 1.

In the following pages, you will find your diary in advance. Pay special attention to each day. Ride with the tide. Be observant in connection with subtle nuances. And find out once and for all whether or not your love is reciprocated.

Now let us begin your daily adventure in the year 2003!

CHAPTER 19

Eighteen Months of Day-by-Day Predictions—July 2002 to December 2003

All times are calculated for EST and EDT.

JULY 2002

Monday, July 1 (Moon in Pisces to Aries 3:48 p.m.)
Travel indications are strong this month. Talk about this possibility with someone close to you, including your mate or partner. The Pisces moon stirs creative juices. You no longer will be satisfied with the status quo. Predict the future; make it come true!

Tuesday, July 2 (Moon in Aries) You have a lot of fun. Forces are scattered, so don't ignore your resolutions about exercise, diet, and nutrition. Make up for it! Finally, you get back to work, doing something constructive. Gemini and Sagittarius play dynamic roles. Your lucky number is 3.

Wednesday, July 3 (Moon in Aries) You've had fun; now it's time to get your strength back. The moon in your sixth house places emphasis on employment, general health, and the ability to "break the rules" and still survive. Another Scorpio makes a surprise appearance. Confer quietly; employ discretion!

Thursday, July 4 (Moon in Aries to Taurus 4:14 a.m.) The July Fourth holiday! You are called upon to speak, to give opinions on the future. The Aries moon enables you to speak fluently about labor and capitalism. You'll hear these words: "You have made this holiday meaningful, at least for me!" Show your patriotism!

Friday, July 5 (Moon in Taurus)   Focus on family, home, and protection of your property and loved ones. Get rid of leftover fire hazards. You did very well yesterday; now you have the right to be proud. You'll hear these words: "You showed us there is nothing wrong with being patriotic!" Music plays!

Saturday, July 6 (Moon in Taurus to Gemini 2:59 p.m.) There are reports of Unidentified Flying Objects (UFOs). Be receptive; maintain an attitude of curiosity and a willingness to listen and learn. Avoid self-deception. Exude an aura of intrigue; don't tell all; don't confide or confess. Pisces and Virgo will play fascinating roles.

Sunday, July 7 (Moon in Gemini)   Once again a request is granted for more responsibility. The pay scale also rises. The pressure is on, and you will be up to it. Some people tell you, "You should not be so intense." You know where to tell them to go! A Capricorn, in search of truth, will consult you.

Monday, July 8 (Moon in Gemini to Cancer 10:34 p.m.) On this Monday, you breathe a sigh of relief. There was a mix-up or a mistake, and some fingers pointed to you. However, your innocence was proven. When you think about it, you breathe that sigh of relief. Finish what you start. Aries and Libra will be on your side.

Tuesday, July 9 (Moon in Cancer)   On this Tuesday, with the moon leaving Gemini, you can anticipate good fortune within 24 hours. Focus on original thinking, independence, and serious consideration of travel. Some people are for it; others close to you are not so enthusiastic. Have luck with number 1.

Wednesday, July 10 (Moon in Cancer to Leo 3:06 a.m.) New places, sensations, and experience would be desirable.

The moon in Cancer, your ninth house, tells of a new interest in philosophy, astrology, and theology. You ask yourself, "Where do I fit in, why am I here?" The spotlight is on partnership, cooperative efforts, and your marital status.

Thursday, July 11 (Moon in Leo)   You are drawn once more to mystery and intrigue. Allow your intuitive intellect to provide the answers. Once again there is serious discussion about a possible "name change." Gemini and Sagittarius will play raucous roles. Gemini curiosity is put to the test. Amusing and mystifying!

Friday, July 12 (Moon in Leo)   Get your priorities in order. Solve a jigsaw puzzle. Relatives display temperament and mood swings. Maintain your own emotional equilibrium. Taurus, Leo, and another Scorpio will play "sensational" roles. With Taurus, attention will center on partnership, legal agreements, and marital status.

Saturday, July 13 (Moon in Leo to Virgo 5:39 a.m.)
On this Saturday, get ready for change, travel, and variety. The Leo moon relates to your career, business accumen, and ability to transform the ordinary into the extraordinary. Read, investigate, report, and teach. Sharing knowledge is very important. Know it, and act accordingly. Your lucky number is 5.

Sunday, July 14 (Moon in Virgo)   On this 14th day of July, you come to terms with yourself regarding your career, ambitions, and marriage. You demand the facts, and you get them. Now, what are you going to do about it? Confer with your family. Don't forget it is French Independence Day. Dinner with a loved one is appropriate.

Monday, July 15 (Moon in Virgo to Libra 7:38 a.m.)
As July wanes, your spirit rises. This is because of the Virgo moon in your eleventh house. You provide encouragement for others. You win the friendship of "very important people." Maintain an aura of exclusiveness. Don't give up your valuable privacy to those who don't appreciate it. Meditate!

Tuesday, July 16 (Moon in Libra)   What you start out to do will not turn out that way. It will turn out better! Keep your hopes up. Refuse to be discouraged by "little people." A detour in the road will be found, and you will be pleased by your own progress. Cancer and Capricorn play dynamic roles.

Wednesday, July 17 (Moon in Libra to Scorpio 10:12 a.m.)   On this Wednesday, you could have good fortune by sticking with number 9. Participate in a language class. Remember that "knowledge is power." Someone you trust will prove worthy. Libra and Aries figure in today's lively scenario. You live and learn!

Thursday, July 18 (Moon in Scorpio)   The moon is in your sign; therefore, circumstances are turning in your favor. You exude personal magnetism and sex appeal. Some people ask you to "slow down!" It might not be too bad an idea, but heed your own counsel. Leo and Aquarius shine through with new, fresh ideas.

Friday, July 19 (Moon in Scorpio to Sagittarius 2:01 p.m.)   Your cycle continues high. You'll be at the right place at a special moment. Question your direction, motivation, and meditation. Consider seriously proposals that include partnership and marriage. A decision you make involves distance and separation from familiar ground.

Saturday, July 20 (Moon in Sagittarius)   On this Saturday, the emphasis is on fun, games, and rollicking humor. You'll be telling yourself, "This most certainly has been a lively Saturday night!" People comment on your timing. Some ask, "How did you know to be here?" Gemini and Sagittarius play outstanding roles. Your lucky number is 3.

Sunday, July 21 (Moon in Sagittarius to Capricorn 7:27 p.m.)   On this Sunday, people put their money where their opinions are, and you could benefit considerably as a result. What starts out to be a boring task turns out to be creative and exciting. Time to tear down for the ultimate purpose of rebuilding. Taurus plays a dramatic role.

Monday, July 22 (Moon in Capricorn) Loosen the reins on your intellectual curiosity. Ask questions; be persistent in going after truth. A Capricorn relative invites you for a short trip. Be sure you are not getting involved in a wild-goose chase! The list of grievances is shorter—read them without becoming too involved.

Tuesday, July 23 (Moon in Capricorn) Family confusion revolves around "how to divide money." Stand aloof, without appearing arrogant. Keep your plans flexible. No one knows exactly what to do. A welter of indecision exists. You might finally be asked to "name names." Libra plays a top role.

Wednesday, July 24 (Moon in Capricorn to Aquarius 2:39 a.m.) At the track: post position special—number 1 p.p. in the seventh race. Hot daily doubles: 2 and 2, 4 and 8, 3 and 7. Later, be entertained by a visitor who thinks a great deal of you. Pisces and Virgo will be in this picture. Avoid self-deception.

Thursday, July 25 (Moon in Aquarius) You could be involved in a financial scandal, but you emerge unscathed. You will be cleared entirely, and possibly promoted. Deal gingerly with a Capricorn who may be holding a grudge. A land deal will be coming up sooner than you anticipated. Have luck with number 8.

Friday, July 26 (Moon in Aquarius to Pisces 12:04 p.m.) Look beyond the immediate. Within 24 hours, you will be hearing from someone in a distant land, perhaps overseas. Let others know that you understand what is going on and will proceed accordingly. Aries and Libra will play cards close to the chest.

Saturday, July 27 (Moon in Pisces) Secrets are involved. A Leo takes you into his or her confidence. Plan a strategy that enables you to travel, yet leave someone in charge. An Aquarius also will figure prominently. The Pisces moon is in your fifth house—a love relationship could make you impulsive. Young persons are involved.

Sunday, July 28 (Moon in Pisces to Aries 11:38 p.m.)
The fast track could be dangerous—you learn from experience. The focus continues to be on partnership and marital status. Capricorn and Cancer figure in this dramatic scenario. You'll be saying to yourself, "I would hardly know it is Sunday!" A seafood dinner is on the menu tonight!

Monday, July 29 (Moon in Aries) Separation from a loved one is temporary. Know it, and respond accordingly. If you wait and see, you'll be doing the "right thing." Gemini and Sagittarius will back you to the hilt. Check your wardrobe; prepare a routine aimed at making people laugh.

Tuesday, July 30 (Moon in Aries) A mathematical problem will be solved. Your work methods improve. Another Scorpio could become your "true ally." You are drawn to Aries, but it appears that nothing will come of it. Do not be too sad; you cannot have everything! Taurus announces, "I'm here!"

Wednesday, July 31 (Moon in Aries to Taurus 12:15 p.m.) Lucky lottery: 5, 9, 10, 12, 19, 32. A romantic relationship is fun, but sooner or later, you must face reality. Read and write, learn and teach. The "other party" is possibly an Aries—you learn that love and romance are a two-way street.

AUGUST 2002

Thursday, August 1 (Moon in Taurus) You will be facing the music in connection with participation in a community project and with marriage. The Taurus moon relates to commitment and the ability to withstand legal pressure. Before the day is finished, you'll find ways to avoid the obvious. Some claim you are lucky—you respond, "The harder I work, the luckier I get!"

Friday, August 2 (Moon in Taurus to Gemini 11:44 p.m.)
Pressures in various areas continue. You will be up to it, if you handle details and do some basic research. Be willing to revise, rewrite, and rebuild—regard this as your "makeover" day. Taurus, Leo, and another Scorpio figure in this fascinating scenario.

Saturday, August 3 (Moon in Gemini) The reins are loosened. You will read and write, and will express your "true feelings." Some people say, "You are not your old self!" You respond: "No, I am not my old self; I am new, vibrant, independent, and sensual!" A romantic interlude lends spice, and could be just what you need!

Sunday, August 4 (Moon in Gemini) On this Sunday, you reunite with people who mean the most in your life. Focus on domestic harmony and decisions involving where you live and with whom. Your marital status continues to be a "bone of contention." Beautify your surroundings, decorate and remodel, and choose quality. Libra is in the picture.

Monday, August 5 (Moon in Gemini to Cancer 8:00 a.m.)
Look beyond the immediate; avoid self-deception. Help a Pisces who seems to have "lost the way." Maintain your aura of mystery and intrigue. Don't tell all; don't confess or confide—let others play guessing games. Pisces and Virgo will play fascinating roles.

Tuesday, August 6 (Moon in Cancer) A long-distance communication relates to a possible journey. Stand firm on beliefs, without being unduly stubborn. You receive good news; it boosts your morale. Don't quit now. Don't change horses in midstream. Capricorn and Cancer will not let you forget an obligation.

Wednesday, August 7 (Moon in Cancer to Leo 12:25 p.m.) On this 7th day of August, your creative juices stir. Get ready for change, travel, and a variety of sensations and experiences. Those who say you are "not fit" are themselves less than perfect. Aries and Libra will be in a fighting mood. Have luck with number 9.

Thursday, August 8 (Moon in Leo)   Stress individuality, take the lead, and don't follow others. Avoid heavy lifting, if possible. Listen to your heart; it will lead you in the right direction. The new moon in Leo equates to leadership, extra responsibility, and a promotion. Aquarius is in the picture.

Friday, August 9 (Moon in Leo to Virgo 2:02 p.m.)   A relative talks about "where I would like to go." Be understanding; curb a tendency to make a sharp remark. Cancer, Leo, and Aquarius play interesting roles. The focus will be on direction, motivation, and the necessity for meditation. Luck with number 2.

Saturday, August 10 (Moon in Virgo)   Join in the fun and games. The Virgo moon relates to your eleventh house. Your popularity is on the rise. Some people comment, "You are different today; we like you much better this way!" In truth, you *are* different. You win friends and influence people. Lucky lottery: 3, 12, 13, 16, 30, 46.

Sunday, August 11 (Moon in Virgo to Libra 2:37 p.m.) On this Sunday, you emerge confident, dynamic, creative, and sexy. Don't waste time debating with those who know better, but want to put you down a level. Stand tall; refuse to be concerned with envious people. Taurus, Leo, and another Scorpio figure in this dramatic scenario.

Monday, August 12 (Moon in Libra)   You could receive a unique honor as a result of the written word. Those who are envious and want you to fail will be disappointed. You are lively, alert, and willing to fight if the cause is right. Gemini, Virgo, and Sagittarius play outstanding roles. Have luck with number 5.

Tuesday, August 13 (Moon in Libra to Scorpio 4:00 p.m.)   You will be very conscious of the appearance of your home—your concept of color coordination will be tested. A domestic adjustment is featured. You will be amazed at the results obtained through little effort. Taurus, Libra, and another Scorpio figure in the dynamic scenario.

Wednesday, August 14 (Moon in Scorpio)　　Your cycle is high, but don't press your luck! You will be at the right place at a special moment almost effortlessly. Pisces and Virgo will play "sensational" roles. All is not what appears on the surface—obviously, all that glitters is not gold!

Thursday, August 15 (Moon in Scorpio to Sagittarius 7:25 p.m.)　　Past efforts pay dividends. You exude personal magnetism, which can be translated into sex appeal. Be able to communicate feelings. Don't break too many hearts. At the very least, offer tea and sympathy. Wear bright colors; let others know, "Here I am; you get what you see!"

Friday, August 16 (Moon in Sagittarius)　　The emphasis is on travel, and the ability to project yourself into a situation that draws international attention. Do not shy away from a challenge. Money is involved. You will retrieve losses and thus gain prestige. Aries and Libra will play significant roles.

Saturday, August 17 (Moon in Sagittarius)　　Make a fresh start in a new direction. You will be offered the "same old thing." Be diplomatic, but reject it. Instead, present your own format and concept. The more "original" you are today, the better. Important: Avoid heavy lifting if possible. Have luck with number 1.

Sunday, August 18 (Moon in Sagittarius to Capricorn 1:15 a.m.)　　Be close to loved ones; highlight spiritual values. What you felt was lost will reappear in a dramatic way. You'll be saying, "This is one Sunday I won't soon forget!" The spotlight is on cooperative efforts and the ability to make a marriage work.

Monday, August 19 (Moon in Capricorn)　　No Blue Monday! Relatives communicate. You gain information which can be valuable. Don't ask for too much at once. Digest what you have; find out what to do about it. Gemini and Sagittarius will play dynamic, youthful roles. Your lucky number is 3.

Tuesday, August 20 (Moon in Capricorn to Aquarius 9:16 a.m.)   Don't expect too much at once! Take time to be thorough. Rewrite, rebuild, and review lessons. Strive to "look unique." Some people comment on your "difference." Realize within that the "different look" is positive and works on your behalf. Taurus is in the picture.

Wednesday, August 21 (Moon in Aquarius)   At the track: post position special—number 2 p.p. in the fifth race. Hot daily doubles: 3 and 5, 5 and 5, 2 and 6. Later, do some rewriting on a special program or thesis. You have things going for you, if you don't let them get away. Gemini plays a role.

Thursday, August 22 (Moon in Aquarius to Pisces 7:10 p.m.)   The full moon in Aquarius is in your fourth house, so emphasize land, real estate, and durability. Insist on quality. Reject the flimsy. Pay for what you want, and want what you can afford. Taurus, Libra, and another Scorpio will play fantastic roles.

Friday, August 23 (Moon in Pisces)   Maintain an aura of mystery and intrigue. Your creative juices stir, so trust yourself, let yourself try something "far-out." Pisces and Virgo will play memorable roles and have these letters or initials in their names: G, P, Y.

Saturday, August 24 (Moon in Pisces)   The moon remains in your fifth house in Pisces—that spells impulsiveness, creativity, children, challenge, and a variety of sensations. Many come forward to say, "I don't care what others think. I am for you all the way!" Your response: "I won't let you down. I'll do my best and I will win if possible!"

Sunday, August 25 (Moon in Pisces to Aries 6:47 a.m.)
On this Sunday, you sense that events are changing in your
life. Work methods are transformed, you have your way,
and you have help. A health report is encouraging. Look
beyond the immediate. Finish a project started two months
ago. Aries plays a significant role.

Monday, August 26 (Moon in Aries)   On this Monday,
you start anew. People say, "How can you get everything
right, since it is so new to you!" You answer: "I don't
know, I just do!" Leo and Aquarius will play colorful roles.
The Aries moon relates to your sixth house of health, work,
and achievement.

Tuesday, August 27 (Moon in Aries to Taurus 7:30 p.m.)
Your marital status figures prominently on this Tuesday.
You might ask yourself, "What am I working for? What
do I hope to gain by it?" You'll get cooperation from one
who previously opposed you. Continue along the same
path. You are doing good and the right thing!

Wednesday, August 28 (Moon in Taurus)   Lucky lottery: 6, 14, 16, 28, 40, 46. The element of luck rides with
you. You come to public attention. The spotlight is on proposals—business, career, and marriage. A surprising Taurus
asserts, "I go for you in a big way!" Don't give up something of value for nothing.

Thursday, August 29 (Moon in Taurus)   Check the details. Solve a mathematic problem. Be sure of "measurements." Questions loom large about cooperative efforts,
legal rights, and your marital status. Taurus and another
Scorpio figure prominently. What you want is not as far
away as you might expect. You're getting close, so don't
quit now!

Friday, August 30 (Moon in Taurus to Gemini 7:44 a.m.)
Someone close confides in you about his or her marital
discord. Offer the best advice you can, without becoming
directly involved. Don't take things for granted; some peo-

ple really do not know where they are going and are not eager to find out. Virgo is in this picture.

Saturday, August 31 (Moon in Gemini)   Don't let pandemonium break loose. A family member relies upon your judgment—don't disappoint him. Some people want to give up, to throw caution to the wind. Don't permit that to happen—maintain a steady pace, and do what the doctor ordered in connection with your health.

SEPTEMBER 2002

Sunday, September 1 (Moon in Gemini to Cancer 5:13 p.m.)   On this first day of September, strive to keep your emotional equilibrium. Forces are scattered, and it seems each person has his own idea of what you should be doing. What must be done is to attend to details, to "fix" computer errors.

Monday, September 2 (Moon in Cancer)   During this month you have a legitimate opportunity to win friends and influence people. Today, you should read and write, teach and learn. Let people know who you are and give them a chance to test your ideas. Gemini, Virgo, and Sagittarius will figure prominently.

Tuesday, September 3 (Moon in Cancer to Leo 10:34 p.m.)   The day will be memorable. The moon in your ninth house equates to spirituality, philosophy, theology, and travel. Publish and advertise. You are far ahead of competitors; know it, and act accordingly. Fix things at home. Make an intelligent concession during a domestic dispute.

Wednesday, September 4 (Moon in Leo)   Within 24 hours, questions will loom large about legal affairs, a partnership, and marriage. You are on the precipice of creative action that could lead to fame and fortune. Don't stunt your own growth! Give yourself room to think and act, to travel, and to give yet another chance to romance.

Thursday, September 5 (Moon in Leo) Many of your views will be verified. The Leo moon in your tenth house equates to promotion, production, prestige, and possible fame. People continue to ask, "How do you do it?" Your best answer: "The harder I work, the luckier I get!" Capricorn plays the top role.

Friday, September 6 (Moon in Leo to Virgo 12:14 a.m.) Stress universal appeal. Peer into the future and come up with predictions you can make come true. It should be obvious to you by now that you are unusual and that you don't belong with the crowd. Remain high; don't let jealous people make you lose confidence.

Saturday, September 7 (Moon in Virgo to Libra 11:56 p.m.) A bright surprise is due for you this Saturday. Many of your hopes and desires can be fulfilled—be sure you believe it, and do something about it. The moon in your eleventh house means that your popularity is on the rise. You can win friends and influence people. Lucky lottery: 1, 11, 14, 18, 22, 33.

Sunday, September 8 (Moon in Libra) Be close to a family member who of late has been "feeling low." Focus on steps forward, and fixing things at home. Be especially attentive to plumbing. What seemed out of reach could actually be at your doorstep. Cancer and Capricorn play major roles.

Monday, September 9 (Moon in Libra to Scorpio 11:48 p.m.) On this Monday, your spirits rise—what was lost will be recovered. Don't make a federal case of it; this means don't ask too many questions. Behind-the-scenes activities are taking place fast and furious. Do what must be done; let others know you expect the same from them.

Tuesday, September 10 (Moon in Scorpio) A long-distance call will verify your views. The Libra moon is in your twelfth house—that emphasizes the need to visit someone temporarily confined to home or hospital. Your cycle moves up, so you will be at the right place at a special moment. Another Scorpio plays a dramatic role.

Wednesday, September 11 (Moon in Scorpio)   At the track: post position special—number 5 p.p. in the third race. Hot daily doubles: 3 and 5, 3 and 6, 1 and 7. Later, be sensitive to sound; pay attention to a family member who "wants to sing." Gemini, Virgo, and Sagittarius will play featured roles.

Thursday, September 12 (Moon in Scorpio to Sagittarius 1:44 a.m.)   On this Thursday, with the moon in your sign, wear bright colors and make many contacts. Don't hold back. Take the initiative. Let people know you are here to stay and to finish what you start. Taurus, Libra, and another Scorpio will play exciting roles.

Friday, September 13 (Moon in Sagittarius)   This day can be lucky for you, even though it is Friday the 13th. An element of deception is present, so protect yourself in emotional clinches. Be especially wary of a Pisces who promises everything verbally, but puts nothing in writing. Be alert and on the ready!

Saturday, September 14 (Moon in Sagittarius to Capricorn 6:47 a.m.)   This could be your power play day, especially where your earning potential is concerned. What was lost will be recovered. Open lines of communication— somebody wants to "tell you something." Don't look a gift horse in the mouth! Capricorn and Cancer play outstanding roles.

Sunday, September 15 (Moon in Capricorn)   On this Sunday, maintain a universal outlook. Read and write; express your opinions about the nation and the world. Let go of an obligation you should not have assumed in the first place. Focus on travel and romance. Aries and Libra will figure prominently.

Monday, September 16 (Moon in Capricorn to Aquarius 2:54 p.m.)   Don't waste time trying to convince others.

Accent original thinking, stress independence of action. Do not follow others, let them follow you. Avoid heavy lifting, if possible. Leo and Aquarius grab the spotlight, and will make the most of it.

Tuesday, September 17 (Moon in Aquarius)   Focus on motivation, desires, and meditation. Most of your problems can be solved if you heed your "inner voice." The spotlight is on proposals, business and career, as well as marriage. Cancer and Capricorn could dominate this scenario. Enjoy a seafood dinner tonight!

Wednesday, September 18 (Moon in Aquarius)   Lucky lottery: 3, 18, 26, 29, 30, 42. Organize a social gathering which could result in a "clash of ideas." You are and have been the central figure—don't forget it! Gemini and Sagittarius will play active roles. Make inquiries; give full rein to your intellectual curiosity.

Thursday, September 19 (Moon in Aquarius to Pisces 1:17 a.m.)   Be aware of the fine print and details; realize there is a mathematical puzzle and you are capable of solving it. Within 24 hours, your creative juices stir—you will make your mark and be the subject of admiration as a result. You're on solid ground!

Friday, September 20 (Moon in Pisces)   Give full rein to your intellectual curiosity—investigate, ask questions, read, write, and teach. Suddenly, so it seems, new opportunities beckon. Answer the call. You're going to enjoy travel, romance, style, and achievement. A flirtation could get serious!

Saturday, September 21 (Moon in Pisces to Aries 1:10 p.m.)   On this Saturday, with the full moon in Pisces, which is your fifth house, expect plenty of activity, challenges, and the tapping of creative resources. You might be asking yourself, "Am I a new person?" This spotlight is on your home, family, and beautifying your surroundings. Have luck with number 6.

Sunday, September 22 (Moon in Aries)   During this Sunday, play your cards close to the chest. Don't give away any secrets. Get promises in writing. Avoid self-deception. Someone has an elaborate scheme, and asks you to participate. Play the waiting game. The "scheme" actually flirts with the law.

Monday, September 23 (Moon in Aries)   A remarkable comeback! You'll have more responsibility. The pressure will be on, but you will be up to it. The spotlight is on production and distribution. On a personal level, a relationship is "hot and heavy." Don't ask for more than you can handle, you will receive what you request.

Tuesday, September 24 (Moon in Aries to Taurus 1:53 a.m.)   Questions arise concerning distance, travel, and communication. Within 24 hours, there will be proposals which require legal clarification. Money is involved, so hold tight to your possessions. Refuse to give up something of value for nothing. The Aries moon "warns" there is work ahead.

Wednesday, September 25 (Moon in Taurus)   You are a romantic figure! The moon in Taurus is in your seventh house, and your numerical cycle number is 1. All of this adds up to creativity, style, personal magnetism, and sex appeal. Questions loom large about cooperative efforts, partnership, and marriage. Your lucky number is 1.

Thursday, September 26 (Moon in Taurus to Gemini 2:25 p.m.)   Face the music early. Don't feel that everything necessary to do will merely fade away. Overcome a temptation to brood by transforming any such tendency into a positive meditation. A family member tells of love for you. This should elevate your morale and brighten your day.

Friday, September 27 (Moon in Gemini)   You possess a "mysterious" quality. Let others try to figure it out. Don't confide, confess, or tell all. Attend a social gathering where you can make valuable contacts. Gemini and Sagittarius will play instrumental roles. Give full play to your intellectual curiosity.

Saturday, September 28 (Moon in Gemini)   On this Saturday, overcome a temptation to take the "cold plunge." Test temperatures and other measurments. Taurus, Leo, and another Scorpio will play dominant roles. Deal gingerly with them. Make this your "makeover" day. Tear down in order to rebuild—read and write; learn through the process of teaching others.

Sunday, September 29 (Moon in Gemini to Cancer 12:59 a.m.)   On this Sunday, there will once again be talk of possible "name changes." Out of a welter of confusion will arise a definite program. Don't stop in midstream; continue your progress. Be aware of accounting procedures; don't cheat yourself!

Monday, September 30 (Moon in Cancer)   On this last day of September, make a decision concerning staying at home or traveling. If you travel, combine business with pleasure. If remaining at home, make a domestic adjustment which will satisfy dissenters. Taurus, Libra, and another Scorpio will figure prominently.

OCTOBER 2002

Tuesday, October 1 (Moon in Cancer to Leo 7:56 a.m.)
During October, much that was behind the scenes and out of sight will become visible. You'll also discover subtle character flaws in those who mean much to you. The moon in Cancer today represents your house of travel. Discover how the "other half" lives.

Wednesday, October 2 (Moon in Leo)   The moon in Leo represents your tenth house. This means you are accepting more responsibility and having the appearance of leadership. Attention also revolves around your home, family, and the giving and receiving of gifts. Lucky lottery: 6, 12, 13, 15, 40, 51.

Thursday, October 3 (Moon in Leo to Virgo 10:50 a.m.)
Your numerical cycle today equates to Neptune—be careful that you are not the victim of self-deception. What appears to be love could be lust, and that isn't so bad either. Remember all that glitters is not gold. Pisces and Virgo will play major roles.

Friday, October 4 (Moon in Virgo)   The moon in Virgo represents your eleventh house—that section of your horoscope relates to hopes, wishes, and fulfillment. The numerical cycle number 8 equals a power play! This is the time to "bellow out loud" what you want and demand. Capricorn and Cancer figure in this exciting scenario.

Saturday, October 5 (Moon in Virgo to Libra 10:50 a.m.)
Look beyond the immediate. Peer into the future—you have done it in the past, and can do it again. "What goes around comes around." You've been here before and are becoming aware of it. Aries and Libra play instrumental roles. Your lucky number is 9.

Sunday, October 6 (Moon in Libra)   Make a fresh start in a new direction. Don't worry about what people think or like—attempting to please everyone is a sure road to madness. "Physician, heal thyself." Please yourself first. Leo and Aquarius are capable of putting on a show. They prove it!

Monday, October 7 (Moon in Libra to Scorpio 9:57 a.m.)
Slow down on this Monday—questions arise about your ultimate destination, materials required, and marital status. Focus on balance, emotional equilibrium, and the sound of music. Permit yourself to smell the flowers, to relax and enjoy life. A Cancer is involved.

Tuesday, October 8 (Moon in Scorpio)   Your cycle is high, so you could shine at a social affair. There's a strange transformation—instead of being in awe or frightened of you, people express a desire to be with you. Some persons vie for the privilege of wining and dining you. Accept this change gratefully and graciously.

Wednesday, October 9 (Moon in Scorpio to Sagittarius 10:21 a.m.)   Your cycle remains high, so attend to questions and problems which previously eluded you. Revise, review, and tear down in order to rebuild. Don't be discouraged by someone who seems bewildered. Taurus, Leo, and another Scorpio are in the picture, and attempt to take over.

Thursday, October 10 (Moon in Sagittarius)   Refuse to give up something of value for nothing—request that promises be put in writing. Don't be bothered by those who try to make you feel guilty; they are merely envious. Gemini, Virgo, and Sagittarius insist on posing questions to which even they do not know the answers.

Friday, October 11 (Moon in Sagittarius to Capricorn 1:45 p.m.)   Money is involved. A lost article is recovered. Strive to understand who you are, what you want, and why you are here. Some people say, "That is metaphysics." Don't be afraid of that word—follow your instincts and your heart. Doors will open— opportunity knocks!

Saturday, October 12 (Moon in Capricorn)   On this Saturday, with number 7 "in power" and the moon in Capricorn, you undergo many moods. Some people will attempt to persuade you that it is all in your mind. People you respect give opposite opinions—it is best to let them form their own conclusions. Pisces is featured.

Sunday, October 13 (Moon in Capricorn to Aquarius 8:51 p.m.)   You could be saved from disaster in the nick of time. Be gallant and brave, but don't tempt fate. Almost as if by magic, you will be at the right place at a special moment. A power play! People in roles of authority are on your side. You have won them over almost effortlessly.

Monday, October 14 (Moon in Aquarius)   Within 24 hours, you will know where you stand in connection with a "land deal." Let go of an obligation you should not have assumed in the first place. Free yourself to travel, investigate, write, and publish. A reunion with a loved one tonight will provide "creative drama sparks."

Tuesday, October 15 (Moon in Aquarius)   People accommodate you. Someone who has "held office" for some time will look your way and favor your efforts. Your "light" shines bright, and results in enlightenment in areas previously dark. Don't follow others; let them follow you, if they so desire. Your lucky number is 1.

Wednesday, October 16 (Moon in Aquarius to Pisces 8:51 p.m.)   At the track: post position special—number 6 p.p. in the second race. Hot daily doubles: 4 and 2, 3 and 3, 5 and 2. Later, make a domestic adjustment that could lead to contentment and happiness. Money lost or won will play a significant role. A Cancer is in the picture.

Thursday, October 17 (Moon in Pisces)   You will have reason to celebrate. A social gathering proves important where contacts are concerned. Remember recent resolutions about exercise, diet, and nutrition. Your personality provides winning ways. Some clothes are too tight, so do something about it by keeping those diet resolutions!

Friday, October 18 (Moon in Pisces to Aries 7:12 p.m.) The Pisces moon in your fifth house relates to creativity, sensuality, and sex appeal. Be careful. Know when to say, "Enough is enough!" Taurus, Leo, and another Scorpio figure prominently in your scenario, and could have these letters in their names: D, M, V.

Saturday, October 19 (Moon in Aries)   A lively Saturday! Today's scenario highlights change, travel, and a variety of sensations. Express your feelings and impressions in writing. You actually learn by teaching—share knowledge; consult someone who has earned your respect. A Gemini figures prominently.

Sunday, October 20 (Moon in Aries)   An Aries helps you "fix things." You are on more solid ground, so express confidence. Don't go to a meeting with hat in hand. You will be praised and consulted. You could get a raise in pay and more pressure and responsibility. Stop hiding your light under a bushel.

Monday, October 21 (Moon in Aries to Taurus 7:55 a.m.) Pisces and Aries continue to play major roles in your scenario. They get away with a lot by saying they are the only ones who truly understand you. Make it crystal clear you have had enough of that—you want your orders followed. Have luck with number 7.

Tuesday, October 22 (Moon in Taurus) Your attention will be riveted on financial transactions. Also, you locate a lost article, and deal gingerly with a Capricorn member of the opposite sex. Relatives are involved. Rumors go spinning forth. A Cancer who has played a behind-the-scenes role will step forward, demanding added recognition.

Wednesday, October 23 (Moon in Taurus to Gemini 8:16 p.m.) Lucky lottery: 2, 9, 12, 19, 22, 47. Stress universal appeal; participate in political or charitable campaigns. Finish what you start; make your dreams come true. Aries and Libra will play memorable roles. Open lines of communication with someone living in a distant land.

Thursday, October 24 (Moon in Gemini) Within 24 hours, the moon will be in Gemini, your eighth house. Emphasize your aura of mystery and intrigue. Find out more about money and how it gets that way. The spotlight is on accounting procedures and methods. Leo will play a paramount role. Have luck with number 1.

Friday, October 25 (Moon in Gemini) You're on familiar ground, but among strangers. Strive to make yourself known; spend money where necessary. There's a gourmet dinner tonight; invite Cancer to share the succulent fare. Pay attention to proposals that include partnership, career, and marriage.

Saturday, October 26 (Moon in Gemini to Cancer 7:09 a.m.) Luck rides with you; your timing is honed to razor-sharpness. If at the track, choose number 3 post position in the fifth race. Later, find out where you stand in a relationship that has become "complicated." Gemini and Sagittarius will play dynamic, dramatic roles.

Sunday, October 27—Daylight Saving Time Ends (Moon in Cancer)   On this Sunday, attend to details, and line up priorities in such a way that you immediately recognize them. Another Scorpio attempts to interfere, but should be told, "No go!" The favorable lunar position equates to travel plans that include a foreign land.

Monday, October 28 (Moon in Cancer to Leo 2:18 p.m.)   You will be at the right place at the right time almost effortlessly. Let a Cancer know you appreciate his efforts, even if you don't always show it. A painful confrontation can be avoided if you toss your pride aside and make a friendly gesture. A Virgo figures prominently.

Tuesday, October 29 (Moon in Leo)   There will be a serious discussion about "names." Use your intuitive intellect. Reach beyond the orthodox. Strive for mystery and originality. A domestic adjustment is necessary and will result in beautifying your home. Taurus and Libra figure in this quixotic scenario.

Wednesday, October 30 (Moon in Leo to Virgo 6:58 p.m.)   Today's scenario features mystery, intrigue, and deception. Someone "at the top" displays envy and wants to "take you down a peg." Maintain your aplomb; be gracious, and let it be known you fear nothing and will not back down from your principles. Pisces and Virgo are featured.

Thursday, October 31 (Moon in Virgo)   This is Halloween for most persons, but for those interested in magic, it will be National Magic Day in memory of Harry Houdini. Within 24 hours, the moon will be in your eleventh house— that means you'll win friends and influence people. Your popularity is on the rise. Capricorn is involved.

Friday, November 1 (Moon in Virgo to Libra 8:27 p.m.)
On this Friday, the first day of November, you survey past
and present and feel, "I haven't done so poorly after all!"
Your morale gets a boost. You receive a "letter of com-
mendation." Leo and Aquarius "work their way" into featured roles.

Saturday, November 2 (Moon in Libra)   On this Saturday, some people insist on "playing games." Participate if
you like, but don't be cajoled into revealing secrets. Go
slow; play the waiting game. A favorable moon aspect favors long-distance communication. Pisces figures prominently.

Sunday, November 3 (Moon in Libra to Scorpio 8:09 p.m.)
Contact made 24 hours ago will cause "ripples." You are
doing just fine—know it, and don't be discouraged by "naysayers." The emphasis is on promotion, production, and in
your personal life, sure knowledge that your love is not
unrequited. Capricorn plays a top role.

Monday, November 4 (Moon in Scorpio)   The new
moon in your sign coincides with your ability to "beat the
odds." In matters of speculation, stick with number 9. At
the track: pick six—3, 6, 8, 4, 1, 2. Hot daily doubles: 4 and
4, 2 and 1, 2 and 8. Later, finish what was started and then
abandoned. You'll have better luck with that project today.

**Tuesday, November 5 (Moon in Scorpio to Sagittarius 8:01
p.m.)**   Take the initiative, and make contacts. Imprint
style; do not follow others. Display your pioneering spirit.
Go where they say angels fear to tread. You are on the
brink of beginning a new adventure. You exude personal
magnetism and sex appeal. Leo could fall heavily!

Wednesday, November 6 (Moon in Sagittarius)   Lucky
lottery: 2, 5, 12, 18, 22, 33. Attention revolves around your
financial and marital status. The two go together today.
You'll find that out and will be able to do something con-

structive about it. Cancer and Capricorn will play memorable roles.

Thursday, November 7 (Moon in Sagittarius to Capricorn 10:00 p.m.)   There are fun and games today if you so permit. The Sagittarius moon relates to your ability to locate lost articles and to increase your income potential. You have given a lot, much of yourself; now it is your time to receive and don't feel guilty about it. Gemini is in the picture.

Friday, November 8 (Moon in Capricorn)   Dig deep for information. A relative who once took you on a joy ride again seeks your company. Let it be known you have things to do, places to go. Be polite, but make certain it is understood you have no time now for frivolity. Taurus is represented.

Saturday, November 9 (Moon in Capricorn)   On this Saturday, realize you have a lot to learn and require needed material. Once this is done, your cycle continues to rise, and you with it. Someone of the opposite sex declares, "You fascinate me, I can hardly keep my hands off you!" What a boost to your morale!

Sunday, November 10 (Moon in Capricorn to Aquarius 3:27 a.m.)   Someone who once declared, "I never want to see you again!" will be knocking at your door. Don't throw salt in their wounds. Be generous; show the spirit of forgiveness. By so doing, your character strengthens in the eyes of those who really care for you. Libra is involved.

Monday, November 11 (Moon in Aquarius)   Maintain your aura of mystery—don't tell all. Don't confide or confess. An Aquarius can be your valuable adviser. You did what you were supposed to do—now stop worrying! Pisces and Virgo figure in today's dynamic, dramatic scenario.

Tuesday, November 12 (Moon in Aquarius to Pisces 12:41 p.m.)   Within 24 hours, the moon will be in Pisces, your fifth house—this stirs up creative juices. Walk and talk with confidence. Don't go hat in hand. Focus on results, production, distribution, and promotion. Capricorn and Cancer will play amazing roles.

Wednesday, November 13 (Moon in Pisces)   Today's emphasis is on universal appeal. A solid suggestion is made in connection with travel to a foreign land. You are told, "You need representation!" There may be more truth than poetry in that assertion. You do require someone to speak up for you, to promote you. Aries is involved.

Thursday, November 14 (Moon in Pisces)   What was started 24 hours ago can be completed if you follow through. You have so much to offer that you sometimes overlook essentials in favor of superficial contributions. Someone who speaks a foreign language talks to you in a frank, sincere way. It's best to listen!

Friday, November 15 (Moon in Pisces to Aries 12:37 a.m.) Make a concession to a family member. Also make promises you intend to keep. An Aries behind the scenes works on your behalf, even if not so effectively. The emphasis is on cooperative efforts, partnership, and your marital status. Cancer and Capricorn play key roles.

Saturday, November 16 (Moon in Aries)   On this Saturday, make people laugh. It is a gift you have and you should use it. In truth, Scorpio, you are a charming individual, but often hide that charm under a brusque manner. Gemini and Sagittarius will figure prominently. Have luck with number 3.

Sunday, November 17 (Moon in Aries to Taurus 1:22 p.m.)   Try to relax; you have earned a rest period. Within 24 hours, when the moon enters your seventh house, questions will loom large concerning legal affairs, partnership, and marriage. But for now, see the humor in it all and relax. Taurus will play a sensational role.

Monday, November 18 (Moon in Taurus)   A lively Monday! You'll receive proposals, including career, business, marriage. People want to be with you. Some actually vie to wine and dine you. You have something, Scorpio, so why not bottle and sell it! Gemini, Virgo, and Sagittarius figure in this scenario.

Tuesday, November 19 (Moon in Taurus)   A family discussion concerns money and how to obtain more of it. An art object livens up your home appearance. You will be sensitive to sound, to music—you can dance to your own tune. Libra and another Scorpio could make this a most memorable day.

Wednesday, November 20 (Moon in Taurus to Gemini 1:23 a.m.)   The full moon and lunar eclipse in Taurus fall in your seventh house. You realize, once and for all, that you cannot hide the essentials, so come out in the open and face the music early. Avoid seeing people and places only as you wish they could be. By viewing them in a realistic light, you prevent loss and embarrassment.

Thursday, November 21 (Moon in Gemini)   A powerful day, if you so permit. Discover a possible computer error. Check the interest rates. Get the most for your money and demand top quality in what you purchase. Focus on promotion, production, and distribution. You are going places. Others realize it, and could be envious.

Friday, November 22 (Moon in Gemini to Cancer 11:46 a.m.)   On this Friday, you look back with pleasure—you actually have accomplished more than you realized. Focus on universality, the sure knowledge that what goes around comes around. Be optimistic. You are going to get backing or funding for a favorite project. On a personal level, you are loved!

Saturday, November 23 (Moon in Cancer)   Let others know you are here and that you intend to imprint your style. Stress independence and creativity; do not follow others. Leo and Aquarius will play significant roles. Those who follow you will prove loyal—know it and respond accordingly. Your lucky number is 1.

Sunday, November 24 (Moon in Cancer to Leo 8:01 p.m.)
You might be thinking your "old nemesis" returns. In actuality, you have nothing to fear, so move ahead with confidence. Directions will be made crystal clear. Questions loom large about whether or not to cooperate with someone whose methods often "flirt with the law."

Monday, November 25 (Moon in Leo)   Diversify; stress versatility and intellectual curiosity. On this Monday, a professional superior will politely request your presence. Don't go hat in hand—exude confidence. You have earned respect. Gemini and Sagittarius will play outstanding roles.

Tuesday, November 26 (Moon in Leo)   Attend to details, face the music early, and direct pertinent questions to your superior. Wait a reasonable time for the answers and then repeat the queries. Don't back down, maintain your principles, and insist on clarifications. By so doing, you avoid added complications—deal gingerly with another Scorpio.

Wednesday, November 27 (Moon in Leo to Virgo 1:40 a.m.)   Be analytical. Base decisions on factual data. On a personal level, what begins as a mild flirtation could be transformed into "something else." Don't fight your stars! Gemini, Virgo, and Sagittarius continue to play major roles. Have luck with number 5.

Thursday, November 28 (Moon in Virgo)   On this Thanksgiving, you will enjoy the company of those who do love you. Entertain at home; let others know your true feelings. Give a little talk about the meaning of this holiday. You have money coming to you, which will be a most pleasant surprise. Libra is involved.

Friday, November 29 (Moon in Virgo to Libra 4:53 a.m.)
Something mysterious is going on in your life—you are aware of it, at least on the subconscious level. Your knowledge of Freud surpasses that of most students. As a Scorpio, you dig deep for information and appreciate the works of both Jung and Freud.

Saturday, November 30 (Moon in Libra)   On this last day of November, flex your muscles. You have accomplished a great deal, and you will receive more recognition as a result. Capricorn and Cancer figure prominently and could become valuable allies. In matters of speculation, stick with number 8.

DECEMBER 2002

Sunday, December 1 (Moon in Libra to Scorpio 6:14 a.m.) Your cycle is such that caution is required in business and personal dealings. The emphasis is on legal affairs, your reputation, partnership, and marital status. Pisces and Virgo figure prominently, and could have these letters or initials in their names: G, P, Y.

Monday, December 2 (Moon in Scorpio)   Your cycle is high, so take the initiative. A promotion is due. More money comes like a bolt out of the blue. The moon in your sign emphasizes your personality, charm, and an ability to get your way, right or wrong. Be sure you are right, then go full steam ahead! Lucky number is 8.

Tuesday, December 3 (Moon in Scorpio to Sagittarius 6:57 a.m.)   On this Tuesday, you will be amazed that the axiom "What goes around comes around" is in motion. You feel as if, "I have been here before!" Aries and Libra figure prominently, and could have these letters or initials in their names: I and R. Go back to square one.

Wednesday, December 4 (Moon in Sagittarius)   The new moon and solar eclipse in Sagittarius fall in your second house. Take the initiative without creating a sensation. Avoid notoriety. Turn on your Scorpio charm and sex appeal. Leo and Aquarius figure prominently, and have these letters in their names: A, S, J. Your lucky number is 1.

Thursday, December 5 (Moon in Sagittarius to Capricorn 8:38 a.m.)   One might say, "Count your blessings!" You have more money than you originally anticipated. Your health is generally good. Your marital status is the way you want it to be. Check priorities, protect assets, and don't give up something of value for nothing. Capricorn is involved.

Friday, December 6 (Moon in Capricorn)   Get ready for a "big weekend." Relatives could be involved. Fun and games are featured. Humor is your mainstay. Show others that you can laugh at your own mistakes and foibles. People are genuinely glad to see you. Gemini and Sagittarius figure in this scenario.

Saturday, December 7 (Moon in Capricorn to Aquarius 12:54 p.m.)   People remember Pearl Harbor—as for you, check the details, and be positive concerning mathematics and measurements. Another Scorpio, a Leo, and a Taurus play featured roles. Above all, don't blame others for possible errors. The third house moon relates to a short trip.

Sunday, December 8 (Moon in Aquarius)   Do plenty of reading, writing, and analyzing. Form your own conclusion concerning "great books." People ask you questions about the Bible and mantic arts and sciences that include the Kabala, number mysticism, and astrology. Gemini is represented.

Monday, December 9 (Moon in Aquarius to Pisces 8:46 p.m.)   Attention revolves around where you live, your marital status, and how you respond to a relative's peace offering. Toss aside false pride. Be diplomatic. Respond in an intelligent way. Music figures in this scenario. You will be sensitive to sound. Taurus figures prominently.

Tuesday, December 10 (Moon in Pisces)   Pangs of emotion strike, along with pangs and romance and love. You feel all "mixed up." Give yourself time to regain your emotional equilibrium. Pisces and Virgo figure in this dynamic scenario. An element of dishonesty is present—do not fall victim to self-deception.

Wednesday, December 11 (Moon in Pisces)   The moon in Pisces relates to the stirring of creative juices. The lunar emphasis is on children, challenge, change, and a variety of sensations. Find out where you are going, then do something about it. A period of delay is finished; now is the time for action. Have luck with number 8.

Thursday, December 12 (Moon in Pisces to Aries 7:57 a.m.) Finish what you start; you might not realize it, but you are on the precipice of fame and fortune. Act as if you're aware of it; don't go anywhere hat in hand. In truth, you are in the driver's seat. Open the lines of communication; someone in a distant land wants to relate something of importance to you.

Friday, December 13 (Moon in Aries)   Despite the fact that it is Friday the 13th, this could be your lucky day. You get the job done; you pay more attention to recent resolutions about exercise, diet, and nutrition. You also perform genuine service for a friend and coworker. Leo is involved.

Saturday, December 14 (Moon in Aries to Taurus 8:42 p.m.)   The focus is on how you relate to the "outside world." A Cancer-born individual could be the love of your life and you should be happy about it. The spotlight is on the public, publicity, and attention you have long deserved in connection with your work, home, and family.

Sunday, December 15 (Moon in Taurus)   Questions about cooperative efforts, City Hall politics, and your marital status will loom large. Within 24 hours, the moon will be in Taurus, your seventh house, the "house of marriage." Gemini and Sagittarius want to display loyalty and want also to provide pleasure for you.

Monday, December 16 (Moon in Taurus)   Practical matters demand your attention—check legal papers, whether or not you have rights and permissions. You are charming today, but also should be correct in what you assume, what you intend to achieve. A Taurus figures prominently.

Tuesday, December 17 (Moon in Taurus to Gemini 8:41 a.m.) Your cycle is such that you can afford to play the waiting game. All facts are not in; if you wait, you win. Get ready for a change of itinerary. Personal magnetism will be transformed into sex appeal. Gemini, Virgo, and Sagittarius will play astonishing roles.

Wednesday, December 18 (Moon in Gemini) Lucky lottery: 6, 15, 32, 44, 46, 48. A restless family member attempts to be diplomatic, but fails. Enmity is aroused, so control your own temper. As a Scorpio, you can hit hard if you so desire. Taurus, Libra, and another Scorpio figure in today's dynamic, dramatic scenario.

Thursday, December 19 (Moon in Gemini to Cancer 6:29 p.m.) The full moon in Gemini relates to your eighth house—be aware of a possible computer error, accounting procedures, and the occult. You attract unusual conditions and people. Steer clear of self-deception. Pisces and Virgo figure in this unique scenario.

Friday, December 20 (Moon in Cancer) Communicate with those in foreign lands. Locate a representative for your talent and product. Your key word should be "expansion." Another way of putting it, "Don't be satisfied with the status quo." You are designed to grow, so live up to your potential.

Saturday, December 21 (Moon in Cancer) Look beyond the immediate; find out where you stand, where you will live and with whom. Aries and Libra figure prominently and ·could have these letters or initials in their names: I and R. Stress universal appeal, and participate in charitable political activities.

Sunday, December 22 (Moon in Cancer to Leo 1:47 a.m.) Make a fresh start in a new direction. Shake off your emotional lethargy. Imprint style. Don't follow others. You have a rare opportunity to show others that you belong at the top and intend to get there and stay there. Leo and Aquarius make crystal clear they are on your side.

Monday, December 23 (Moon in Leo) Focus on partnership, cooperative efforts, and your marital status. A leadership role is practically handed to you; do not reject it! Be aware of priorities. Realize you have plenty to offer of value. Cancer and Capricorn will play instrumental roles. Your lucky number is 2.

Tuesday, December 24 (Moon in Leo to Virgo 7:04 a.m.) On this Christmas Eve, the spotlight will be on generosity, and the pleasure of giving. The Leo moon points to color, showmanship, and the ability to praise others and to help them regain confidence. Promoting the spirit of the holiday will be largely up to you. A Sagittarius is in the picture.

Wednesday, December 25 (Moon in Virgo) On this Christmas Day, the moon in Virgo is in your eleventh house. That is all to the good. It means you attract positive vibrations in the form of friends, and that you will be well liked. Taurus, Leo, and Scorpio figure prominently, and could have these initials in their names: D, M, V.

Thursday, December 26 (Moon in Virgo to Libra 10:52 a.m.) You feel good following the holiday. Your vitality returns; you had expected a "letdown." But this did not happen—instead, you feel that your energy has come back and that you are far from being "knocked out." Gemini, Virgo, and Sagittarius play amazing roles. The lucky number is 5.

Friday, December 27 (Moon in Libra) Stick close to home, if possible. The Libra moon means your twelfth house is involved—in turn, that means that "something is going on" behind the scenes. Attention revolves around your family relationships, home, income potential, and marital status. Libra plays a role.

Saturday, December 28 (Moon in Libra to Scorpio 1:40 p.m.) Play the waiting game. Something happened, and you must not permit yourself to be the "victim" of surprise. Instead, find out what it's all about. Some people, well meaning, are doing something that possibly they should not have planned in the first place. Pisces is involved.

Sunday, December 29 (Moon in Scorpio)   A power play day. Your cycle is high. You can have things your way, but be willing to make intelligent concessions. A Capricorn relative appears to be in an argumentative mood. Have none of it—walk away, or just say, "When you are this way, I don't really appreciate it!"

Monday, December 30 (Moon in Scorpio to Sagittarius 4:00 p.m.)   Look beyond the immediate; review New Year's Eve plans; let go of past grievances; make this a New Year in reality. Aries and Libra figure in today's scenario and should be consulted about the "where and when" of a celebration. Have luck with number 9.

Tuesday, December 31 (Moon in Sagittarius)   Make this New Year's Eve a time of hope, love, and the ability to "create your own future." You'll be dealing with temperamental people who need to be catered to, but not to extremes. Many discussions revolve around payments, collections, income, money, and the nation's economy. Leo plays a dynamic role.

HAPPY NEW YEAR!

JANUARY 2003

Wednesday, January 1 (Moon in Sagittarius to Capricorn 6:42 p.m.)   Count your change! People tend to be "careless" with your money. Get ready for a variety of exciting experiences. A flirtation could move from fun to serious. Focus on a possible change of residence or marital status. Libra is involved.

Thursday, January 2 (Moon in Capricorn)   The new moon in Capricorn, which is your third house, means you will have plenty to do with relatives and short trips as well as decisions involving a change of mind and direction.

Avoid self-deception. It is fine to dream, but don't get carried away to the degree that could cause accidents.

Friday, January 3 (Moon in Capricorn to Aquarius 10:57 p.m.)   It is near the end of the week, but suddenly you could receive an assignment requiring overtime. Focus on organization and recognition of priorities. Relationships intensify; don't play games with emotions, your own or others'. Capricorn figures prominently.

Saturday, January 4 (Moon in Aquarius)   At the track: post position special—number 3 p.p. in the sixth race. Hot daily doubles: 1 and 8, 3 and 6, 4 and 7. Away from the track, finish what you start. Look beyond the immediate; take charge of your own fate. Libra plays a fantastic role.

Sunday, January 5 (Moon in Aquarius)   Your spiritual values surface. A young person looks to you as a role model. Emphasize original thinking, your pioneering spirit, and willingness to make a fresh start in a new direction. Your creative juices stir. A different kind of love could be featured. Don't be taken for granted!

Monday, January 6 (Moon in Aquarius to Pisces 5:56 a.m.)   The emphasis is on cooperative efforts and decisions relating to a partnership or marriage. Focus also on structure, design, and removal of fire hazards. Decide on direction, motivation, and the need for meditation. A Cancer makes an offer that's hard to refuse.

Tuesday, January 7 (Moon in Pisces)   Look behind the scenes. Something is going on behind your back. Give full play to your intellectual curiosity. Someone you meet at a social gathering may have ulterior motives. Don't scatter your forces. Have fun without being careless. Lucky number is 3.

Wednesday, January 8 (Moon in Pisces to Aries 4:14 p.m.)   Lucky lottery: 4, 12, 7, 22, 18, 15. The Pisces moon is in your fifth house; that represents creative projects, children, change, and a variety of experiences. Avoid self-deception; see relationships as they exist. Obtain a definition of terms.

Thursday, January 9 (Moon in Aries)   Keep resolutions about your general health. The employment picture ties in with the way you feel. As a passionate Scorpio, you never do things halfway, so be sure you are in condition to win your way. Gemini, Virgo, and Sagittarius figure in this scenario.

Friday, January 10 (Moon in Aries)   Stay close to home, if possible. You learn about a secret meeting. Don't be upset. You're talked about in a kind way. A domestic adjustment is essential, which could include decorating or remodeling. Taurus and Libra will play significant roles.

Saturday, January 11 (Moon in Aries to Taurus 4:47 a.m.) Slow the pace. Strive to perfect techniques, making life easier for yourself. Gain is indicated if you're willing to play the waiting game. Time is on your side. You receive a "revelation." Accent mystery and intrigue. Don't make yourself too available.

Sunday, January 12 (Moon in Taurus)   Lie low. Additional facts are required concerning a legal arrangement. A mysterious stranger enters your life. Be careful; don't be overly impressed by parlor tricks. Capricorn and Cancer figure in this fascinating scenario. Money comes your way!

Monday, January 13 (Moon in Taurus to Gemini 5:06 p.m.)   Focus on proposals that include business, career, and marriage. With the moon in Taurus, your seventh house, it is best to wait, listen, and observe. Don't be cajoled into making a snap decision. You require more information concerning legal rights and permissions.

Tuesday, January 14 (Moon in Gemini)   You get the proverbial second chance. Someone who once broke a promise concerning funding will now live up to his obligation. Dig deep for information, much of which could be found in arcane literature. Leo and Aquarius play dramatic roles.

Wednesday, January 15 (Moon in Gemini)   Settle financial differences with your partner or mate. Make your living room comfortably attractive. If married, an in-law could pay a surprise visit. Married or single, be positive concerning the cheerfulness of your home atmosphere. A Cancer is in the picture.

Thursday, January 16 (Moon in Gemini to Cancer 2:54 a.m.)   Within 24 hours, you obtain the answers to questions involving a possible journey. On this Thursday night, be with people who stimulate you intellectually. You will teach that learning can be fun. Your popularity zooms—you will feel fulfilled as a result.

Friday, January 17 (Moon in Cancer)   Details unravel in connection with a long-range project. Reach beyond the immediate. Take charge of your own fate. Steer clear of those who take you for granted. Taurus, Leo, and another Scorpio figure in today's dynamic scenario. Write and rewrite!

Saturday, January 18 (Moon in Cancer to Leo 9:27 a.m.) The full moon in Cancer, its own sign, equates to your ninth house. This means the emphasis will be on communication via advertising, publishing, and lecturing. Express your views in a forthright way, without being domineering. Have luck with number 5.

Sunday, January 19 (Moon in Leo)   A family member shares the good news. A promotion is involved, which means more money will be coming in. Be diplomatic, without being weak. Make an intelligent concession, without abandoning your principles. Taurus and Libra will play exciting roles.

Monday, January 20 (Moon in Leo to Virgo 1:30 p.m.)   Define terms. Learn more about a real estate proposal. The Leo moon relates to your tenth house; that could mean a promotion and an ability to "climb up the ladder." Avoid self-deception. See people, places, and relationships as they are, not merely as you wish they could be.

Tuesday, January 21 (Moon in Virgo)   What had been "held back" will be released in your favor. You can win friends and influence people. Your persuasive abilities are heightened. You could win a contest and could have luck with number 8. An older individual tells you, "You most certainly are going places!"

Wednesday, January 22 (Moon in Virgo to Libra 4:24 p.m.)   Within 24 hours, your cycle moves up. Circumstances that had been less than favorable will turn in a way that elevates your morale. Think on a universal level; perceive opportunities in a foreign country. Aries and Libra will help inform you.

Thursday, January 23 (Moon in Libra)   What had been dark and depressing will receive the benefit of more light, largely as a result of your efforts. You will be surrounded by an aura of romance—maintain your emotional equilibrium. A romantic Leo enters your life, providing cheer.

Friday, January 24 (Moon in Libra to Scorpio 7:08 p.m.) What was missing will be replaced. Someone who had been hiding something will confess. Don't be harsh; show that you can be understanding. The spotlight is on your home, income potential, and marital status. Capricorn and Cancer will play substantial roles.

Saturday, January 25 (Moon in Scorpio)   This could be a lively Saturday! Focus on humor, diversity, versatility. You'll be asked questions about fashions and restaurants. Gemini and Sagittarius play provocative roles, and have these letters in their names: C, L, U. Lucky number is 3.

Sunday, January 26 (Moon in Scorpio to Sagittarius 10:25 p.m.)   Your cycle moves up; you will be at the right place at a special moment. What you have been waiting for will happen. Circumstances move in your favor; puzzle pieces fall in place. You will be very attractive, but don't break too many hearts. Taurus is in this picture.

Monday, January 27 (Moon in Sagittarius)   You will experience more freedom of thought and action. The moon is in Scorpio, your sign, which means you will be in the spotlight and could be the "talk of the town." On a personal level, there will be a flirtation. Your creative juices stir. What you write could result in profit.

Tuesday, January 28 (Moon in Sagittarius)   What could have been a family crisis will be settled amicably. A lost article is located. What you own is worth more than you originally expected. Add to a unique collection. Share your interests with someone born under Cancer.

Wednesday, January 29 (Moon in Sagittarius to Capricorn 2:29 a.m.)   What at first seemed impossible can be obtained. You don't have the complete story, so be careful. Look behind the scenes. Be discreet and maintain an aura of mystery. This means, don't tell all, don't confide, don't confess. Pisces is represented.

Thursday, January 30 (Moon in Capricorn)   A communication is received from a relative. It contains good news. Focus on trips, visits, and ideas that can be developed into viable concepts. You have the right cards, so play them with confidence. Capricorn and Cancer figure in this scenario.

Friday, January 31 (Moon in Capricorn to Aquarius 7:44 a.m.)   On this last day of January, reach beyond the immediate. Certain people have been waiting to hear from you; let them "hear," but on your terms. Exude confidence. Help others, but don't neglect your own needs. An Aries figures prominently.

FEBRUARY 2003

Saturday, February 1 (Moon in Aquarius)   Be wary about promises and propositions relating to real estate deals. A run-down shack could be represented as "the latest thing." Avoid self-deception, especially where romance is concerned. The new moon tends to make the ordinary appear extraordinary. Protect yourself in close quarters.

Sunday, February 2 (Moon in Aquarius to Pisces 2:54 p.m.) On this Sunday, remain on familiar ground. Focus on organization; plan ahead to meet the competition. News is received concerning promotion, production, and distribution. You will have more responsibility. The pressure is on, and you will be up to it.

Monday, February 3 (Moon in Pisces) On this Monday, you awaken with a dream that can come true. A communication from a relative could be garbled. Work out this puzzle. You need not take everything seriously. Aries and Libra will play major roles, and have these letters in their names: I and R.

Tuesday, February 4 (Moon in Pisces) Don't follow others. Imprint your own style; feature original thinking. You exude personality and sex appeal. Be kind to those attracted to you; don't break hearts. Wear bright colors when you make personal appearances. You could invent an object that might lead to riches.

Wednesday, February 5 (Moon in Pisces to Aries 12:44 a.m.) What had been a matter of speculation will be transformed into a reality. Focus on cooperative efforts, direction and motivation, and your marital status. Keep resolutions about diet. A seafood dinner tonight will prove delicious. Capricorn is involved.

Thursday, February 6 (Moon in Aries) Avoid scattering your efforts. Don't attempt to do the impossible just to please everyone. Diversify! Demonstrate versatility, giving full play to your intellectual curiosity. Gemini and Sagittarius play pertinent roles. Have luck with number 3.

Friday, February 7 (Moon in Aries to Taurus 12:58 p.m.) Give full attention to the job at hand. A coworker seems to want you to do two jobs. Don't be taken for granted. Attend to details and repairs at home. Revise and review; rebuild structure. Taurus, Leo, and another Scorpio will play featured roles.

Saturday, February 8 (Moon in Taurus)   Get ready for change, travel, and a variety of experiences. A flirtation could get out of hand. Be careful about your signature; don't permit others to "borrow" it. Focus on handwriting, reading, and teaching. Lucky lottery: 5, 12, 9, 13, 33, 4.

Sunday, February 9 (Moon in Taurus)   A family discussion concerns the value of your possessions. Offers are received, but don't give up something of value for nothing. Beautify your surroundings, including your home. A Libra will demonstrate musical ability; show appreciation, without being obsequious.

Monday, February 10 (Moon in Taurus to Gemini 1:44 a.m.)   The feeling of being restricted or deceived is temporary. By tomorrow, you learn more about who is lending money and interest rates. You will be accused by some of being in the playground of the occult. A romantic relationship could get hot and heavy.

Tuesday, February 11 (Moon in Gemini)   You will be drawn to the mantic arts, including astrology. Follow your intuition. Einstein once said that intuition is more important than knowledge. A partner or mate discloses vital information. Capricorn and Cancer will play "mysterious" roles.

Wednesday, February 12 (Moon in Gemini to Cancer 12:17 p.m.)   Look beyond the immediate. A project once rejected could now be accepted. Put the finishing touches on a presentation. On a personal level, romance blossoms. Accent idealism. Don't lower your standards. Participate in humanitarian activities. You will be remembered for kind, generous deeds.

Thursday, February 13 (Moon in Cancer)   Find your own rhythm. March to your own tune. Long-range prospects can be clarified to your advantage. Make a fresh start. Don't follow others; let them follow you. Leo and Aquarius play outstanding roles, and have these letters in their names: A, S, J. Lucky number is 1.

Friday, February 14 (Moon in Cancer to Leo 7:03 p.m.)   On this day, you receive many cards featuring romance and love. Someone at a distance gets "in touch." There is a suggestion that a long-lost love could be revived. Maintain your emotional equilibrium. The question of your marital status will loom large.

Saturday, February 15 (Moon in Leo)   At the track: post position special—number 3 p.p. in the third race. Hot daily doubles: 3 and 3, 5 and 7, 2 and 1. Away from the track, arrange a social get-together and permit ideas to flow freely. Gemini and Sagittarius play provocative roles, and have these letters in their names: C, L, U.

Sunday, February 16 (Moon in Leo to Virgo 10:23 p.m.)   The full moon in Leo is in your tenth house—the house of career. An emotional entanglement could occur with one who is your professional superior. Be careful. During this phase of the moon people tend to be ultrasensitive, and some act in a "crazy way." Another Scorpio is involved.

Monday, February 17 (Moon in Virgo)   Read and write. Written words are ultraimportant. You could start a diary. Express yourself freely; no one else need read it. A flirtation could lead to something serious—be careful. Protect yourself in emotional clinches.

Tuesday, February 18 (Moon in Virgo to Libra 11:47 p.m.)   A domestic adjustment is featured, which could include a change of residence or marital status. The Virgo moon relates to your eleventh house. Many of your hopes and wishes could be fulfilled. In matters of speculation, stick with number 6. Your powers of persuasion are heightened; you can, at this time, convince anybody of anything!

Wednesday, February 19 (Moon in Libra)   Blend altruism with practicality. Some people want to deceive you for no good reason. Protect yourself. Be on guard, but also realize that romantic illusions can be fulfilled. Define terms, outline boundaries. Lucky lottery: 7, 14, 32, 5, 25, 18.

Thursday, February 20 (Moon in Libra)   You get results! Step right in where angels fear to tread. You will learn secrets and can make practical use of them. In entering buildings, be sure you know where the exit signs are located. The spotlight is on distribution, production, and getting your priorities in order.

Friday, February 21 (Moon in Libra to Scorpio 1:09 a.m.)   Be finished with someone who takes you for granted. You learn about a person who talks behind your back; don't brood about it. Don't make yourself too available. Maintain your self-esteem. Be in control of a creative project. A long-distance communication verifies your opinions; be pleased.

Saturday, February 22 (Moon in Scorpio)   On this Saturday, new interests enter your life, including romance. Your lunar cycle is high, so timing and the element of luck ride with you. Take the initiative; don't follow others. Your judgment and intuition are on target. Know it, be confident, and act accordingly. Fortunate number is 1.

Sunday, February 23 (Moon in Scorpio to Sagittarius 3:45 a.m.)   Stick close to home. The spotlight will be on your marital status. You will be at the right place at a special moment, almost effortlessly. Take the initiative; arrange future appointments. What you thought was moribund will show signs of "coming back to life."

Monday, February 24 (Moon in Sagittarius)   The element of luck enables you to possibly win a contest. Focus on payments, collections, and your income potential. You get most of what you want by displaying your sense of humor. Keep plans flexible. Cooperate with a Sagittarius who of late has felt neglected.

Tuesday, February 25 (Moon in Sagittarius to Capricorn 8:10 a.m.) Rewrite and rebuild. This could be your "makeover" day. People who took you for granted will take a second look and feel slightly ashamed. Taurus, Leo, and another Scorpio figure prominently, and could have these letters or initials in their names: D, M, V.

Wednesday, February 26 (Moon in Capricorn) Lucky lottery: 5, 10, 12, 18, 30, 40. An excellent day for getting your thoughts on paper, perhaps starting a diary. If single, you could meet your future mate. If married, the spark that brought you together will reignite. A short journey is indicated in connection with a relative.

Thursday, February 27 (Moon in Capricorn to Aquarius 2:24 p.m.) Attention revolves around your home, music, and romance. Take special care in traffic. People around you, including drivers, tend to be careless. A worried relative will be able to laugh off the matter. Taurus, Libra, and another Scorpio will play dramatic roles.

Friday, February 28 (Moon in Aquarius) On this last day of February, you will find that you are more secure than you originally anticipated. Define terms; get your promises in writing. Maintain an aura of mystery and intrigue. Don't be too available! Above all, avoid self-deception. Face facts as they exist.

MARCH 2003

Saturday, March 1 (Moon in Aquarius to Pisces 10:25 p.m.) This is the start of a creative, romantic month. A powerful Saturday to get organized and put your priorities in the proper place. Focus on land, real estate, solid structure. Get rid of safety hazards. Let people know that you mean business. A relationship is intensified!

Sunday, March 2 (Moon in Pisces) Within 24 hours, your creativity will be activated. Find your own rhythm and style. Today, finish what you started two months ago. Look beyond the immediate. Predict your future and make it come true. Aries and Libra play "stunning" roles.

Monday, March 3 (Moon in Pisces) The new moon began last night in Pisces, and represents your fifth house. This means creativity, romance, style, and passion. If you are merely playing games, it would be best to move on. You are capable of overwhelming people. Don't hurt others or break hearts. Leo is involved.

Tuesday, March 4 (Moon in Pisces to Aries 8:29 a.m.) Someone who played a romantic role in your life could make a surprise appearance. Be sure this person understands that your time is valuable, that your self-esteem has been elevated. Focus on direction, motivation, and the need of privacy for the purpose of meditation.

Wednesday, March 5 (Moon in Aries) Diversify! Accent your humor and versatility. Be willing to engage in social activities. More people understand you and are getting to "like you." On this Wednesday, you will find that Gemini and Sagittarius play outstanding roles. Lucky number is 3.

Thursday, March 6 (Moon in Aries to Taurus 8:35 p.m.) A family member who has been restless and moody will "settle down." Don't fear the unknown; make it known as a result of personal investigation. Communicate with someone temporarily confined to home or hospital. Another Scorpio will play a fascinating role.

Friday, March 7 (Moon in Taurus) On this Friday, be especially discreet. Ignore the pleadings of someone who insists, "I must know the secret!" There will be a "changing of the guard." You receive a written notice, which is favorable. Gemini, Virgo, and Sagittarius play top roles. Have luck with number 5.

Saturday, March 8 (Moon in Taurus) Domestic tranquillity is restored. If diplomatic, you get almost everything you wish. Restrain an impulse to make demands. No unconditional surrender! Legal prospects will brighten. Taurus and Libra play unusual roles.

Sunday, March 9 (Moon in Taurus to Gemini 9:36 a.m.) Your spiritual values surface. You will hear many "sob stories." Know when to say, "Enough!" You do not possess the necessary information, so play the waiting game; do not equate delay with defeat. Someone who intrigues could also be deceptive.

Monday, March 10 (Moon in Gemini) You discover an unusual source of income. The moon in your eighth house equates to mystery—perhaps the financial status of someone close to you. You will wonder why you were not told, but don't make a federal case of it. Capricorn and Cancer play "productive" roles.

Tuesday, March 11 (Moon in Gemini to Cancer 9:10 p.m.) At the track: post position special—number 1 p.p. in the seventh race. Hot daily doubles: 1 and 1, 3 and 7, 4 and 6. Away from the track, let go of a burden not rightly your own in the first place. You discover the secret of "universal appeal."

Wednesday, March 12 (Moon in Cancer) Make a fresh start. Show your pioneering spirit. Emphasize original thinking. What had been restricted will be released. You will be complimented on your ability to handle confidential matters. Classification is up; it has been long deserved.

Thursday, March 13 (Moon in Cancer) A young person confides, "I rely upon your judgment." Focus on a communication that includes advertising or publishing. A philosophical discussion with a Cancer proves beneficial. Questions about partnership and marriage will loom large.

Friday, March 14 (Moon in Cancer to Leo 5:05 a.m.) Diversify, experiment! Bring together people of opposing political views. Your sense of humor and your fitness will "rule the day." Gemini and Sagittarius play fantastic roles, and could have these letters in their names: C, L, U. Lucky number is 3.

Saturday, March 15 (Moon in Leo)   Be willing to tear down in order to rebuild. Your superiors will be impressed; you will receive accolades. Overcome minor details; skip over pressure points that really don't concern you. Taurus and another Scorpio will play dramatic roles.

Sunday, March 16 (Moon in Leo to Virgo 8:51 a.m.) Write your thoughts. Your ideas will be especially appreciated if you put them in writing. You will meet someone who is attractive and intelligent. Express your feelings, but maintain your emotional equilibrium. Gemini is represented.

Monday, March 17 (Moon in Virgo)   On this St. Patrick's Day, avoid someone who has overindulged. You can celebrate, but go easy on adult beverages. Include a family member in your get-together. A domestic adjustment relates to beautifying your home, to entertaining and being entertained.

Tuesday, March 18 (Moon in Virgo to Libra 9:42 a.m.) The full moon in Virgo in your eleventh house means your romantic interests are heightened. You could have luck in matters of speculation by sticking with number 7. A feeling of being restricted is only temporary. Pisces figures prominently.

Wednesday, March 19 (Moon in Libra)   Puzzle pieces fall into place. What had been a secret will be revealed to your advantage. Don't fear the unknown. Get off the bench and into the game, the game of your life. Organize your priorities. Assume the role of leadership. Do things your way!

Thursday, March 20 (Moon in Libra to Scorpio 9:37 a.m.) Don't hold on to a losing proposition. Refuse to be taken

243

for granted. Participate in a humanitarian project. As events unfold, you might be asking, "Is this déjà vu?" Today's scenario features familiar places and faces. Aries plays an astounding role.

Friday, March 21 (Moon in Scorpio)   Emphasize independence of thought and action. Even as you read these words, circumstances are turning in your favor. Don't follow others. Express yourself! Wear bright colors. A different kind of romance will beckon. Leo figures in this scenario.

Saturday, March 22 (Moon in Scorpio to Sagittarius 10:33 a.m.)   At the track: post position special—number 6 p.p. in the second race. Hot daily doubles: 2 and 8, 1 and 5, 4 and 4. Away from the track, the question of your partnership, cooperative efforts, and marital status will figure prominently.

Sunday, March 23 (Moon in Sagittarius)   The light touch wins. What you want will be presented to you. A lost article is located. Emphasize humor and versatility. Maintain your self-esteem. Your political views will be sought; be frank, but realize that there is a tomorrow. Sagittarius is involved.

Monday, March 24 (Moon in Sagittarius to Capricorn 1:48 p.m.)   On this Monday, you awaken to learn of a financial opportunity. Open the lines of communication. What appears to be a defeat will boomerang in your favor. A recent investment will pay dividends. Wear your hair in a different style; wear a hat in a "jaunty" way.

Tuesday, March 25 (Moon in Capricorn)   Today's scenario highlights trips, visits, and your intellectual curiosity. What begins as a mild flirtation could get too hot to handle. Be aware and alert; don't give up something of value for nothing. Gemini, Virgo, and Sagittarius play practical roles.

Wednesday, March 26 (Moon in Capricorn to Aquarius 7:50 p.m.)   Lucky lottery: 6, 10, 12, 18, 33, 9. In dealing with a temperamental family member, be gentle. You get surprising news—no finger-pointing! Play the role of "mediator." Taurus, Libra, and another Scorpio figure in this scenario.

Thursday, March 27 (Moon in Aquarius)   An inquiry you made nine days ago will finally be answered, to your satisfaction. A relative has been the source of deception, deliberate or otherwise. Slow your pace; play the waiting game. Legal clearance could be obtained, if you are persistent.

Friday, March 28 (Moon in Aquarius)   On this Friday, your lunar cycle moves up. This coincides with your popularity, your ability to be at the right place at a special moment. You will be on solid ground, despite naysayers who actually are envious and resentful. You made a good bargain!

Saturday, March 29 (Moon in Aquarius to Pisces 4:25 a.m.)   Stick close to home base, if possible. Someone wants to tell you something about the beginning or ending of a job or of a relationship. Focus on romance and passion, but maintain your emotional equilibrium. Aries figures prominently.

Sunday, March 30 (Moon in Pisces)   Express your views in an original, dynamic way. The Pisces moon relates to your fifth house, which equates to children, challenge, change, and a variety of experiences. Don't be daunted by those who lack imagination. Wear bright colors; heed your own counsel.

Monday, March 31 (Moon in Pisces to Aries 3:04 p.m.)   On this last day of March, come to terms with your partner or mate. Your creative juices stir. You can afford to be generous. A word of caution: There is a difference between generosity and extravagance. People want to be with you; a special person expresses feelings.

APRIL 2003

Tuesday, April 1 (Moon in Aries)   Don't participate in an April Fools' prank; it could actually be dangerous. The new moon in Aries represents your sixth house; that places emphasis on your general health, employment, and getting the job done. Aries and Libra play major roles.

Wednesday, April 2 (Moon in Aries)   Make a fresh start; show that you are not a "Johnny One-note." Original thinking is the key. Imprint your own style. Don't follow others; follow your heart. Your intuitive intellect is heightened. You attract romance and love, if you so desire. Lucky number is 1.

Thursday, April 3 (Moon in Aries to Taurus 3:19 a.m.) Be willing to wait and win. Don't let others cajole you into making snap decisions. Protect your property and home. If single, you could meet your future mate. If married, there could be speculation about an addition to the family.

Friday, April 4 (Moon in Taurus)   Focus on direction, social activity, and getting your life in proper perspective. Maintain your emotional equilibrium. Have luck with number 3. Gemini and Sagittarius play fascinating roles, and have these letters in their names: C, L, U.

Saturday, April 5 (Moon in Taurus to Gemini 4:23 p.m.) Those who say you are behind the times or ahead of your time are envious and frustrated. You are right on time, so build on a solid structure. Refuse to be discouraged by those who lack talent or money. Taurus, Leo, and another Scorpio figure in this scenario.

Sunday, April 6—Daylight Saving Time Begins (Moon in Gemini)   Spend more time with your family. Discuss ambitions and prospects for the future. Make your home beautiful. Read and write; start a diary. People are curious about your thoughts and feelings. Get to the heart of matters in expressing yourself.

Monday, April 7 (Moon in Gemini)   Dig deep for information! What you find will be surprising, ultimately beneficial. You could discover a "love letter." Let the past be the past; don't revive old grudges. Taurus and Libra are in this picture, and have these letters in their names: F, O, X.

Tuesday, April 8 (Moon in Gemini to Cancer 5:35 a.m.) Advise one close to you that character means doing the right thing when no one is looking. Remember: Jealousy is the only vice from which no pleasure is received in return. Avoid self-deception. Highlight a relationship with Pisces. Be near water, if possible.

Wednesday, April 9 (Moon in Cancer)   Focus on organization, priorities, and the pressure of extra responsibility; you will be up to it and will prosper. An older individual expresses confidence, assuring you, "I will be on your side." Capricorn and Cancer are in this scenario. Lucky number is 8.

Thursday, April 10 (Moon in Cancer to Leo 2:52 p.m.) On this 10th day of the month, you find that a family member finally agrees to a special education course. Focus on universal appeal as well as a possible journey. Publish your findings. You deserve more than you are getting. Aries plays an astonishing role.

Friday, April 11 (Moon in Leo)   Emphasize showmanship, drama, and color coordination. A promotion is due, despite objections by jealous associates. Make a fresh start in a new direction. Do things your way; don't follow others. This message will become crystal clear tonight.

Saturday, April 12 (Moon in Leo to Virgo 8:05 p.m.) Evaluate your dreams. Properly interpreted they could be doorways to the future. If married, family planning is necessary. Capricorn and Cancer play significant roles. Have luck with number 2.

Sunday, April 13 (Moon in Virgo)   What had been depressing could now be transformed into a reason for celebrating. Someone in a position of authority takes note of

247

your accomplishments and talent. Your popularity increases; social life accelerates. Gemini figures prominently.

Monday, April 14 (Moon in Virgo to Libra 9:40 p.m.) Revise, review, and, if necessary, rebuild. Suddenly your powers of persuasion are heightened; you win friends and influence people. Your explanations and analysis will be provocative, exciting, dramatic. Another Scorpio is in this picture.

Tuesday, April 15 (Moon in Libra) Get ready for a change of itinerary; written instructions will be revised. Take a leadership role. Be creative; don't fall into the trap of merely wanting to be popular. Before you retire tonight, this message becomes crystal clear. Virgo is represented.

Wednesday, April 16 (Moon in Libra to Scorpio 9:15 p.m.) The full moon in Libra represents your twelfth house; this means you could find romance in a secluded area. Focus on family responsibilities—a chance to prove your loyalty. Maintain your emotional equilibrium; give logic equal time with impulsive urges.

Thursday, April 17 (Moon in Scorpio) Discretion truly is the better part of valor; those words will tumble in your mind. Keep confidential matters private; overcome the temptation to tell all. Define terms. Avoid self-deception. Maintain an aura of mystery and intrigue.

Friday, April 18 (Moon in Scorpio to Sagittarius 8:51 p.m.) Get ready for a weekend that places you in the center of attraction. Some very important people want your attention and will be obvious about it. Capricorn and Cancer play outstanding roles. Get your priorities in order; required financing will be obtained.

Saturday, April 19 (Moon in Sagittarius) You can do almost anything you want. Your lunar cycle and number 9 keynote both point to achievement. Focus on giving and receiving love; refuse to be taken for granted. Elevate your self-esteem. Aries and Libra play outstanding roles.

Sunday, April 20 (Moon in Sagittarius to Capricorn 10:21 p.m.) New ways of increasing your income are featured. Emphasize original thinking. Take the initiative; don't follow others. Your way for you will be the best way. Today's scenario highlights travel and excitement; Leo and Aquarius will play scintillating roles.

Monday, April 21 (Moon in Capricorn) Improved family life can be attributed to the fact that your home is more beautiful and comfortable. If single, you could meet your future mate. Married or single, there will be a "glow" in knowing you are loved. A Cancer will play a mysterious role.

Tuesday, April 22 (Moon in Capricorn) Maintain your emotional equilibrium and sense of humor. Today's scenario features trips, visits, relatives, and a tendency to scatter your forces. People want to be with you because you make them laugh, if even through their tears. Sagittarius is in this picture.

Wednesday, April 23 (Moon in Capricorn to Aquarius 2:58 a.m.) At the track: post position special—number 4 p.p. in the fourth race. Hot daily doubles: 1 and 3, 5 and 4, 6 and 2. Away from the track, attend to details, read the fine print, tend to repairs at home. Taurus is involved.

Thursday, April 24 (Moon in Aquarius) People you care about could be undergoing a crisis. Focus on the sale or purchase of property, helping one who "desperately" needs your aid. Gemini and Sagittarius play entertaining roles. Be analytical; find reasons for recent happenings.

Friday, April 25 (Moon in Aquarius to Pisces 11:02 a.m.) A family member says, "You did what needed to be done and I thank you!" Focus on domesticity, music, style. Keep up with fashion news. Wear shades of blue. Be with one temporarily confined to home or hospital. Libra figures prominently.

Saturday, April 26 (Moon in Pisces)   Pursue a creative project. Define terms. See people and relationships in a realistic light. Trust your hunch. You can see without seeing—you undergo a mystical experience. Pisces and Virgo play major roles, and have these initials in their names: G, P, Y.

Sunday, April 27 (Moon in Pisces to Aries 9:54 p.m.) Focus on production, distribution, and creative ways of promoting a project. Use color coordination in advertising; obtain a display for your talent or product. You might be saying, "I have played the waiting game long enough, now I am going to act!"

Monday, April 28 (Moon in Aries)   Accent universal appeal. Finish what you start. Help a young person to get bearings. Look beyond the immediate to perceive future potential and make dreams come true. Within 24 hours, a mystery will be solved to your benefit.

Tuesday, April 29 (Moon in Aries)   Provide enlightenment in areas dark with fear, doubts, and suspicions. Display the courage of your convictions. Act in an independent way. Waiting for others would be an error. Leo and Aquarius play astonishing roles, and have these letters in their names: A, S, J.

Wednesday, April 30 (Moon in Aries to Taurus 10:25 a.m.)   On this last day of April, you journey into an area previously unexplored. Focus on cooperative efforts and proposals of partnership or marriage. Keep resolutions about exercise and nutrition. Capricorn and Cancer will play helpful roles.

MAY 2003

Thursday, May 1 (Moon in Taurus)   The new moon is in Taurus, your seventh house. You make friends and become aware of those who oppose you. Focus on legal rights, partnership, and marriage. Leo and Aquarius play exciting roles. You learn much that is encouraging.

Friday, May 2 (Moon in Taurus to Gemini 11:26 p.m.)
The spotlight falls on where you live and with whom. Take time to analyze. Refuse to be cajoled into a snap decision. Be positive you are on the right side of the law. Capricorn and Cancer play dynamic roles, and could have these initials in their names: B, K, T.

Saturday, May 3 (Moon in Gemini) Forces are scattered. Bring order out of chaos. Your popularity is on the rise. You will be invited to join a unique group. Within 24 hours, you could discover oil or money. People want to be with you because you make them laugh. Have luck with number 3.

Sunday, May 4 (Moon in Gemini) A rebuilding process is under way. A missing link is discovered. You could receive a reward. What had been rejected will be accepted, if you are willing to do some rewriting. Taurus, Leo, and another Scorpio will play exciting roles.

Monday, May 5 (Moon in Gemini to Cancer 11:40 a.m.)
Delve deep into a mysterious area. Someone has been holding out on you. This could be a money problem. Use your extrasensory perception. Your intuitive intellect is honed to razor-sharpness. Writing and traveling will figure prominently. Virgo is represented.

Tuesday, May 6 (Moon in Cancer) A domestic adjustment is necessary, so make an intelligent concession. A long-distance communication verifies your views and makes you feel better. Music will play. Dance and march to your own tune. Taurus, Libra, and another Scorpio play key roles. Lucky number is 6.

Wednesday, May 7 (Moon in Cancer to Leo 9:44 p.m.)
Don't trip while walking or running. Focus on a communication that includes advertising and publishing. You attract foreign trade. Don't stop now; push ahead on an interna-

251

tional scale. Don't deceive yourself; Pisces and Virgo play intriguing roles.

Thursday, May 8 (Moon in Leo) What had been delayed will arrive. Make this your power play day! Focus on taking a "poetic" approach to situations and people. Within 24 hours, you learn where you really stand in connection with a love relationship. Don't fret; it could be good!

Friday, May 9 (Moon in Leo) Look beyond the immediate. You could fall in love with someone from a foreign nation. The Leo moon is in your tenth house, which emphasizes career and business, perhaps a promotion. Let go of a burden that does not really belong to you.

Saturday, May 10 (Moon in Leo to Virgo 4:29 a.m.) Answer: Affirmative. Stress independence, take charge, make a fresh start in a new direction. A love relationship could "sizzle." If it is getting too warm for you, move on. Leo and Aquarius will play dramatic roles, and have these letters in their names: A, S, J.

Sunday, May 11 (Moon in Virgo) Regard this as a "new day." During this Sunday, spiritual values surface. The lunar position highlights your ability to make wishes come true. What at first appeared to be a setback will boomerang in your favor. A Cancer is involved.

Monday, May 12 (Moon in Virgo to Libra 7:41 a.m.) Diversify. Give full play to your intellectual curiosity. You get what you ask for, so be careful. Don't ask for more than you can handle. You have luck today in matters of speculation; stick with number 3. A Sagittarius acts in a surprising way, which is excellent for you.

Tuesday, May 13 (Moon in Libra) Rebuild what had been dismantled three months ago. The moon in your twelfth house means protect confidential information. Your powers of persuasion are utilized during a "sales talk." No matter, be discreet and keep a secret. A Taurus figures prominently.

Wednesday, May 14 (Moon in Libra to Scorpio 8:12 a.m.)
Lucky lottery: 5, 15, 18, 33, 22, 9. Read and write, learn by
teaching. You will have access to classified information. Use
it, but don't exploit it. People will look to you for enlightenment. Gemini, Virgo, and Sagittarius figure in this scenario.

Thursday, May 15 (Moon in Scorpio)   Be sweet to people you care about. An important domestic adjustment
takes place which will favor you. Brighten your home. Use
your knowledge of color coordination. Don't let anyone
remove your wonderful, comfortable chair. Libra is represented.

Friday, May 16 (Moon in Scorpio to Sagittarius 7:42 a.m.)
Late last night's full moon and lunar eclipse fell in your
sign of Scorpio. There will be a shake-up in your plans, so
keep your options open. Maintain an aura of mystery; don't
tell all. Let others play a guessing game. Strange things
could be happening on earth; inclement weather adds to
your discomfort. This shake-up could be more than symbolic.

Saturday, May 17 (Moon in Sagittarius)   On this Saturday, you enter areas mostly prohibited. A relationship
could get too hot to handle. Find a quiet place with someone you are drawn to; be positive of privacy and then "pour
out your heart." Capricorn figures prominently.

***Sunday, May 18 (Moon in Sagittarius to Capricorn 8:03
a.m.)***   Look beyond the immediate. You could discover
ways to increase your income. What had been lost will be
recovered. Add to your collection. Don't be discouraged
by philistines. Plan ahead for a possible journey. Aries and
Libra play important roles.

Monday, May 19 (Moon in Capricorn)   The answer to
your question: Yes, this is the time to take the initiative,
to do things your way, to make a fresh start. A short trip
involves a relative. That is fine, but don't get caught up in a
wild-goose chase. Leo and Aquarius figure in this scenario.

Tuesday, May 20 (Moon in Capricorn to Aquarius 11:01 a.m.)   Focus on direction, motivation, and ways of increasing your earning power. If single, you could meet your future mate. Married or single, a domestic adjustment is necessary. Make room for an additional family member in the not-too-distant future!

Wednesday, May 21 (Moon in Aquarius)   Highlight diversity, sensitivity, intellectual curiosity. The sale or purchase of property could be featured. Check safety rules and regulations. Read the fine print. Be aware of "minor points." Gemini and Sagittarius will play key roles.

Thursday, May 22 (Moon in Aquarius to Pisces 5:40 p.m.) Revise, review, rewrite. A phenomenon occurs—you learn by teaching. You will be approached by another Scorpio who says, "Why waste your time here, come with me!" Your answer could be, "Thanks, but no thanks!"

Friday, May 23 (Moon in Pisces)   You experience more freedom of thought and action. A romantic interlude lends spice. You will be exuding personal magnetism and sex appeal. Don't break any hearts! Find an outlet for your creative force. People you admire will be watching and will expect great things from you.

Saturday, May 24 (Moon in Pisces)   Attention revolves around your home, painting, and musical tones. Focus on diplomacy, making intelligent concessions without abandoning your principles. You could change your residence or marital status. Don't permit pride to deter your progress or happiness.

Sunday, May 25 (Moon in Pisces to Aries 3:58 a.m.) Let your spiritual values surface. What had been an exciting relationship need not end. Give the other person time to breathe! Focus on youth, vigor, ambition, variety. Pisces and Virgo will play dramatic roles.

Monday, May 26 (Moon in Aries)   Get organized! Recognize your priorities and what to do about them. Focus on intensity, putting ideas across concerning distribution. Capricorn and Cancer play outstanding roles and have these initials in their names: H, Q, Z.

Tuesday, May 27 (Moon in Aries to Taurus 4:31 p.m.)
You'll be engaged in a discussion about "time." You will agree, "It is mysterious." People are claiming to invent "time machines." You have within you an "inner clock." You know what time it is without consulting your watch. Aries plays a role.

Wednesday, May 28 (Moon in Taurus) Lie low—wait and listen, observe and be aware of subtle innuendos. The question of a legal contract will arise; watch for hidden clauses. You are not being selfish by insisting on your fair share. Follow your own intuitive intellect. Leo is involved.

Thursday, May 29 (Moon in Taurus) You could be traveling a perilous road; be alert for signals of caution. One who would be your partner or mate makes known views in a "quiet" way. Your marital status figures prominently. Get down to brass tacks about a business arrangement.

Friday, May 30 (Moon in Taurus to Gemini 5:30 a.m.)
The emphasis continues on getting legal clearance. By tomorrow, you'll know for sure that you are right, that others are wrong. With your Scorpio passion, some people will be overwhelmed. Make repairs at home, also pursue artistic projects. Lucky number is 3.

Saturday, May 31 (Moon in Gemini) There is a blue moon and a solar eclipse in Gemini, your eighth house. Mysterious things happen. You might wonder if there are such things as poltergeists. Financial backing is coming, but not as much as you desire and not as soon. Taurus and another Scorpio are featured.

JUNE 2003

Sunday, June 1 (Moon in Gemini to Cancer 5:26 p.m.)
Get into your own rhythm. Events happen that will prove
favorable for you. Emphasize independence of thought and
of action; hold fast to your ideals. You will do very well in
any debate. Capricorn and Cancer figure in this scenario.

Monday, June 2 (Moon in Cancer)   Focus on a variety
of sensations and experiences. The moon in your ninth
house coincides with communication, publishing, being "on
line" with someone in a foreign nation. Social activities
accelerate. A political discussion becomes hot and heavy.

Tuesday, June 3 (Moon in Cancer)   Repair work at
home is necessary. Dismantle in order to rebuild. Another
Scorpio is in this picture, and attempts to force views. Be
aware of necessary adjustments, including plumbing. You
excel today in word games, especially crossword puzzles.

Wednesday, June 4 (Moon in Cancer to Leo 3:23 p.m.)
News comes regarding tasks at home and employment duties. The focus is also on general health, fitness, exercise.
Be aware of your diet and nutrition. You'll make progress,
if you write your thoughts. A recent dream will prove prophetic; take notes.

Thursday, June 5 (Moon in Leo)   Accent diplomacy.
Let a family member know you really care, then do something to prove it. The focus is on music, romance, a unique
gift. Your voice is different today, clear and melodious.
Taurus and Libra play dynamic roles.

Friday, June 6 (Moon in Leo to Virgo 10:49 a.m.)
Define terms, play the waiting game. All is not what appears on the surface, including job and career offers. Wait
and observe; additional facts will be coming in. Pisces and
Virgo play astounding roles, and have these letters or initials in their names: G, P, Y.

Saturday, June 7 (Moon in Virgo)   This could be your "power play" day! The moon in your eleventh house in Virgo means you will articulate desires, beliefs, and commitments. Your powers of persuasion are heightened. Your passion, recently suppressed, will "find a way out." Capricorn is involved.

Sunday, June 8 (Moon in Virgo to Libra 3:28 p.m.) Look beyond the immediate. Take time to meditate, to take charge of your own fate. If you have been wishing to travel, your wish is almost certain to come true. Open the lines of communication. Even in a foreign country, there is someone who "speaks your language."

Monday, June 9 (Moon in Libra)   On this Monday, you wake up realizing that your vigor has made an amazing comeback. The spotlight is on creativity, originality, and a willingness to go your own way. Behind-the-scenes activity will be revealed. Encourage enlightenment where there has been darkness.

Tuesday, June 10 (Moon in Libra to Scorpio 5:38 p.m.) What had been hidden will be revealed. This will include the "hidden desires" of your partner or mate. There's special emphasis on home, security, and your marital status. Turn on your Scorpio charm; people will take for granted "your passion." Cancer is involved.

Wednesday, June 11 (Moon in Scorpio)   In matters of speculation, stick with number 3. Elements of timing and luck ride with you. Don't get in your own way. Select the best! Don't lower your standards, even for a physical attraction. Gemini and Sagittarius will play fascinating roles.

Thursday, June 12 (Moon in Scorpio to Sagittarius 6:11 p.m.)   Your lunar cycle is high. Therefore, your judgment and intuition are on target. Handle details adroitly. Refuse to be intimidated by someone who claims to "know it all." Taurus and another Scorpio edge their way into this scenario, and have these letters in their names: D, M, V.

Friday, June 13 (Moon in Sagittarius)   You'll have luck, but not bad luck. You gain enlightenment. People who attempt to stop you will be overruled. Take note of your experiences and dreams. Don't be satisfied to know merely that something happened—find out why it occurred.

Saturday, June 14 (Moon in Sagittarius to Capricorn 6:37 p.m.)   The full moon is in Sagittarius, your second house. Romantic talk blends with information about finances. A lost article is returned. Guard your valuables; don't give up something "rare" for a mere promise. Lucky lottery: 6, 15, 31, 32, 2, 12.

Sunday, June 15 (Moon in Capricorn)   Romance lends spice. Don't expect much more than a mere thrill. The focus is also on trips, visits, and relatives. You find out something humorous, so laugh at your own foibles. Pisces and Virgo will play memorable roles.

Monday, June 16 (Moon in Capricorn to Aquarius 8:41 p.m.)   What started out on a negative tone will boomerang in your favor. Keep plans flexible. Someone from your past makes a surprise appearance. Have fun, but don't attempt to relive the past. Capricorn presents a fantastic offer.

Tuesday, June 17 (Moon in Aquarius)   A relative helps straighten out a legal complication. Show gratitude, without being obsequious. What you are up against could be an "obscure law." People are on your side. Your popularity is on the rise. There is a mix-up concerning the time of an appointment or date. Don't make a federal case of it.

Wednesday, June 18 (Moon in Aquarius)   At the track: post position special—number 1 p.p. in the fifth race. Hot daily doubles: 8 and 1, 3 and 7, 4 and 6. Away from the track, make a fresh start. Take care of your garden; get an estimate on the value of land. Wear bright colors when you make personal appearances.

Thursday, June 19 (Moon in Aquarius to Pisces 1:57 a.m.)
Some of your ideals in connection with home and romance will be fulfilled. The focus is on direction, motivation, and meditation. Avoid overeating. A meal tonight will feature seafood. Cancer and Capricorn play outstanding roles.

Friday, June 20 (Moon in Pisces) You will feel ultra-attractive. At least one person confides, "I can hardly keep my hands off you!" Your morale surges upward as a result. Display talent and humor. Gemini and Sagittarius play top roles, and could have these letters in their names: C, L, U.

Saturday, June 21 (Moon in Pisces to Aries 11:05 a.m.)
This could be a lively Saturday night. Your creative juices stir. Participate in an exciting event. Hurdle obstacles; don't be stopped by foolish rules. You win your way, despite attempts to block your progress. Another Scorpio is involved.

Sunday, June 22 (Moon in Aries) Obey safety regulations in connection with work and employment. Be especially careful when handling sharp objects. Be ready for change, travel, and a variety of sensations. Take notes, especially of your dreams. A Gemini figures prominently.

Monday, June 23 (Moon in Aries to Taurus 11:14 p.m.)
Be diplomatic. Make an intelligent concession to a family member. Focus on the sound of your voice, music, flowers. A coworker shares your interests, and could become a friend. Taurus, Libra, and another Scorpio play intriguing roles. Lucky number is 6.

Tuesday, June 24 (Moon in Taurus) Time is on your side, so don't be cajoled into making a snap decision. What appears on the surface is not what actually exists: all that glitters is not gold. Maintain an aura of intrigue, be discreet. Someone who once deceived you will try it again.

Wednesday, June 25 (Moon in Taurus) A relationship intensifies, which could lead to marriage. If married, there's an addition to your family in the not-too-distant future.

Focus on power, production, distribution, and promotion. Check legal rights and permissions. Lucky number is 8.

Thursday, June 26 (Moon in Taurus to Gemini 12:11 p.m.)   Let go of a situation that is not on the right side of the law. You receive proposals concerning business, career, and marriage. Check measurements and attend to details. No need to rush! You will be at the finish line. A romantic interlude lends spice. Don't start anything if not serious.

Friday, June 27 (Moon in Gemini)   Pressure is relieved. Show independence of thought and of action. Wear bright colors and imprint your personal style; don't follow others. Accept a leadership role; get legal clearance. You experience a new kind of love, which applies whether married or single.

Saturday, June 28 (Moon in Gemini to Cancer 11:50 p.m.)   Delve deep into a mysterious area. You could learn that your partner or mate is in a better financial position than you expected. An interest in the occult is stimulated; it will work out to your advantage. Cancer and Capricorn will play unusual roles.

Sunday, June 29 (Moon in Cancer)   On this Sunday, your spiritual values become very much in evidence. Joy and laughter are featured. You will celebrate being free of a serious situation. Highlight your versatility, humor, and intellectual curiosity. A Gemini figures prominently.

Monday, June 30 (Moon in Cancer)   On this last day of June, a long-distance communication will verify your views. Be aware of safety measures, especially when working with tools. Correct a recent error; someone overlooked the essential details. You'll emerge as a hero. Taurus plays a featured role.

Tuesday, July 1 (Moon in Cancer to Leo 9:11 a.m.) On this first day of July, your creative juices stir. You'll be especially attractive. There could be a reason for celebration. Your popularity is on the rise. People want to be with you, and vie to see if they can wine and dine you. Sagittarius is involved.

Wednesday, July 2 (Moon in Leo) Revise, review, rebuild. Someone in a position of authority is on your side, and a promotion is due as a result. Taurus, Leo, and another Scorpio play key roles, and could have these letters or initials in their names: D, M, V. Have luck with number 4.

Thursday, July 3 (Moon in Leo to Virgo 4:15 p.m.) At the track: post position special—number 1 p.p. in the fifth race. Hot daily doubles: 1 and 5, 3 and 2, 4 and 1. Away from the track, a secret is revealed; you'll be asked to "write about it." A flirtation is serious, but maintain your emotional equilibrium.

Friday, July 4 (Moon in Virgo) Attention revolves around your home, repairs, decorating, and remodeling. Celebrate this holiday by recalling the American Revolution and talking about the significance of the Declaration of Independence. Taurus, Libra and another Scorpio will play prominent roles.

Saturday, July 5 (Moon in Virgo to Libra 9:19 p.m.) What appears to be a defeat will be transformed into a rousing victory. The lunar position emphasizes your ability to make wishes come true. Avoid self-deception; see people and places as they are, not merely as you wish they could be.

Sunday, July 6 (Moon in Libra) On this Sunday, hold tight to what you recently gained. Someone wants to take from you something of value while giving nothing in return. Be on guard. Maintain your balance. Realize your own worth. A Cancer is involved.

Monday, July 7 (Moon in Libra)   This could mark the beginning or the ending of a romance or major project. Look behind the scenes. A secret arrangement is being made behind your back. You are not being neurotic, merely protecting your interests. A Pisces figures prominently.

Tuesday, July 8 (Moon in Libra to Scorpio 12:42 a.m.) Provide enlightenment. Encourage someone temporarily confined to home or hospital. Don't fear the unknown. Take the initiative! Be a role model for those who are reticent. Display the courage of your convictions. Let it be known you are not afraid and do not intend to "go away."

Wednesday, July 9 (Moon in Scorpio)   Lucky lottery: 2, 8, 12, 16, 33, 4. Make a fresh start. Your lunar cycle is high, so you will be at the right place at a special moment where the action occurs. The emphasis is also on your home, marital status, direction, and motivation. Capricorn is represented.

Thursday, July 10 (Moon in Scorpio to Sagittarius 2:47 a.m.)   Your cycle continues high. Take the initiative; don't follow others. There will be a reason for celebrating. You emit personal magnetism and sex appeal. Protect yourself in emotional clinches. Do not lower your standards. Have luck with number 3.

Friday, July 11 (Moon in Sagittarius)   What appeared to be an immovable object will finally cease to be a problem. This is your makeover day; dress differently, change your appearance. People comment, "You look different; you could be a movie star!" Leo plays a dramatic role.

Saturday, July 12 (Moon in Sagittarius to Capricorn 4:20 a.m.)   Money is earned via the written word. Take notes; record thoughts and dreams. Good news: A lost article is located. It has sentimental value. Gemini, Virgo, and Sagittarius play instrumental roles, and have these letters in their names: E, N, W. Lucky number is 5.

Sunday, July 13 (Moon in Capricorn) The full moon is in Capricorn, which is your third house. That coincides with short trips, visits, entertaining guests at home. A domestic adjustment is necessary, and could include a change of residence or marital status. Libra plays the top role.

Monday, July 14 (Moon in Capricorn to Aquarius 6:37 a.m.) Outline boundaries. Estimate your property value. What seemed a "sure thing" will turn out to be something entirely different. Focus on diversity and versatility. Expand your social horizons. Pisces and Virgo will play fantastic roles.

Tuesday, July 15 (Moon in Aquarius) You'll be surprised at the amount of money invested in home or property. You will be told, "If you want it done right you will have to spend money!" Maintain your emotional equilibrium. Cancer and Capricorn will play "steadying" roles.

Wednesday, July 16 (Moon in Aquarius to Pisces 11:14 a.m.) Let go of a situation that drains you financially or emotionally. You deserve more freedom of thought and of action. Someone takes you for granted and thus takes advantage. Have no more of it! Aries and Libra figure in this scenario.

Thursday, July 17 (Moon in Pisces) Focus on creativity, variety, romance. Imprint your style, wear bright colors; don't follow others. Original thinking is the key to success and happiness. A romantic Leo could win your heart. Be careful. You deserve the best; make sure you get it!

Friday, July 18 (Moon in Pisces to Aries 7:19 p.m.) A family member confides, "I am in love and don't know what to do about it!" Don't get caught up in a love triangle; be sympathetic, but remain neutral. An excellent dinner tonight will help heal frayed nerves. A Cancer is involved.

Saturday, July 19 (Moon in Aries) What begins as an "impossible task" will turn out to be easy, even fun. Your property value is subject to change. An Aquarius plays a key role in this area. Gemini and Sagittarius will also be involved. Accept an invitation to a prestigious social affair. Lucky number is 3.

Sunday, July 20 (Moon in Aries)   Start a conditioning program; keep resolutions about exercise and diet. As obstacles are overcome, spiritual values surface. Energy makes a dramatic comeback. You are going to emerge victorious despite the odds. Taurus is represented.

Monday, July 21 (Moon in Aries to Taurus 6:47 a.m.) Time is on your side. Refuse to be rushed into making a snap decision. Take notes; read and write, perhaps start a diary. Gemini, Virgo, and Sagittarius will play outstanding roles, and have these initials in their names: E, N, W. Lucky number is 5.

Tuesday, July 22 (Moon in Taurus)   Remain close to home. Repairs are required. Decorate and remodel. Today's scenario also features flowers, music, romance—your love is not unrequited. A family member needs you and says so. Libra and Taurus play mysterious roles.

Wednesday, July 23 (Moon in Taurus to Gemini 7:41 p.m.)   At the track: post position special—number 1 p.p. in the seventh race. Hot daily doubles: 3 and 4, 1 and 5, 6 and 2. Away from the track, see people and relationships as they are and not merely as you wish they could be. Pisces is in this picture.

Thursday, July 24 (Moon in Gemini)   Money comes from a surprise source. You are involved with a financial transaction and very much involved in a relationship. You will be told in no uncertain terms: "This is your life!" Focus on distribution, promotion, and more harmonious dealings with superiors.

Friday, July 25 (Moon in Gemini)   Someone you care about seems suddenly to have become invisible. Be patient; finish what you start. Answers are found in arcane literature. An interest in the mantic arts will increase. You will find astrology of immense help.

Saturday, July 26 (Moon in Gemini to Cancer 7:22 a.m.)
Lucky lottery: 1, 4, 33, 12, 18, 22. Make a new start. Exercise independence, creativity, and original thinking. A love relationship blossoms. Make an important concession here, and be ready to take a chance on romance. This applies no matter what your chronological age.

Sunday, July 27 (Moon in Cancer)   Focus on your home, family, and marital status. No matter how far you go from home, you will be called back. Don't neglect details, especially plumbing. Cancer and Capricorn will play instrumental roles. Get legal papers in order.

Monday, July 28 (Moon in Cancer to Leo 4:15 p.m.)
Be sure your roofing can "withstand" inclement weather. The spotlight is on direction, motivation, and the need for meditation. Look beyond the immediate. Attend a social gathering where you could meet someone destined to play an important role in your life.

Tuesday, July 29 (Moon in Leo)   The new moon in Leo is in your tenth house; this relates to your career and dealings with authorities, perhaps governmental representatives. Stress showmanship. Let it be known that you are alive and kicking. Leo, Taurus, and another Scorpio will play astounding roles.

Wednesday, July 30 (Moon in Leo to Virgo 10:25 p.m.)
By writing, you gain prestige and a possible promotion. Someone of the opposite sex could be bold enough to state, "There are times when I can hardly keep my hands off you!" Don't believe everything you hear. Lucky number is 5.

Thursday, July 31 (Moon in Virgo)   On this last day of July, the emphasis will be on public relations, your reputation, and legal rights. If single, you could meet your future mate. Married or single, you need to cooperate with some-one familiar with rules and regulations.

AUGUST 2003

Friday, August 1 (Moon in Virgo)   Despite objections by some who lack faith, you move ahead and hurdle the obstacles. Taurus, Leo, and another Scorpio become your strong allies. Read the fine print; be aware of the hidden clauses in any agreement. Display strength of your convictions.

Saturday, August 2 (Moon in Virgo to Libra 2:46 a.m.) Get ready for change, travel, and a variety of sensations. A discovery is made by entering an area previously prohibited. Communicate with someone you care about who is confined to home or hospital. Written material is important, providing an outlet for your creative surge.

Sunday, August 3 (Moon in Libra)   Attention revolves around your home and family as well as a romantic interlude that lends spice. A family member has been keeping a secret; you will learn about it tonight. Don't fear the unknown. Stand tall, have courage. Libra is involved.

Monday, August 4 (Moon in Libra to Scorpio 6:11 a.m.) Define terms. Insist on answers, not evasions. Your cycle moves up, and circumstances take a dramatic turn in your favor. Choose quality; don't accept secondhand goods. Pisces and Virgo play outstanding roles. Have luck with number 7.

Tuesday, August 5 (Moon in Scorpio)   You'll have things your way. So you have to ask yourself, "What is my way?" Accent your personality, make new contacts, wear bright colors. Elements of timing and luck ride with you. Don't get in your own way. Capricorn is involved.

Wednesday, August 6 (Moon in Scorpio to Sagittarius 9:10 a.m.)   Lucky lottery: 9, 12, 18, 13, 33, 22. Look beyond the immediate. You have the ability to predict the future, especially your own. Steer clear of those who take you for granted. A love relationship gets warm, if you can stand the heat!

Thursday, August 7 (Moon in Sagittarius)   What you learned 24 hours ago will be put to use tonight. Focus on original thinking, independence, and the courage of your convictions. Leo and Aquarius play astonishing roles, and have these letters or initials in their names: A, S, J. Lucky number is 1.

Friday, August 8 (Moon in Sagittarius to Capricorn 12:02 p.m.)   On this Friday, the question of your marital status could loom large. The moon is in your second house, which has to do with personal possessions and locating lost articles. An opportunity will exist to increase your income. Cancer is involved.

Saturday, August 9 (Moon in Capricorn)   Highlight your versatility and intellectual curiosity. Be with people who are not afraid to state their views on politics. Ignore someone who attempts to "put you down." Gemini and Sagittarius will play encouraging roles. Have luck with number 3.

Sunday, August 10 (Moon in Capricorn to Aquarius 3:23 p.m.)   You will be dubbed an "indispensable person." Prove your worth by attending to details overlooked by others. Taurus, Leo, and another Scorpio play major roles. A relative requests that you join in a short trip to retrieve your legal papers.

Monday, August 11 (Moon in Aquarius)   Get ready for the unusual! Read and write. A flirtation will lend spice. Examine claims in connection with real estate. Don't get caught up in a whirlwind of illusion. Gain is indicated by writing your experiences.

Tuesday, August 12 (Moon in Aquarius to Pisces 8:18 p.m.)   The full moon in Aquarius is in your fourth house, relating to where you live. A romantic involvement gets serious. If single, it could lead to marriage. If married, there could be an addition to your family quite soon. Taurus is in this picture.

Wednesday, August 13 (Moon in Pisces)   At the track: post position special—number 3 p.p. in the fifth race. Hot daily doubles: 1 and 7, 3 and 5, 1 and 1. Away from the track, avoid self-deception. Maintain your emotional equilibrium. You could find yourself in the throes of a hot romance.

Thursday, August 14 (Moon in Pisces)   Money is involved— invest in your own capabilities. Going into business for yourself would be a good idea. Get priorities in order. Let it be known, "I am running things!" Capricorn and Cancer will play significant roles.

Friday, August 15 (Moon in Pisces to Aries 3:59 a.m.) Keep resolutions about health. Be friendly with a coworker who shares your basic interests. Let go of a losing proposition. Welcome the chance for a reunion with a loved one. In any color scheme, involve red. A long journey provides a way to reorganize priorities.

Saturday, August 16 (Moon in Aries)   The Aries moon relates to an "aggressive" coworker. Focus on creativity as well as a different kind of love. Let it be known, "I am not to be taken for granted!" Leo and Aquarius will play mysterious roles. Have luck with number 1.

Sunday, August 17 (Moon in Aries to Taurus 2:52 a.m.) Play the waiting game. Don't be too available. Let others play a guessing game. Focus on giving service, fulfilling basic needs. Be creatively selfish. This means raise your self-esteem. The emphasis is on cooperative efforts and proposals of partnership or marriage.

Monday, August 18 (Moon in Taurus)   Give full play to intellectual inquiries, especially those involving legalities. The question of your marital status will loom large. Check legal rights and permissions. Social activities accelerate. Avoid scattering your forces.

Tuesday, August 19 (Moon in Taurus)   Don't ask for more than you can handle. Details have yet to be ironed out. Focus on public relations, learning who really is your friend and otherwise. If single, the question of marriage could be raised yet again. Taurus is involved.

Wednesday, August 20 (Moon in Taurus to Gemini 3:40 a.m.)   Lucky lottery: 5, 3, 35, 18, 22, 1. The emphasis is on a variety of experiences and an ability to express yourself in writing. A flirtation lends spice, but be ready to move on. Gemini, Virgo, and Sagittarius play major roles.

Thursday, August 21 (Moon in Gemini)   Attention revolves around the necessity for remaining on familiar ground. This is not the time for "getting away." A family member needs you, and will say so. If you do go away, you will be called back. Check interest rates, and be wary concerning investments.

Friday, August 22 (Moon in Gemini to Cancer 3:43 p.m.)   Avoid self-deception. Someone attempts to pull the wool over your eyes. Within 24 hours, you learn about a proposed journey that could include a foreign land. Communicate via advertising and publishing; Pisces plays a significant role.

Saturday, August 23 (Moon in Cancer)   On this Saturday, get ready for a "lively night." A relationship intensifies, and could get too hot not to cool down. The lunar aspect promotes sensuality, creativity, and romance. Capricorn and Cancer figure in this scenario. Lucky number is 8.

Sunday, August 24 (Moon in Cancer)   A very hot relationship could get under way. No fooling around! If not serious, move on. The "other person" wants it to last. Aries and Libra will play substantial roles. You will know them by the initials I and R in their names. Lucky number is 9.

Monday, August 25 (Moon in Cancer to Leo 12:46 a.m.)
Everything points to creativity, imprinting your own style.
Don't follow others; let them follow you. Emphasize original thinking and the courage of your convictions. Your professional superior wants to consult with you. It results in promotion and more responsibility.

Tuesday, August 26 (Moon in Leo) The Leo moon is
in your tenth house. This relates to promotion, distribution,
and taking charge of a huge operation. A family member
expresses the desire to redecorate and remodel in order to
make the home beautiful. Agree, if at all possible.

Wednesday, August 27 (Moon in Leo to Virgo 6:25 a.m.)
The new moon in Virgo relates to your eleventh house;
many of your hopes and wishes can be fulfilled. You win
friends and influence people. Arrange a social gathering
among those who have a sense of humor and intellectual
curiosity.

Thursday, August 28 (Moon in Virgo) An obstacle that
appeared to be immovable will move due to your efforts.
You will have luck in matters of speculation by sticking
with number 4. Rewrite, review, rebuild; this is your makeover day. Taurus is in this picture.

Friday, August 29 (Moon in Virgo to Libra 9:40 a.m.)
Within 24 hours, mysterious happenings take place. Look
behind the scenes; do not fear the unknown. Read and
write, express feelings, publicize charitable events. Gemini,
Virgo, and Sagittarius will boost your morale.

Saturday, August 30 (Moon in Libra) A secret is revealed. Follow subtle clues that could lead to riches. You
require "private time" in order to meditate. What once
"disappeared" will make a dramatic reappearance. Taurus
and Libra figure in this scenario.

Sunday, August 31 (Moon in Libra to Scorpio 11:59 a.m.)
On this last day of August, see people and relationships in
a realistic light. The moon in your twelfth house means

temporary confinement, an aura of mystery, intrigue. People want to know everything about your personal life. Don't tell all; don't confide or confess.

SEPTEMBER 2003

Monday, September 1 (Moon in Scorpio)   On this first day of the month, your cycle is high. Read, write, learn by teaching. Others find you attractive, but you could get involved in a "complicated flirtation." If only playing games, you will pay the price. Know it and respond accordingly.

Tuesday, September 2 (Moon in Scorpio to Sagittarius 2:31 p.m.)   A domestic adjustment is featured. This could involve a possible change of residence or marital status. Almost effortlessly, you will be at the right place at a special time. Your judgment and intuition are on target. Taurus is featured.

Wednesday, September 3 (Moon in Sagittarius)   Lucky lottery: 6, 13, 7, 4, 14, 12. Lie low, play the waiting game. Time is on your side, so don't equate delay with defeat. Someone wants to trip you up—don't give them the satisfaction. Be sure shoes fit well; don't let your vanity cause discomfort.

Thursday, September 4 (Moon in Sagittarius to Capricorn 5:50 p.m.)   There are ways to increase your income—you will find them! Focus on promotion, more responsibility, and ways of distribution. Someone you care about will seek advice. Give it without taking sides. Walk a fine line between being helpful and going where you don't belong.

Friday, September 5 (Moon in Capricorn)   Be finished with someone who takes you for granted. Today's scenario highlights trips, visits, and relatives who feel they know best how to live your life. Finish what you start. Participate in an idealistic project. Aries plays a dramatic role.

Saturday, September 6 (Moon in Capricorn to Aquarius 10:14 p.m.)   Answer: Affirmative. It is time for a new start in a different direction. A short trip is necessary to obtain a legal document. Refuse to be held back by the lack of a "signed paper." Imprint your style; don't follow others. Have luck with number 1.

Sunday, September 7 (Moon in Aquarius)   Within 24 hours, you locate what you have been looking for in connection with your property or home. Stick to rules and regulations. By so doing, you avoid future complications. Taurus, Leo, and another Scorpio will play featured roles.

Monday, September 8 (Moon in Aquarius)   Your property will look wonderful, but could be "too shaky." Spread your emotional wings, but know where and why you are flying. Don't scatter your forces. Gemini and Sagittarius will help you when most needed. Lucky number is 3.

Tuesday, September 9 (Moon in Aquarius to Pisces 4:06 a.m.)   Be willing to revise, review, rewrite, and rebuild. This is your "makeover" day. Wear your hair in a different style. People will comment, "You look different; everything about you is wonderful!" Taurus, Leo, another Scorpio play key roles.

Wednesday, September 10 (Moon in Pisces)   At the track: post position special—number 3 p.p. in the second race. Hot daily doubles: 2 and 3, 5 and 5, 4 and 6. Away from the track, play with passion. The full moon in Pisces is in your fifth house, which equates to creative projects, a variety of sensations, and intense romance.

Thursday, September 11 (Moon in Pisces to Aries 12:09 p.m.)   During this time, you could change your residence or marital status. Focus on change, travel, and unusual experiences. Maintain creative control while you share your skill and talent. The "right people" take notice. You could be knocking on doors of fame and fortune.

Friday, September 12 (Moon in Aries)   Keep resolutions about your general health. Revise work methods. Don't lose sleep over a minor problem. Define terms. Avoid self-deception. Someone you trust could mean well, but lacks financing. Maintain an aura of mystery and intrigue.

Saturday, September 13 (Moon in Aries to Taurus 10:49 p.m.)   You are doing it correctly! Some people, feeling they know more than they actually do, will tell you otherwise. This is your power play day. Do things your way; it will be the right way. Capricorn and Cancer will play involved roles.

Sunday, September 14 (Moon in Taurus)   A legal document could arrive tomorrow. Complete a project you have been working on. What you finish could have international implications. The prospect of a journey overseas is a distinct possibility. A reunion tonight is with someone you once loved.

Monday, September 15 (Moon in Taurus)   The emphasis is on partnership or marriage. You will be closely observed concerning legal rights and permissions. Accent original thinking. Take a chance on romance. There will be spice in your life, which will mark an end to boredom. A Leo figures prominently.

Tuesday, September 16 (Moon in Taurus to Gemini 11:31 a.m.)   Check your property rights. A family member is sincere, but could be sincerely misinformed. Focus on local politics, cooperative efforts, and proposals of partnership or marriage. You can afford to play the waiting game.

Wednesday, September 17 (Moon in Gemini)   Lucky lottery: 3, 5, 35, 22, 18, 16. Avoid trying to please everyone; that is the sure road to madness. Arrange a social gathering that includes those with definite political views. A clash of ideas will prove exciting and informative.

Thursday, September 18 (Moon in Gemini) Rebuild. Find out where financial backing can be made available. Many answers are found by studying arcane literature. Keep an open mind without being naive. A romantic rendezvous is fun, but could prove expensive. Maintain your emotional equilibrium.

Friday, September 19 (Moon in Gemini to Cancer 12:06 a.m.) Someone you once loved is now becoming a pest. Know when to say, "Enough!" A romantic interlude has run its course. If you stop now, there will be no ill feelings and no one will be hurt. Your Scorpio passion surfaces; don't let go!

Saturday, September 20 (Moon in Cancer) A long-distance communication verifies your opinions. Find someone who can represent your talent or product in a foreign nation. Keep your plans flexible. Read and write; learn through the process of teaching others. Your popularity rises—people want to wine and dine you.

Sunday, September 21 (Moon in Cancer to Leo 10:00 a.m.) A favorable lunar aspect coincides with philosophy, psychology, and theology. A family member has much to tell you; show that you are willing to listen. A long journey could mark the conclusion of a search. Pisces and Virgo play fascinating roles.

Monday, September 22 (Moon in Leo) This could be your lucky day, especially if you stick with number 8. Focus on promotion, distribution, and added recognition. On a personal level, you might become involved in a relationship that goes all the way, including marriage. Capricorn is represented.

Tuesday, September 23 (Moon in Leo to Virgo 4:03 p.m.) A chance exists for international recognition as well as participation in a humanitarian project. Look beyond the immediate. Advertise and publish. A relationship begins or ends. By tonight, the answers become crystal clear.

Wednesday, September 24 (Moon in Virgo)   At the track: post position special—number 7 p.p. in the first race. Hot daily doubles: 6 and 3, 1 and 7, 3 and 5. Away from the track, wear bright colors so that people know you are alive and kicking. A new kind of love requires that you maintain your emotional equilibrium.

Thursday, September 25 (Moon in Virgo to Libra 6:48 p.m.)   Refuse to be limited by those who lack talent or faith. Look beyond the immediate. You can perceive the future and make it come true. Analyze published material, which could provide the answer to a dilemma. A Cancer is involved.

Friday, September 26 (Moon in Libra)   Give full play to your intellectual curiosity. Late last night's new moon in Libra represents your twelfth house. This relates to theaters, hospitals, institutions, and secrets. You gain a new way of looking at people and places; what was previously hidden is revealed. Gemini is involved.

Saturday, September 27 (Moon in Libra to Scorpio 7:51 p.m.)   Don't let details elude you. What was held back will be released; there are flaws not previously detected. Let others know that you are "in the know." Once this is established, you could gain access to pertinent data. Taurus is involved.

Sunday, September 28 (Moon in Scorpio)   Keep your mind open to ideas concerning theology. Your lunar cycle is high. You live and learn, and find there is spice in your life. Write your thoughts; take note of dreams. Tonight's dream, properly interpreted, could be a guidepost to the future.

Monday, September 29 (Moon in Scorpio to Sagittarius 8:56 p.m.)   On this Monday, a domestic adjustment is necessary. Make intelligent concessions, without abandoning your principles. The moon in your sign emphasizes your personality and sex appeal. Don't break any hearts. The heart you break could be your own. Libra is involved.

Tuesday, September 30 (Moon in Sagittarius)　On this last day of September, be sure to visit someone temporarily confined to home or hospital. Define terms. Get commitments in writing. A money promise will be paid following a delay. There is a "hidden matter" you can learn about tonight.

OCTOBER 2003

Wednesday, October 1 (Moon in Sagittarius to Capricorn 11:21 p.m.)　Money that had been held back will be released. Yes, you waited and won. A domestic adjustment could include an actual change of residence or marital status. You should be dealing with or corresponding with people in distant cities and foreign lands.

Thursday, October 2 (Moon in Capricorn)　Within 24 hours, you will feel, "I have the right to enjoy success!" Focus on exclusivity, without making yourself too available. Maintain your aura of mystery, of intrigue. Be selective; choose top quality. Virgo is involved.

Friday, October 3 (Moon in Capricorn)　This can be your power play day, if you so permit. The waiting game is over. Get your fair share, and let others know you mean business. On a personal level, a relationship is hot and heavy. A short trip involves a relative who needs your cooperation.

Saturday, October 4 (Moon in Capricorn to Aquarius 3:45 a.m.)　Keep plans flexible. You could get a sudden notice that travel is imminent. Look beyond the immediate, but finish what you start. A romantic involvement lends spice. Refuse to give up something of value for nothing. Lucky number is 9.

Sunday, October 5 (Moon in Aquarius)　You are on more solid ground, so let go of preconceived notions. Create, invent! Give and receive love. You will be with talented, temperamental people—maintain your own emotional equilibrium. Make personal appearances.

Monday, October 6 (Moon in Aquarius to Pisces 10:20 a.m.) Focus on where you live and the need to decorate or remodel. The feeling of being confined is only temporary. You get solid backing. Your family will be on your side. The emphasis is on proposals that include partnership or marriage.

Tuesday, October 7 (Moon in Pisces) The emphasis is on social activity and creative projects. You will be flattered by a special member of the opposite sex. You will entertain and be entertained. Today's scenario highlights the excitement of change, travel, and variety. Have luck with number 3.

Wednesday, October 8 (Moon in Pisces to Aries 7:07 p.m.) Lucky lottery: 4, 7, 12, 17, 6, 26. Be willing to revise, review, rewrite; this could be your "makeover" day. The moon in Pisces represents your fifth house, which relates to children and a variety of sensations. Taurus is in the picture.

Thursday, October 9 (Moon in Aries) Keep resolutions about diet and exercise. Your energy level will soar, if you so permit. The employment picture will be clarified. Let things run at home as well as at work. Gemini, Virgo, and Sagittarius will play featured roles.

Friday, October 10 (Moon in Aries) Focus on beauty, art, music, and the ability to make your home attractive. The full moon in Aries represents your sixth house, which relates to your ability to persevere in the job at hand. Someone who shares your interests will pay a meaningful compliment.

Saturday, October 11 (Moon in Aries to Taurus 6:04 a.m.) Don't get emotionally involved with one who takes you for granted and would like to "take you." Define terms. Know when to say, "Enough!" An aura of deception exists, deliberate or otherwise. Pisces and Virgo figure in this scenario.

Sunday, October 12 (Moon in Taurus)   Lie low, play the waiting game. Be careful about signing a document. You do not have a clear picture now. If you wait, you will ultimately win. Don't be cajoled into making a snap decision. Cancer and Capricorn play major roles.

Monday, October 13 (Moon in Taurus to Gemini 6:44 p.m.)   A legal agreement might be over when you thought it was just beginning. You discover hidden clauses; what appeared on the surface was not the complete story. Remember once again, "All that glitters is not gold." Aries and Libra will play outstanding roles.

Tuesday, October 14 (Moon in Gemini)   A mystery is solved, to your advantage. You learn where the money is and how it got that way. Wipe the slate clean. Get rid of preconceived notions. Maintain creative control. It is your style and talent people want. Leo is represented.

Wednesday, October 15 (Moon in Gemini)   Look beyond the immediate. Decide on your future direction and motivation. Many answers will be available, if you meditate. Focus on cooperative efforts, partnership, and marriage. Keep diet resolutions; tonight you will enjoy a seafood dinner.

Thursday, October 16 (Moon in Gemini to Cancer 7:39 a.m.)   Your cycle moves up. What had blocked your way will be removed. A contact made at a recent social gathering will prove valuable. Give full play to your intellectual curiosity. Gemini and Sagittarius play mysterious roles. Lucky number is 3.

Friday, October 17 (Moon in Cancer)   Long-range plans crystallize. Focus on advertising and publishing; be sure your material is circulated in a foreign land. By rewriting, you will be assured of acceptance. Taurus and another Scorpio figure in this scenario.

Saturday, October 18 (Moon in Cancer to Leo 6:40 p.m.)   Written material brings recognition. On a personal level, there will be spice in your life. Someone of the opposite sex declares, "I can hardly keep my hands off you!" This elevates your morale, but don't believe everything you hear. Sagittarius is involved.

Sunday, October 19 (Moon in Leo)   Blend your career with domestic life. Make an intelligent concession, but don't abandon your principles. If single, you could meet your future mate. Married or single, make your home more comfortable and attractive. Another Scorpio is involved.

Monday, October 20 (Moon in Leo)   Define terms. Insist on answers, not evasions. Someone in a position of authority seeks a meeting. Display your knowledge of showmanship. You will be counted on to draw a crowd, so wear bright colors. See people and relationships in a realistic light.

Tuesday, October 21 (Moon in Leo to Virgo 1:59 a.m.) You might be saying, "It seems impossible, but my wishes are being fulfilled!" Elements of timing and luck ride with you. In matters of speculation, stick with number 8. A relationship is hot and heavy. You'll be involved, more than originally expected.

Wednesday, October 22 (Moon in Virgo)   A project will be completed according to your specifications. A romance grows. Don't make promises you cannot keep. Long-range expectations are closer to fulfillment than might be anticipated. Aries plays a spectacular role.

Thursday, October 23 (Moon in Virgo to Libra 5:26 a.m.)   The answer to a question: Yes, this is the time to try something new. Emphasize innovativeness—your ability to invent, to create. Wear bright colors that include yellow and gold. Let others know you are alive and kicking. Leo and Aquarius figure in this scenario.

Friday, October 24 (Moon in Libra)   What had been hidden will be revealed. This could relate to where you live and with whom. The focus is on your partnership or marital status. Keep health resolutions, especially in connection with your diet. Cancer and Capricorn will play amazing roles.

Saturday, October 25 (Moon in Libra to Scorpio 6:07 a.m.)   The new moon in your sign emphasizes the possibility of a "new love." Circumstances are turning in your favor, even as you read these lines. Diversify! Highlight versatility and intellectual curiosity. Lucky lottery: 3, 12, 2, 20, 14, 17.

Sunday, October 26—Daylight Saving Time Ends (Moon in Scorpio)   On this Sunday you will know that your love is not unrequited. Details relating to responsibility will become crystal clear. Check your plumbing and electricity. Be willing to rebuild, to rewrite, to make this your makeover day.

Monday, October 27 (Moon in Scorpio to Sagittarius 4:54 a.m.)   You receive a written notice that you have additional funds coming to you. It is important to budget assets. Your cycle continues high. You will be at the right place at a special moment. A Sagittarius will prove of immense help. Your lucky number is 5.

Tuesday, October 28 (Moon in Sagittarius)   At the track: post position special—number 3 p.p. in the fifth race. Hot daily doubles: 3 and 7, 4 and 6, 1 and 1. Away from the track, make a domestic adjustment that includes beautifying your surroundings. Libra plays a helpful role.

Wednesday, October 29 (Moon in Sagittarius to Capricorn 5:36 a.m.)   A relative could involve you in a wild-goose chase, if you so permit. Be sure of what is expected of you. Be flexible, but don't scatter your forces. Avoid self-deception; see relationships in a realistic light. Pisces is represented.

Thursday, October 30 (Moon in Capricorn) You get results based on previous efforts. Take special care in traffic; people tend to be careless at the wheel during this cycle. What you thought was finished will be revived. A relationship could run its course; Capricorn plays a key role.

Friday, October 31 (Moon in Capricorn to Aquarius 8:41 a.m.) Steer clear of a bibulous individual. No matter what the costume, you won't be able to hide who you are. Know it and have fun, but don't attempt to deceive. Get rid of preconceived notions. On this Halloween, you can predict your future.

NOVEMBER 2003

Saturday, November 1 (Moon in Aquarius) Attention revolves around real estate, especially the sale or purchase of property. See people and relationships in a realistic light. Someone may want to deceive you; protect yourself in emotional clinches. Pisces and Virgo play mysterious roles.

Sunday, November 2 (Moon in Aquarius to Pisces 2:52 p.m.) A payoff day when you get results of recent efforts, which can bring a substantial payment. Capricorn and Cancer will play outstanding roles. Spiritual values surface. Heed "inner messages." Refuse to be overwhelmed by a "salesperson."

Monday, November 3 (Moon in Pisces) You'll be dealing with children who are restless, creative, and demanding. Let go of a losing proposition. Set the pace. Take charge of your destiny. A reunion tonight involves a romantic interlude. Libra plays a fantastic role.

Tuesday, November 4 (Moon in Pisces) Your powers of persuasion peak. Focus on the fulfillment of desires. Be careful what you ask for—you are likely to get it. Creative juices stir. You could be in love! Leo and Aquarius will "show the way." Lucky number is 1.

Wednesday, November 5 (Moon in Pisces to Aries 12:02 a.m.) Attention revolves around your home, family, and marital status. By meditating, answers will come from within. Keep recent diet resolutions. A seafood dinner tonight will be delicious and nourishing. Cancer is involved.

Thursday, November 6 (Moon in Aries) The emphasis is on getting the job done as well as stabilizing your sleep pattern. Highlight versatility. Bring together those of opposing political views. Gemini and Sagittarius play top roles, and could have these letters or initials in their names: C, L, U.

Friday, November 7 (Moon in Aries to Taurus 11:28 a.m.) At the track: post position special—number 3 p.p. in the fifth race. Hot daily doubles: 2 and 5, 4 and 4, 3 and 1. Away from the track, attend to details and study the fine print. The employment picture is emphasized; you'll be told what is upcoming.

Saturday, November 8 (Moon in Taurus) Lucky lottery: 5, 7, 12, 13, 18, 43. Get ready for a change of direction. Keep your options open. A flirtation gets hot and heavy; know when to say "enough!" Gemini, Virgo, and Sagittarius play sensational roles, and have these initials in their names: E, N, W.

Sunday, November 9 (Moon in Taurus) Last night's full moon and lunar eclipse fell in Taurus, your seventh house. The spotlight is on partnership or your marital status. Be sure legal affairs are in order. A verdict or judgment will be upset. Domestic adjustment could result in a change of residence as well as marriage plans.

Monday, November 10 (Moon in Taurus to Gemini 12:13 a.m.) Pay attention to what you see out of the corner of your eye. You could discover deception, deliberate or otherwise. Lie low; play the waiting game. Pisces and Virgo will edge their way into this scenario.

Tuesday, November 11 (Moon in Gemini)   A discovery is made concerning the financial status of someone close to you. Dig deep for information. Don't fear the occult. You're in the driver's seat, so act accordingly. Capricorn and Cancer play amazing roles. Have luck with number 8.

Wednesday, November 12 (Moon in Gemini to Cancer 1:09 p.m.)   Unless you obtain facts, let go of a situation. Let it be known you have had enough evasions. Communication is received from a distant city or foreign land. Your views will be verified. Aries and Libra will play major roles.

Thursday, November 13 (Moon in Cancer)   Your lucky number is 1. Creative juices stir. Physical attraction is much in evidence. Give logic equal time. Don't be swept off your feet. Stress independence and original thinking. A "different" kind of romance is on the horizon.

Friday, November 14 (Moon in Cancer)   Focus on your home, marital status, and decisions concerning direction and motivation. Keep diet resolutions. Consider where you are to live and with whom. Avoid brooding; accent meditation. A gift is received from a family member who had been anything but friendly.

Saturday, November 15 (Moon in Cancer to Leo 12:46 a.m.)   Diversify! Give full rein to your intellectual curiosity. Participate in social activities. You will meet someone destined to play an important role in your life. Gemini and Sagittarius act in a mysterious way. Lucky number is 3.

Sunday, November 16 (Moon in Leo)   Good news is received; you passed a test with flying colors. A promotion is due; you could be in a position of authority. A passionate relationship runs its course, unless you do something about it. Taurus, Leo, and another Scorpio figure in this scenario.

Monday, November 17 (Moon in Leo to Virgo 9:34 a.m.) The written word is important, so get thoughts and concepts on paper. A member of the opposite sex confides, "At times, I can hardly keep my hands off you!" Don't believe everything you hear. Maintain your emotional equilibrium. Virgo is represented.

Tuesday, November 18 (Moon in Virgo)   A wish comes true in connection with your home or marital status. Music plays; march to your own tune. Beautify your quarters, including flowers and art. Taurus and Libra will play fantastic roles. If diplomatic, you win. If you force issues, you come up empty-handed.

Wednesday, November 19 (Moon in Virgo to Libra 2:40 p.m.)   Lucky lottery: 6, 13, 5, 22, 18, 1. Define terms. Ask for what you need; you will receive a gift of a luxury item. Avoid self-deception. Refuse to be taken for granted. Perfect techniques and streamline procedures. Pisces plays a role.

Thursday, November 20 (Moon in Libra)   A secret meeting works to your advantage. What was kept confidential will be revealed. You'll be trusted to be discreet. Don't tell all; don't confide or confess. You gain prestige and a promotion. A Capricorn figures prominently.

Friday, November 21 (Moon in Libra to Scorpio 4:22 p.m.)   Today's Libra moon represents your twelfth house. Focus on institutions, hospitals, the theater. Get "in touch" with one temporarily confined to home. You will receive valid counsel. A reunion with someone you once loved is scheduled tonight.

Saturday, November 22 (Moon in Scorpio)   Don't hesitate to express your doubts or suspicions. Insist on proof in writing. You are due for a fresh start in a new direction. Avoid heavy lifting. Leo and Aquarius play significant roles, and could have these letters in their names: A, S, J. Have luck with number 1.

Sunday, November 23 (Moon in Scorpio to Sagittarius 4:02 p.m.)   The new moon and solar eclipse fall in your sign. A change of scene occurs. You undergo a personality transformation. A personal relationship could be upset, which might work out to your advantage. Steer clear of explosives as well as heavy-drinking individuals.

Monday, November 24 (Moon in Sagittarius)   A money situation is solved. A young person has much to do with it. Be independent, not arrogant. Make an appointment to see someone in authority. But don't go hat in hand. Exude confidence. Today you have an abundance of sex appeal.

Tuesday, November 25 (Moon in Sagittarius to Capricorn 3:31 p.m.)   Funds that had been tied up will be released. A lost article is located. Your earning power increases. A family member confides, "I will need more than I originally requested!" Taurus, Leo, and another Scorpio figure in this scenario.

Wednesday, November 26 (Moon in Capricorn)   A short trip is necessary. A relative is involved. A legal document has been misplaced, but will be found on a shelf. Be prepared for a variety of experiences. Don't take a flirtation too lightly! Read and write; perhaps you should start a diary.

Thursday, November 27 (Moon in Capricorn to Aquarius 4:48 p.m.)   Be with your family, if possible. A relative visits to share the holiday. Inject humor into the proceedings. A traditional dinner will be fine. You will receive compliments. Enjoy this Thanksgiving. Taurus and Libra play meaningful roles.

Friday, November 28 (Moon in Aquarius)   Attention revolves around real estate, including the sale or purchase of a home. Be aware of the fine print, and attend to details that include plumbing. Someone attempts to deceive you—protect yourself at close quarters. Pisces and Virgo will play stunning roles.

Saturday, November 29 (Moon in Aquarius to Pisces 9:26 p.m.)   Money changes hands—you play an instrumental role. A relationship sets hot and heavy. If merely playing games, look out! The other person is serious, and expects a legal commitment. Capricorn and Cancer play fascinating roles, and have these letters in their names: H, Q, Z.

Sunday, November 30 (Moon in Pisces)   Look beyond the immediate. A new, exciting relationship is on the horizon. If married, the spark that brought you together reignites. If single, you fall in love with your future mate. Aries and Libra will play "prophetic" roles.

DECEMBER 2003

Monday, December 1 (Moon in Pisces)   You get off to a roaring start on this first day of the month. Your creative juices are activated. Highlight original thinking as well as new ways of distribution. Capricorn and Cancer play amazing roles, and have these initials in their names: H, Q, Z.

Tuesday, December 2 (Moon in Pisces to Aries 5:55 a.m.) Your creative project will succeed—it could be known internationally. Look beyond the immediate in connection with a personal relationship. Don't carry someone else's burden. Refuse to be taken for granted.

Wednesday, December 3 (Moon in Aries)   Keep recent resolutions about your health. Be careful about your diet. Make a fresh start. Emphasize original thinking. Be independent in thought, and action. Wear bright colors that include yellow or gold. Have luck with number 1.

Thursday, December 4 (Moon in Aries to Taurus 5:29 p.m.)   Blend work methods with domestic duties. The focus is on your home, especially emotional security with a partner. You'll be asked to cooperate in a local political situation. Proposals received include partnership or marriage. A Cancer is involved.

Friday, December 5 (Moon in Taurus)   Accept a social invitation. You will receive news about a legal document. Be amiable, but stick to your principles. Legal affairs dominate—take nothing for granted where the law is concerned. A Sagittarius plays a role.

Saturday, December 6 (Moon in Taurus)   Legal pitfalls are present, so be thorough and aware of hidden clauses. Someone tells you something—it is not the entire truth. See people and relationships as they actually exist. Revise, review, rewrite. Another Scorpio is involved.

Sunday, December 7 (Moon in Taurus to Gemini 6:25 a.m.)   Be analytical. Find out why something occurred. Your marital status figures prominently. A frank discussion with someone who would be your partner is necessary. Gemini, Virgo, and Sagittarius play unusual roles, and have these letters in their names: E, N, W.

Monday, December 8 (Moon in Gemini)   The full moon in Gemini represents your eighth house. Emotions take over, and you feel you really are in love. Be careful—you could be involved in a "triangle." Maintain your emotional equilibrium. Taurus, Libra, and another Scorpio figure in this scenario.

Tuesday, December 9 (Moon in Gemini to Cancer 7:10 p.m.)   Promised funding has not been canceled, so don't equate delay with defeat. What you need will be forthcoming. Play the waiting game. Time is on your side. Mysterious circumstances are involved—someone who attempts deception will be caught red-handed.

Wednesday, December 10 (Moon in Cancer)   Don't mix up fiction with fact. Dig deep for information about the financial status of someone who makes grandiose promises. An individual who wants to be your representative should show proof of capabilities. Capricorn and Cancer play astounding roles.

Thursday, December 11 (Moon in Cancer)   An intense relationship is featured—this could be the beginning or the end. Check your travel plans. It is not unlikely that you could be visiting a foreign nation. Participate in a humanitarian project. Aries figures in this scenario.

Friday, December 12 (Moon in Cancer to Leo 6:39 a.m.)
Emphasize original thinking and independence. Insist on maintaining creative control. You are due for a new start in a different direction. Don't follow others. Create your own tradition! A romance gets too hot not to cool down. Leo is involved.

Saturday, December 13 (Moon in Leo) A Capricorn who wants to "sign you up" should be told, "Show me the money!" Keep your options open. Don't be cajoled into making a snap decision. Your marital status figures prominently; have documents at hand, including a birth certificate.

Sunday, December 14 (Moon in Leo to Virgo 4:05 p.m.)
Spiritual values surface. Someone you admire will return the compliment. You are on your way to "bigger things," if you so permit. Don't give up something of value for nothing. A passionate relationship puts you on edge. Strive to maintain your emotional equilibrium.

Monday, December 15 (Moon in Virgo) Be willing to tear down in order to rebuild. What you "imagine" could be transformed into reality. Be analytical. Also be careful what you ask for, because you are very likely to receive it. Elements of timing and luck ride with you; stick with number 4.

Tuesday, December 16 (Moon in Virgo to Libra 10:44 p.m.) At the track, choose horses and jockeys with these letters in their names: E, N, W. Post position special—number 5 p.p. in the third race. Hot daily doubles: 1 and 6, 5 and 7, 3 and 8. Away from the track, read, write, and learn through the process of teaching.

Wednesday, December 17 (Moon in Libra) A family secret will be out in the open. Don't make a federal case of it. No finger-pointing, please! Be diplomatic, remain calm.

Money will be replaced. Music plays, so dance to your own tune. Make your home beautiful by decorating and remodeling.

Thursday, December 18 (Moon in Libra)   Be discreet. Don't tell all; don't confide or confess. You will have access to classified information. Get a definition of terms, also be sure promises are in writing. Deception could be involved, deliberate or otherwise. A secret meeting occurs tonight.

Friday, December 19 (Moon in Libra to Scorpio 2:18 a.m.)   Get ready for a lively weekend! The lunar cycle is high, so you will be at the right place at a special moment almost effortlessly. Your personality sparkles. Others find you sexually attractive. Don't fall head over heels. Keep your balance; don't go below your station.

Saturday, December 20 (Moon in Scorpio)   Finish what you start. Imprint your style. Stress original thinking. A promise has not been broken; a delivery was delayed. Wear bright colors as you make personal appearances. Your cycle continues high; therefore, people want to read what you write and hear what you say.

Sunday, December 21 (Moon in Scorpio to Sagittarius 3:14 a.m.)   Spiritual values are much in evidence. State your beliefs, speaking from the heart. Leo and Aquarius will be very much attuned. As your creative juices stir, you could undergo a "revelation." Guard your possessions; you receive news that a lost article has been located.

Monday, December 22 (Moon in Sagittarius)   A special collection turns out to be worth more than you originally expected. Luck rides with you, if you stick to home base. Pay attention to a minor digestive problem; keep resolutions about your diet. Capricorn is involved.

Tuesday, December 23 (Moon in Sagittarius to Capricorn 2:55 a.m.)   The new moon in Capricorn represents your third house. Take special care in traffic. Arrange a new deal with a relative. There's social activity tonight. Laugh at your own foibles so that others will also laugh at their foolishness.

Wednesday, December 24 (Moon in Capricorn) On this Christmas Eve, you receive gifts that are heavy in weight. You will enjoy the holiday and recognize some of its real meaning. Taurus, Leo, and another Scorpio figure in this scenario. Puzzle pieces will unravel.

Thursday, December 25 (Moon in Capricorn to Aquarius 3:13 a.m.) Stay close to home. Celebrate the holiday with your family. Written material is important. Write and read your thoughts about the "greatest story ever told." That "heavy" gift turns out to be something you wanted but could not afford.

Friday, December 26 (Moon in Aquarius) Attention revolves around your home and the ability to beautify your surroundings. Music is involved. Your voice is different. Some comment, "It is melodious." Romance figures prominently. What you yearned for will come true.

Saturday, December 27 (Moon in Aquarius to Pisces 6:09 a.m.) Look beyond the immediate. Be sure it is love and not mere infatuation. Keep your options open, because instructions and directions are subject to sudden change. You undergo a variety of sensations. You will be assured that your love is not unrequited. Pisces is involved.

Sunday, December 28 (Moon in Pisces) Someone who disappointed you in the past will more than make up for it tonight. Be open-minded, but not naive. Give and receive love. Remember it is human to err, but divine to forgive. Capricorn and Cancer will play dramatic roles.

Monday, December 29 (Moon in Pisces to Aries 1:09 p.m.) Get ready for New Year's Eve. You could be the life of the party, but go easy on adult beverages. Steer clear of heavy drinkers. Stay with someone who takes you seriously and would not hurt you for the world. Aries is represented.

Tuesday, December 30 (Moon in Aries) Keep resolutions about your general health, exercise, and diet. Check the invitation list—don't forget someone who will arrive from out of town. A splendid celebration, if you stick to home base. Leo and Aquarius liven things, and do care about you!

Wednesday, December 31 (Moon in Aries) The accent is on moderation. Be with family, if possible. You receive proposals that involve business and marriage. If married, make a resolution that you will remain together. If single, you could meet your future mate. A Cancer plays an important role.

HAPPY NEW YEAR!

ABOUT THE AUTHOR

Born on August 5, 1926, in Philadelphia, Sydney Omarr was the only person ever given full-time duty in the U.S. Army as an astrologer. He also is regarded as the most erudite astrologer of our time and the best known, through his syndicated column (300 newspapers) and his radio and television programs (he was Merv Griffin's "resident astrologer"). Omarr has been called the most "knowledgeable astrologer since Evangeline Adams." His forecasts of Nixon's downfall, the end of World War II in mid-August of 1945, the assassination of John F. Kennedy, Roosevelt's election to the fourth term and his death in office . . . these and many others are on the record and quoted enough to be considered "legendary."

ABOUT THE SERIES

This is one of a series of twelve
Day-by-Day Astrological Guides
for the signs of 2003
by Sydney Omarr.

The Ultimate Guide to Love, Sex,
and Romance

SYDNEY OMARR'S ASTROLOGY, LOVE, SEX, AND YOU

SYDNEY OMARR

Whether your goal is a sexy seduction, finding your
soulmate, or spicing up a current relationship, this all-
in-one volume will guide you every step of the way—
with a little help from Sydney and the stars.

Includes:
- An in-depth description of each sign for men and women
- Compatibilty forecasts
- A fantastic section on romantic dinners for two, featuring
a complete kitchen-tested menu for each sign
- Myths and symbols associated with each sign
- An introduction to each sign's shadow
- Ratings on which signs are the most passionate
- and much more

206932

Available September 2002

To order call: 1-800-788-6262

SYDNEY OMARR'S ASTROLOGICAL GUIDE FOR YOU IN 2003

SYDNEY OMARR

Brimming with tantalizing projections, this amazing single-volume guide contains advice on romantic matters, career moves, travel, even finance, trends and world events. Find year overviews and detailed month-by-month predictions for every sign. Omarr reveals everything new under the stars, including:

- Attraction and romance
- New career opportunities for success in the future
- Lucky numbers and memorable days for every month of the year
- Global shifts and world forecasts

...and much more! Don't face the future blindly—let the Zodiac be your guide.

206576

Available July 2002

To order call: 1-800-788-6262

THE ASTROLOGY GIFT GUIDE

Constance Stellas

Finding a great gift is as easy as knowing someone's birthday...

INTRODUCING
THE <u>FIRST</u> BUYING GUIDE FOR ALL
SIGNS, OCCASIONS, AND BUDGETS!

This unique gift-buying guide uses individual profiles for each astrological sign to help you choose the perfect gift. **Includes:**

• A vast array of gift ideas, in three price ranges
• Personality profiles for each sign: ruling passion, style, colors, and more
• Shopping lists for men, women, children and teens
• Gift suggestions for every occasion: birthdays, weddings, showers, housewarming, holidays, and much more

Available in October 2002

207262

To order call: 1-800-788-6262